THE ONLINE
ADVERTISING PLAYBOOK

THE ONLINE ADVERTISING PLAYBOOK

Proven Strategies and Tested Tactics
from
The Advertising Research Foundation

JOSEPH PLUMMER

STEVE RAPPAPORT

TADDY HALL

ROBERT BAROCCI

BICENTENNIAL
1807
WILEY
2007
BICENTENNIAL

John Wiley & Sons, Inc.

Published by John Wiley & Sons, Inc., Hoboken, New Jersey.
Published simultaneously in Canada.

Wiley Bicentennial Logo: Richard J. Pacifico

For general information on our other products and services or for technical support, please contact our Customer Care Department within the United States at (800) 762-2974, outside the United States at (317) 572-3993 or fax (317) 572-4002.

Wiley also publishes its books in a variety of electronic formats. Some content that appears in print may not be available in electronic books. For more information about Wiley products, visit our web site at www.wiley.com.

Library of Congress Cataloging-in-Publication Data:

The online advertising playbook : proven strategies and tested tactics from the advertising research foundation / Joe Plummer . . . [et al.].
    p. cm.
  ISBN 978-0-470-05105-4 (cloth)
  1. Internet advertising. I. Plummer, Joe. II. Advertising Research Foundation.
HF6146.I58O55 2007
659.14'4—dc22   2007002550

Printed in the United States of America.

10 9 8 7 6 5 4 3 2

CONTENTS

Bobby J. Calder, Kellogg School of Management
Joanne Bradford, Microsoft
Greg Rogers, TACODA
Rishad Tobaccowala, Denuo
Dan Stoller and Jane Clarke, Time Warner Global
    Marketing
Noel Capon and Jeremy Kagan, Columbia University
Brian McAndrews, aQuantive
David Kenny, Digitas

ACKNOWLEDGMENTS

T he interest and support of the online advertising industry made this book possible. We have so many to thank in every aspect—the advertisers, without whom there would be no industry; the publishers who provide the advertising space; the vendors furnishing infrastructure and a wide variety of technologies; the general and specialized agencies that counsel clients; the research firms that study consumers and ad effectiveness; and the industry associations that tirelessly and imaginatively advance the cause.

Many companies and individuals provided information and wise perspective. Naming names is always chancy, not for the individuals named, but for the risk of not naming all names, the inadvertent oversight. If we overlooked you, please accept our sincerest apologies and contact us right away. We will quickly rectify the error on our companion website.

We thank The ARF board for approving the project and the Playbook Advisory Board. Through their leadership we explored and distilled what we learned about online advertising. This book fulfills their commitment to promoting industrywide discussion and advancing practice for all current and future online marketers.

Marissa Gluck of Radar Research brought deep knowledge and insight to the rapidly evolving field of online measurement. Her draft furnished the basis for that important discussion found in the Appendix.

The authors would like to thank the experts who read and improved key portions of the *Playbook*:

- Brad Lenz, Liz Claiborne
- David Edelman, Digitas
- Don Diforio, ARF
- Gord Hotchkiss, Enquiro
- Jeanniey Mullen, OgilvyOne and Email Experience Council
- Kim Black, CNET Networks

- Lynn Bolger, comScore Networks
- Mickey Wilson, CNET Networks
- Paul Beck, OgilvyOne and Email Experience Council
- Peter Kim, Forrester Research
- Rex Briggs, Marketing Evolution
- Rick Bruner, DoubleClick
- Shar VanBoskirk, Forrester Research
- Stephen Kim, Microsoft
- Stuart Schneiderman, Online Publishers Association

We also would like to thank our staff who spent endless hours finding articles, checking sources, and organizing what we know:

- Annabel Prentice
- Hye-Yeon An
- Maria Ovchinnikova
- Sharon Roopnarine
- Bert Schachter
- Zena Pagán

The *Playbook* distinguishes itself for being data- and case-driven. We reviewed over 1,200 documents—academic articles, research reports, white papers, case studies, trade press articles, columns, newsletters, and blog entries. Every one we used is cited in the references at the end of the book. We urge you to read those to learn the sources, benefit from them, and, if it's right for you, support them with your subscription or purchase.

A number of companies and individuals deserve shout-outs for their interest in and significant commitments to the *Playbook*: Alistair Goodman, Tribal Fusion; Amy Shea Hall, Ameritest; Andy Hunter, GSD&M; Annette Mullin, Insight Express; Bill Harvey, Next Century Research; Dakota Sullivan, BlueLithium; Dana Jones, Ultramercial; David Berkowitz, 360i; Grace Pai, Euro RSCG; Janet McCabe, comScore; Jason Carrillo, WebSideStory; Jeff Mills, eROI; Joe Mandese, MediaPost; Joe Pilotta, BIGresearch; Keith Wardell, Xmplar; Ken Mallon, Dynamic Logic; Kevin Doohan, ConAgra; Kevin Lee, Did-it; Kibibi Springs, Springboard Interactive; Kris Oser, eMarketer; Kristi

Diaz, GSD&M; Liz Lightfoot, CNET Networks; Matt Tatham, Hitwise; Melinda Krueger, Krueger Direct/Interactive; Michelle Mandansky, Yahoo!; Oliver Deighton, Google; Pam Horan, Online Publishers Association; Patricia Balchunas, Fathom SEO; Rene Huey-Lipton, GSD&M; Rick Vandevoorn, Ultramercial; Robert Thibeault, Outsell; Sandy Schlee, Avenue A | Razorfish; Ted Smith, CNET; Todd Tweedy, BoldMouth; Tracy Tang, eMarketer; Van Riley, AOL; Wilma McDaniel, Eyeblaster; and Young-Bean Song, Atlas Solutions. Any errors or misinterpretation of their excellent contributions are entirely our own.

During an intense undertaking like the *Playbook*, we now understand why many authors thank their friends, family, and colleagues; we especially thank our families!

T his book would have been impossible for a nonprofit organization such as The ARF to produce without the generous leadership support of key financial contributors:

Platinum Sponsors

DoubleClick

The Advertising Research Foundation, which for generations has been the standard-bearer for research integrity in traditional advertising, has made a smooth transition into the digital age. DoubleClick has benefited greatly from our collaboration with The ARF, participating in its committees, attending its events, even contracting with it for consultation on our own research methodologies. It has been a privilege to contribute to this *Playbook*, which promises to serve as a definitive resource for many marketers.

—Rick Bruner, Director of Research and
Industry Relations, DoubleClick

DoubleClick enables agencies, marketers, and publishers to work together successfully and profit from their digital marketing investments. Its focus on innovation, reliability, and insight enables clients to improve productivity and results.

Since 1996, DoubleClick has empowered the original thinkers and leaders in the digital advertising industry to deliver on the promise of the rich possibilities of our medium. Today, the company's DART and Performics divisions power the online advertising marketplace. Tomorrow, we will continue to enable clients to profit from opportunities across all digital advertising channels as consumers worldwide embrace them.

advancing conversion™

$$\left[x+1 \right]$$

The ARF has always been a trusted third-party provider of interesting and timely insights to our complicated marketing industry. I often refer to the ARF research in both current client engagements and new business pitches. [x+1] is proud to be participating in this year's *Playbook*.

—Jason Shulman,
Chief Revenue Officer, [x+1]

[x+1] helps marketers simplify their online marketing and achieve greater return on their overall marketing investment. We are reinventing the field of conversion optimization by combining insightful customer service from internet marketing experts with proprietary technology. [x+1]'s tools—Media+1 and Site+1—provide end-to-end conversion optimization as well as continuous reporting and analysis. Our hands-on customer service and consultation reinforce the power of our technology. Leading companies in financial services, telecommunications, online services, and automotive industries have significantly increased message accuracy, customer response, and ROI with [x+1].

WebTrends®

As WebTrends has grown over the past 12 years along with the online advertising industry, we have experienced the excitement and innovation of this rapidly changing marketplace. WebTrends salutes the ARF for providing the valuable insight and direction as we anticipate the next wave of amazing growth in the years to come.

—Tim Kopp, Chief Marketing
Officer, WebTrends

WebTrends is the leading provider of web analytics software and on-demand solutions for web-smart customers including General Mills, IKEA, Microsoft, Reuters, and Ticketmaster. With WebTrends Marketing Lab, the company has expanded its comprehensive analytic platform to offer on-the-fly data exploration, dynamic advertising exploration, and customer targeting solutions fueling relationship marketing. Thousands of enterprises have chosen Web-Trends solutions and consulting services to accurately prove and improve their business and marketing results. For more information, visit www.webtrends.com.

Title Sponsors

As a leading network in the field of online advertising, Casale Media is committed to participating in efforts that will elevate the appeal of this medium for advertisers through education and facilitation. *The Online Advertising Playbook* promises to be just the tool to clarify the common questions that surface around this newest of advertising mediums. We view this as an important knowledge-sharing exercise that will ultimately benefit all those parties involved in the industry.

—Casale Media

Casale Media is a global leader in online media technology. For over a decade, we have been helping advertisers of all varieties strengthen their brands and improve sales through the power of online media. We provide direct access to the web's most trusted media properties and most reliable delivery and optimization technologies, delivering over 25 billion targeted ads monthly to 170+ million consumers worldwide.

ultramercial

Ultramercial is excited to work with our industry's leading research entity. The internet has finally allowed for the measurement of viewer behavior in finite terms, and we welcome the insights and directions that knowledge will bring.

—Dana Jones, President and
Founder, Ultramercial

Ultramercial, LLC markets its patents-pending business model and ad unit that grants internet users free access to premium content (music, news, video on demand, game play, internet access, and more) after choosing to watch and engage with its full-screen multipage commercials. Current Ultramercial viewers metrics: 7% clickthrough rate (CTR); 75% completion rate; 50 seconds of engagement.

Sponsors

Coca-Cola, a global marketer interested in innovation, sponsors this project for the benefit of the industry.

MSN, as a leading global portal, supports the *Playbook* and its contribution to digital advertising practice.

THE ONLINE
ADVERTISING PLAYBOOK

CHAPTER 1

Introduction

Pat McGraw of Gillette started the ball rolling. Sitting down to lunch two years ago he huffed, "I really don't need another highly charged sales pitch on the power of internet advertising. What I would like to know is *how* it works and *why* it works." There were eight people at the lunch table, so the sample was decidedly small, but the consensus that day perked up our ears, and we started snooping around. As our sample expanded, the consensus solidified. A sampling:

- "Marketers cast around on the internet, but it's still a fishing expedition."   —Rance Crain, *Advertising Age*
- "Many marketers do not yet know how to create effective advertising online."   —Greg Stuart, Interactive Advertising Bureau
- "Online advertising offers unique advantages, but what's missing is an *understanding* of which executions will have a desired impact."   —Joe Gillespie, CNET Networks, Inc.
- "Everybody's doing it, but they don't feel confident it's going to produce results."   —Al Ries, consultant

With characteristic flair, and perhaps a bit of hyperbole, Colgate's Jack Haber concluded, "What do we *know* about online advertising? Well, we know that the brand should be present and persistent throughout the ad. Ten years and $15 billion of experience, and that's all we've learned!" Okay, maybe we've learned a bit more, but what? After a decade-plus of experience and a significant amount of spending, *what do we really know* about using the internet to advertise effectively?

Scratching our heads, we at The Advertising Research Foundation (ARF) began to wonder, "Where's the knowledge? What is *known* about using the internet for effective advertising?" Because it is the mission of our foundation to create, aggregate, synthesize, and share the knowledge that marketers require to do their jobs effectively, our interest was more than a passing curiosity.

We began to search for answers.

As with any worthy adventure, there's good news, bad news, and a little luck in the unfolding.

The good news: *Lots* of research has been performed on online advertising.

The bad news: Much of that research is purely confirmatory, with output limited to "it worked," "it didn't work," and shades in between; learning is scattered far and wide in the files of internet providers, advertisers, and researchers.

The luck: Lots of smart leaders, sharing our belief that the power of knowledge increases when it is shared, and willing to share their knowledge to move the industry forward, worked with us to create this book.

Chief among these leaders are the members of *The Online Advertising Playbook*'s Advisory Board, who hail from agencies, media companies, research firms, industry organizations, and advertisers:

Agencies

Brian McAndrews, aQuantive

Clark Kokich, Avenue A | Razorfish

David Verklin, Carat North America

Gerard Broussard, mOne Worldwide

Jonathan Adams, Modem Media

Norman Lehoullier, Grey Interactive Worldwide

Rishad Tobaccowala, Denuo

Sandy Schlee, Avenue A | Razorfish

Stacey Lyn Koerner, Initiative Media

Media Companies

Adam Gerber, Brightcove, Inc

Chris Theodoros, Google Inc.

Murray Gaylord, The New York Times

Rick Bruner, DoubleClick Inc.

Industry Organizations

Greg Stuart, Interactive Advertising Bureau

Michael Donahue, American Association of Advertising Agencies (AAAA)

Pam Horan, Online Publishers Association

Robert Liodice, Association of National Advertisers, Inc. (ANA)

Research Firms

Rex Briggs, Marketing Evolution

Nick Nyhan, Dynamic Logic

Alan Schulman, Brand New World

Advertisers

David Adelman, Johnson & Johnson

Edward Kim, Unilever

Giovanni Fabris, McDonald's

Jack Haber, Colgate-Palmolive Company

Joseph Gillespie, CNET Networks, Inc.

Joy Marcus, Time Warner

Patrick McGraw, Gillette Company

Robert DeSena, Masterfoods USA

Scott McDonald, Condé Nast Publications

Stephen Kim, MSN

Tim Kopp, Coca-Cola

Todd Riley, Volkswagen of America, Inc.

Tom Lynch, ING Group

These leaders did not sit idly with rubber stamps at the ready. Advisors helped us get the story right by providing research content, expert commentary, and painstaking editing. The authors thank them, especially.

Indeed, it was one of the *Playbook*'s advisors who provided the metaphor for this project. In one of those spectacularly rare sports analogies that actually sheds light, Tom Lynch of ING noted, "We're like a bunch of football players before the season starts, studying our

X's and O's and learning all the new plays. Well, all those X's and O's make sense only if you have a good idea for how the game is played— 10 yards for a first down, six points for a touchdown, four quarters in a game, and so on. But we're all out here in the internet advertising world calling plays with no idea of how the game is played: 'Hey, last time we did these five things and they worked pretty well, so let's repeat that approach,' 'I heard that somebody else had success with search optimization, so let's try that, too.'"

The Online Advertising Playbook is The ARF's attempt to clarify how the game is played. More specifically, what we have done is to examine the enormous wealth of research on online advertising—thousands of studies across categories, geographies, and business objectives—some published, but most in private files. We asked specifically what the research tells us about *what we know and how practitioners can use the knowledge to more successfully advertise online.*

Our intended audience is brand managers, their agency counterparts, and company leaders who want to see their business grow: more precisely, as we call them, "the curious fence-sitters," folks who've dabbled enough to pique their interest but who have yet to dive in whole hog or, to put it less metaphorically, who still see online advertising as a bit of a sideshow for the "interactive department" and not a core component of an integrated advertising plan. Their instincts say that this new technology or medium should be a cost-effective way to build their business, but what evidence exists beyond stories in *Advertising Age* about Burger King's Subservient Chicken or press releases announcing today's latest campaigns and novel creative approaches?

Our approach is to let the data speak rather than to theorize baselessly. Fortunately, our research found that quite a bit is *known* about how and why the internet works—how advertising online is evolving with new learning and new technological advances like broadband. It is this knowledge that we share in the book, enabling marketers to use the internet with confidence.

The *Playbook* is designed to be used in two ways:

1. Read it cover to cover for a comprehensive view of what's known.
2. Shoot to a particular chapter based on an immediate need for actionable knowledge.

Consequently, the chapters have been chosen to address the key areas of knowledge need and executive decision making. Or, to put it in a more visceral way, we cataloged the points of discomfort and uncertainty that marketers feel when confronting internet advertising, and we responded by exploring the available research to impart data-based answers.

While research is at the root of the entire book, and we are indebted to all who contributed, the positions expressed are the sole responsibility of the authors. A "hold harmless clause" applies to the innocent.

A final disclaimer and caution: To those who dismissively assert that the marketplace is changing too fast for a book to be of value—not true. We have conducted our research and drafted this book with an eye toward *principles* and proven strategies. There is no question that new tactical opportunities arise daily, but the core principles of effectiveness are more solid, though hardly unchanging. In cases where there is a shelf-life issue, we've tried to highlight those areas with a note.

Additionally, this book has an online "smart" twin that we encourage readers to visit for the latest knowledge and discussion. Go to www.thearf.org for the latest, or email the authors directly: playbook@thearf.org.

Joe Plummer
Steve Rappaport
Taddy Hall
Robert Barocci

CHAPTER 2

Targeting Approaches

A Unique Element in Online Advertising

In our experience," Lee Sherman, Vice President of Global Solutions at Avenue A | Razorfish, relates, "selecting the right audience is a much larger driver of online campaign performance than is . . . creative theme" (Sherman 2004). Creative folks would most likely disagree, but they and Sherman would agree on the fundamental principle: Know the customer.

Today we can routinely track how people connect online, collecting the service providers people use for their on-ramps (e.g., AOL, Earthlink, NetZero); internet protocol (IP) addresses used for internet access; connection types (dial-up, broadband) and speeds; and browser names and versions (e.g., Internet Explorer 5.5, FireFox 1.0, MSN 8, Safari 1.2). Behavioral data gets stored, too: date and time of logins and clicks; pages visited; entry and exit pages; length of time people interact with the ads (relevant for rich media); ads served and their page placement; and cookie-based actions that indicate site visitors' status—prospect, shopper, or buyer. Couple that information with traditional targeting variables, data mine the combination to create rules that personalize ad delivery, and you can see why the industry is excited about online advertising's unique targeting power.

And what is the potential? It's delivering relevant messages more precisely to your customers whenever and wherever they are in the buying process for your product or service. Whether the advertising's goals are direct response, further information through search, or brand building, efficient targeting is, as Sherman says, a critical element of success. We're going to discuss the newer online targeting approaches now—demographic, contextual, behavioral, geographic, daypart, affinity and purchase-based targeting—and review a number of cases in which these targeting strategies were used to achieve specific marketing objectives. These targeting methods can be combined for further fine-tuning. Some focus on the individual (a person's actions, gender, age, location, attitude, desires, and acceptance). Contextual and daypart targeting, by contrast, assume that external factors—the contents on the page or the time of the day/week/year—will serve well to target ads to segments of prospects or customers.

It's worth noting that *ad targeting* is marketer language. From the audience perspective, *relevance* would better describe well-targeted advertising; furthermore, when individuals are presented with ads that speak to them, the relevance is more subtle and in product or service categories they are interested in it tends not be as aggressive as the language of targeting implies.

Expert Insights on Targeting

Lynn D'Alessandro, Vendare

"Targeting isn't an either-or decision, so it's best to mix and match targeting tactics—especially when it comes to educated, prosperous consumers who simply won't respond to messages that aren't personally relevant."

Jim Meskauskas, Underscore Marketing

"Though the media available online stretches out to nigh infinity, the number of hours in the day, or the relevance of a particular product or service to an individual at a particular time in that individual's day, does not. Grocery shopping lacks certain relevance just as I'm arriving to work. Pork resonates more around dinnertime.... It is this kind of additional value that can be extracted from the [online] medium if and when it is packaged in dayparts."

Demographic Targeting

Demographic targeting is, arguably, the longest-running, most widely used concept for targeting advertising. Defining audiences according to their age, gender, income, occupation, and household size is deeply ingrained in marketing. As Jeremy Helfand, a former senior vice president at Advertising.com, wrote for iMedia Connection, "Demographic targeting has its place. It tends to work best for advertisers in broader product categories where links to specific behaviors are less clear. For broad-interest advertisers, such as those selling travel services or consumer electronics, demographic targeting will perform nearly as well as behavioral—and cost less" (Helfand 2005).

Demographic targeting could do a better job when combined with other types of customer characteristics. For example, Microsoft AdCenter offers the ability to serve ads based on consumer demographics, location, or daypart. Google also recently added demographic targeting along with keyword selection to AdWorks, its paid search advertising program. Richer targeting criteria increase the potential for reaching consumers with better-aimed brand advertising.

Contextual Targeting

Contextual targeting is a new concept for targeting, especially online. It places ads on web pages that have a relationship to the content of the page. For example, shampoo ads are placed in the hair care section of health and beauty sites. Financial products are placed on money sites, and hotel ads on travel sites. Well, you get the picture. Collectively, section pages within such properties, called contextual inventory, sell quickly, sometimes years in advance for prime locations.

Contextual targeting's appeal is straightforward—be seen in places where large numbers of shoppers go to catch up on events or news and look for information about a specific product category or activity like traveling or cooking. Contextual locations are like a specialized shopping district, such as those in New York City for diamonds, garments, musical instruments, theater, and restaurant supplies, or auto malls in suburban towns. Concentrating buyers and sellers allows for efficient markets and enables the sellers to understand their customers and differentiate themselves.

Besides the expected business benefits of contextual targeting, such as reaching actively shopping consumers, online advertisers value the context, the location, and the editorial environment their ads appear in. According to an eMarketer study, 43% of online advertisers cited the association of the company's brand with high-quality content as a key benefit (eMarketer 2006f). Figure 2.1 shows what online advertisers think about the benefits of contextual targeting in particular.

Obviously, the great interest in online contextual targeting stems from a belief that it is effective. Over the years, basic research studies have shown that advertising context influences ad effectiveness in offline media. A relevant context matching brand to a related advertising environment is assumed to put shoppers in receptive frames of mind, increasing the potential impact of the brand's message. Offline studies reveal that the credibility of the source in which an ad appears (think *New York Times* versus a supermarket tabloid for advertising diamond jewelry) and the fit between the editorial environment and the ad affect branding measures ranging from recall to purchase intent. Customers and shoppers are more likely to trust ad messages in reputable media that they deem are relevant to their interests and tastes.

Is the same true of online advertising? Little systematic research exists to prove the high value of contextual targeting online. Fortunately, we have some early guidance from Prem Shamdasani and colleagues (2001), who researched the question experimentally.

FIGURE 2.1   Advantages of contextual targeting.

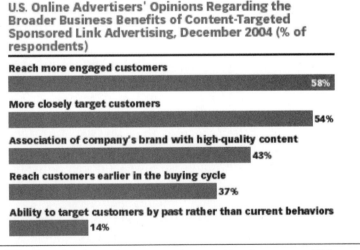

U.S. Online Advertisers' Opinions Regarding the Broader Business Benefits of Content-Targeted Sponsored Link Advertising, December 2004 (% of respondents)

Reach more engaged customers — 58%
More closely target customers — 54%
Association of company's brand with high-quality content — 43%
Reach customers earlier in the buying cycle — 37%
Ability to target customers by past rather than current behaviors — 14%

Note: n = 725 online advertisers who use or are interested in using sponsored links.
Source: JupiterResearch sponsored by Kanoodle, February 2005, data provided by eMarketer (063228).

They tested website reputation, website content, and banner ad placement for two types of products—one consumers thought of as high-involvement (car) and one as low-involvement (sports drink)—on a variety of attitudinal and branding metrics: attitude toward the ad, attitude toward the brand, intention to click, and purchase intention.

For highly involving products like cars, ad effectiveness appears to be relevance-driven: Tight coupling between the ad and web content resulted in better results on all four measures. It matters to consumers that they see car ads on car sites, or dishwasher ads on kitchen sites. Did the website's reputation play a role? Yes. When relevance existed, the halo of website credibility raised scores. But the site's reputation mattered little when the ad and content were disconnected and perceived as irrelevant.

In contrast, advertising effectiveness for low-involving products "appears to be reputation-driven." As website reputation rises, scores improve; relevance matters much less than it does for higher-involving products (Dou and Krishnamurthy 2007). In other words, it may be perfectly fine to advertise paper towels on a car site, so long as the car site is well regarded. When a site's reputation is not well established, consumers then look to relevance as a way to evaluate low-involvement brands.

This study, while preliminary, begins to suggest implications for advertising strategy. When planning contextual advertising, consider both advertising relevance and website reputation as they relate to your brand and its product type. Packaged goods marketers, for example, should strongly consider website reputation first and relevance second. More involving products, such as electronics, fashion, or household appliances, to take a few cases, may be served by a sharp focus on content relevance first, then reputation.

Behavioral Targeting

What happens when you surprise viewers by showing them ads in unexpected places for brands that might be relevant to them? That's the concept behind behavioral targeting, and interest in this targeting approach is building fast. Spending growth more than tripled from $285 million in 2003 to $925 million in 2005, and is forecast to reach $2.1 billion in 2008, according to eMarketer (2006a). Auto advertisers are early adopters.

On sites like NYTimes.com, individuals in different stages of car buying can be reached in areas that do not have a natural affinity for autos but are of interest to auto-shopping consumers based on tracking their site visiting (Meskaukas 2003).

Ad networks' cookie tracking capabilities allow them to trace the patterns of sites, clicks, and pages viewed of people visiting properties across their network. Although the tracking is anonymous—they don't know it's you specifically—the networks detect that you went to the branded site for Automaker X. Then it was on to auto research site Autobytel.com, followed by a niche site for independent music and a quick download. Before leaving this particular network, you visited a child care site for some timely advice on getting a reluctant toddler to take a nap. From these behaviors, networks deduce that you're parenting, you're interested in Automaker X products, and you're an indie music lover. You are much more than a collection of demographic values now; your web behavior has a pattern that has been quantified for targeting purposes.

Advertisers and their strategists use these profiles to serve ads that are relevant to individuals across the various sites they visit. Ads for Automaker X may be shown to you on the music site or child care site, or both. This is different from contextual targeting, where ads of the same type of content or subject appear that directly relate to a specific interest—auto ads on auto sites, music ads on music sites, baby products on child care sites.

Why the Interest in Behavioral Targeting?

Ad buys using contextual targeting can be expensive; inventory on popular sites or networks is often sold out. For example, vertical automotive ad network Jumpstart was completely sold out for 2006 by April of that year (Simpson 2006). With demand outpacing supply, advertisers pay a premium for visibility and communication to large pools of prospects who are actively shopping.

With the right audience data in hand from publishers and ad servers, behavioral targeting strategies can be executed within sites and across most ad networks to reach those potential in-market consumers. Behavioral targeting allows advertisers to create buys from run-of-site inventory and improve the cost-effectiveness of media buys by selecting and adding lower-cost properties into the mix. The industry is responding to advertiser interest. Companies such as 24/7 Real Media, Advertising.com, Revenue Science, and Tacoda Audience

Networks now specialize in behavioral targeting. In the search world, search engine services, like MSN AdCenter, will offer behavioral targeting capability, along with other targeting techniques like daypart and demographic targeting (Smith 2006a).

According to Professor Joseph Turow of the Annenberg School for Communications at the University of Pennsylvania (2006), consumers he surveyed, as part of an ongoing research program by the Annenberg Public Policy Center, are aware that advertisers "have the ability" to collect information on their web behavior (and may use that information to show them ads) and to learn more about them by purchasing additional information on them from database companies. Although consumers expressed several positives about behavioral targeting, notably seeing more relevant ads and products, their concerns run deep about advertiser integrity: Only 17% agreed with the statement "What companies know about me won't hurt me," and 79% agreed that they are "nervous about websites having information on me" (p. 162). Beyond the privacy concerns and ethical use of their personal information, Turow points out that behavioral targeting's ability to offer the same product at different prices to different consumers (usually based on their value to the company) may lead to a new form of economic discrimination, one perpetrated by marketers. As a data-driven and thoughtful critic, Turow's findings and implications for behavioral targeting raise concerns all marketers should find time to address in order to realize the future value of behavioral targeting for their brands.

Results from a study of millions of behaviorally targeted impressions across numerous product categories demonstrated that behaviorally targeted ads delivered out of context showed their power: The click-through rate was 108% higher and the conversion rate was 19% higher than in-context ads. (Conversion is an action of interest taken by a consumer.) However, "overall" does not mean uniform, and the study pointed out that click-through rates and conversion rates varied by category. In some categories, the click-through rates and conversion rates for behaviorally targeted ads were higher when the ads were shown in the same context as a behavior (such as a financial service ad targeted to a prospect who looked at but did not download a brochure or prospectus in the "business and finance" category). In some others, click-throughs and conversions were higher outside their category. For example, the behaviorally targeted ads in the "shoppers" category exhibited the highest click-through rates on "career" sites and the highest conversion rates on "female-oriented" sites, perhaps suggesting that differences exist in reaching browsers and buyers (BL Labs 2006). Advertisers should assess the performance of their ads when shown in context or when shown behaviorally as a "surprise."

Raise Awareness and Brand Knowledge: NTT DoCoMo

Japan's premier mobile communications company, NTT DoCoMo, is somewhat known in the United States, but the company wanted to raise its profile so that its products and services would be more often considered. NTT DoCoMo launched a branding campaign among its target U.S. customers, information technology (IT) and telecom business decision makers, to increase brand awareness. The firm's branding goals derived directly from its company description (NTT DoCoMo 2006):

> NTT DoCoMo is not only Japan's premier mobile communications company, but also an influential force in advancing mobile communications technology on a global scale. In addition to providing voice and data communications to millions in Japan, we create global industry standards and groundbreaking mobile services. . . . Powered by research and development and our "customer-first" philosophy, we are constantly reinventing the concept of mobile communications and pioneering cutting-edge, cost-effective services that make your life richer and more convenient.

The media buy was on the network of the *Financial Times*, FT.com, and split into a run-of-site buy (ads appear on any page within the site) and a behaviorally targeted buy. (See Table 2.1.) Per-

TABLE 2.1   Behaviorally Targeted Ads Raise Brand Attribute Scores

	DoCoMo Attribute Agreement Scores		
	Run of Site	Behaviorally Targeted	% Lift
Pioneer in field of mobile telecommunications	26.9%	49.3%	83.0%
Company with potential for growth	27.0%	45.1%	67.0%
A leader in technology	29.0%	46.0%	59.0%
Innovative mobile phone operator	29.5%	45.8%	55.0%
Reliable company	21.6%	32.7%	51.0%
Company am familiar with	22.4%	32.5%	45.0%

Source: Adapted from Revenue Science, "Case Study: NTT DoCoMo and FT.com," 2005.

haps for proprietary reasons, this case study did not report the exact behavioral targeting criteria, but we can reasonably presume that clicking on stories about mobile communications and visiting the site's "Technology" and "Companies" sections established some of the basis to select prospects. Research firm Dynamic Logic measured branding impacts after exposure, ensuring that differences resulted only from the test condition (Revenue Science 2005b). (Note to readers: You will notice throughout this chapter and sprinkled through some others that Dynamic Logic is referred to quite often. The reason is simple: Many marketing case studies we report utilized Dynamic Logic for their brand research. The ARF is neutral on research methods, and our frequent mentions do not imply an endorsement. We prefer that readers make up their own minds. Readers interested in learning more about Dynamic Logic will find a write-up in the Appendix on measurement.)

Results showed the strength of the behavioral targeting approach. Brand measures for awareness, online ad awareness, and ad recall were 41% to 78% higher than the run-of-site results. And for the key concepts about the company—such as its reliability, innovativeness, and leadership—all brand attribute scores showed gains, which ranged from 45% to 83% over the run-of-site exposed group. Masinori Goto of NTT DoCoMo summed up his experience with these words:

> The results speak for themselves. Behavioral targeting can be an effective and high-performance tool in conveying our message to the right target groups. We are very much satisfied with the outcome of this campaign.

American Airlines: Target Travel Purchase Influencer Segments More Efficiently

Like many air carriers, American Airlines looks to move more action to its website. American's online campaign targeted business travelers who made ticket purchases through an agent or who bought their own tickets. The airline further refined its target by segmenting travelers by the number of trips they took: "one or more" or "five or more" trips per year. That definition led American to select the *Wall Street Journal* Online (www.wsj.com) because its site visitors included sizable air traveler numbers. A run-of-network buy (one where ads appear anywhere on the network) was purchased, with a portion earmarked for behavioral targeting. Dynamic Logic conducted the branding study.

Compared to the run-of-network results, behavioral targeting garnered a more concentrated target audience—indexing 15% to 45% higher. Calculating the costs of the two ad buys, analysis revealed that the behavioral targeting approach for the frequent business traveler group was 32% less expensive than the run-of-network approach, and 18% less expensive for the business traveler group with a minimum of one trip per year.

Convert Shoppers Who Are Researching a Purchase: Vonage

Internet phone company Vonage Marketing, Inc. offers consumers the ability to make low-cost phone calls using Voice over Internet Protocol (VoIP) technology. Vonage and other groundbreaking companies are establishing this new service, and operate in a very competitive marketplace, similar to the early days of cell phones. With the value proposition of this market, consumers who are interested go to Vonage and competitor sites to learn about the service and compare features and pricing. Obviously, the key to growth is converting those visitor-researchers into customers. Over 14 weeks of an online campaign, Vonage ran the first seven weeks using online buys; for the second seven weeks it switched to a behavioral targeting campaign. Results showed that the number of conversions per week increased from an average of roughly 800 to about 1,100, with the biggest jump at the switch-over in targeting approaches; the conversion rate more than doubled (Advertising.com 2005).

Capture Sales from Website Visitors Who Abandoned a Purchase: Lane Bryant

Women's clothing retailer Lane Bryant, like many companies, wants to reduce the number of online shopping cart abandonments, which result when people start a checkout process but don't complete the transaction. By remarketing—targeting people who shopped but didn't buy—Lane Bryant aimed to convert abandoned shoppers into customers. Using behavioral targeting, Lane Bryant served ads offering free shipping on purchases of $50 or more as an incentive. The tactic was successful: Revenue increased by 408% over the goal and the cost-per-sale goal was reduced 85% (Advertising.com 2005).

Geographic Targeting

National advertising gives 100% coverage, but searches for local products and services claim 27% of all searches. Geotargeting, serving ads to particular geographic areas, is a powerful technique for increasing the likelihood that customers see your ads and find them relevant.

The most precise geotargeting uses site or customer registration databases and ties that data back to market descriptors—such as designated market area (DMA), area codes, time zones, or Global Positioning System (GPS) coordinates, for example—or asks that visitors type in a country, state, city, or zip code to specify a location. Internet protocol (IP) addresses provide some geotargeting capability, but their precision varies and they have limited usefulness.

A new addressing scheme is important not only to better handle domestic U.S. traffic, but also to accommodate international visits. While most traffic to U.S. ad networks originates domestically, visitors from Canada and other countries make up about 15% of the total volume—a number likely to increase as internet adoption rises worldwide. Adopting country targeting allows website operators to tailor pages to Canadian or foreign visitors and address any location, pricing, or language issues (Posman 2001). Travel Alberta, for example, fine-tuned its marketing campaign based on visitors' locations that it captured through site registrations. Multiple-currency solution provider E4X Inc. offers its e-commerce customers the ability to provide online pricing in the customers' currency (Carton 2003; Digital Element 2006a). In Sean Carton's words:

> The Web *is* a global medium, but it's becoming increasingly important to think about it as a local medium, too. By adding geolocation and geotargeting to your Web strategy, you can offer higher value to customers and better user experience. These days, those intangibles can provide the competitive advantage.

Because geotargeted buys incur additional expense to set up the buy, geotargeting premiums range from 25% to 35%, depending on the complexity of the target market. Is it worth it? By concentrating reach to areas marketers specify, geotargeting is more efficient and effective. Overall, "geotargeted [advertising] has been shown to produce better click-through rates and costs-per-conversions" than broad un-targeted campaigns (Springs 2006).

Geotargeting Works Best to Drive Business to Local Outlets

Hotels, car rental companies, electronics retailers, mass merchants, and others drive business from their websites to local outlets with geotargeting. Circuit City, Wal-Mart, and Sports Authority provide shoppers the convenience of buying online and picking up at a nearby bricks-and-mortar store, which not only saves consumers shipping costs but can lead to new sales inside the store as shoppers buy accessories or other items. Retailers like CompUSA furnish online shoppers with inventory levels at specific stores to prompt customers to visit or select shipping when a product is not in stock or the store visit is inconvenient.

Looking to increase sales at local dealerships, a premier luxury automaker (unnamed) executed a strategy of directing prospects to dealer websites, and then having them inquire or request information or arrange online for test-drives. This advertiser wanted relevant ads displayed only to people in about 30 carefully selected locations. Working with data mining company [x+1], Inc. (then called Poindexter Systems), which profiled the brand's current customers, and with geotargeting firm Digital Element, ads were served to prospects by zip code or other local market criteria, and customized to include local dealer branding and a call to action for the test-drive. Running for six months, this geotargeted campaign generated 42,000 click-throughs, and 5,000 test-drives. Over 7% of postclick actions led to sales inquiries (Digital Element 2006b).

Local, Directory, and Classified Online Advertising

Local advertisers want to brand and have people in the market "convert," that is, take an action of interest, such as sign up for a newsletter, rent a car, or respond to a job posting. When one of the authors needed to hire a wildlife service to remove some overwintering squirrels, he consulted the Yellow Pages to find a few vendors to call (the conversion action) that were nearby, licensed, and humane, and gave the impression of trustworthiness (branding). Can online local advertising work the same way?

The Interactive Advertising Bureau (IAB) took up the question. They partnered with leading panel research company comScore, publishers, and marketers. They studied conversion, branding, and return on investment (ROI) for very specific tasks: rental car sales through Yahoo! Local, job applications for a Big Four accounting firm and a major international bank through CareerBuilder.com, six categories of local businesses through Verizon SuperPages.com, and leads for car dealers on Cars.com. Seldom do we have a group of case studies that span popular local advertising categories and share a common research methodology (comScore 2006; IAB 2006a).

Let's review the highlights.

Targeting local users makes sense; many potential customers are online looking for information. In any one month in 2005 roughly 74% unique internet visitors used directories, 29% used career verticals, and 32% used auto sites. Like compound interest, value increases over time. Six months later, each site type accumulated a larger audience, enabling advertisers to reach more consumers. Directories led the way at 92%, followed by careers at 51% and autos at 65%. That's a lot of virtual foot traffic and passersby.

Many of those shoppers close deals the old-fashioned way through phone calls, email, or snail mail. Let's look at a few examples. Among Ford Rent-A-Car rentals, 40% of the deals completed offline. On Verizon SuperPages.com overall, 73% of conversions occurred offline. Across specific categories—retail, real estate, hospitality, automotive, and professional services—offline conversion rates ranged from 50% to over 100% higher than online conversions. On CareerBuilder.com, 30% of job applications were offline.

These results reveal a very important point: People who shop online often purchase offline. And while companies would like to move more business transactions online for cost-efficiency, company availability, and related reasons, people still want to speak or communicate directly with advertisers to learn about the service, schedule an appointment, and feel good about the purchase.

Daypart Targeting

Radio introduced the idea of daypart targeting—a widely practiced targeting approach for decades. Radio's morning drive, midday, and evening drive reach most listeners when they're driving to work or

home from work, or during lunch break. Television's myriad dayparts span the full day, from early morning to prime time to late
night. Dayparts vary by medium. Television prime time runs from 8
P.M. to 11 P.M., while radio prime time is the morning and afternoon
drive times.

Each daypart has unique audience size, viewer characteristics,
and product category affinities that advertisers use to target their advertising messages. On television, for example, syndicated talk shows
like *Ellen*, game shows like *The Price Is Right*, and soaps like *General
Hospital* typify the TV daytime daypart, generally targeting consumer
packaged goods advertising to women aged 25 to 54 with a high
school education. The core notion of daypart targeting is timeliness
and cost-efficiency—exposing your message to large numbers of the
target market at the right time. Now think of advertising doughnuts,
floor cleaners, vacations, luxury cars, or beer. Which part of the day
would you choose?

Consumers Use Media Differently Throughout the Day

Media consumption is not monolithic; people choose and use media
throughout the day. Media seemingly, and seamlessly, hand off their
audiences from one to another. The Online Publishers Association
(OPA), with research partner Millward Brown IntelliQuest (MBIQ),
studied patterns of internet usage and traditional media use by sur-
veying consumers who went online the previous day at their workplace (at-work users) and those who did not (non–work users).
Because the internet is frequently used at work for both business and
personal reasons, their study paints a full portrait of consumer media
use of online and traditional media.

Media consumption patterns overall show that at-work online
audiences start their day catching up on news and events. Use ta-
pers off throughout the day as work requires, builds again during
dinner and prime time hours, and then declines as people go to
sleep. That makes sense, doesn't it? Workday rhythms shape online
consumption.

Workers use the internet throughout the workday at higher levels than the other media, and often exclusively. It has become a great
at-work vehicle for reaching executives and white-collar audiences.
Internet usage starts slightly above television in the morning daypart,
but then shoots up to 73% during the first half of the business day as

folks log in to visit sites or prepare for meetings. Afternoon usage exhibits a slight decline, and then drops steadily as people leave work (one-third of internet users can only be reached at work), bottoming out at dinnertime (TV and radio prevail then). Internet usage then spikes in TV prime time, more than doubling to 49%, below television but higher than radio, newspapers, and magazines. The type of usage changes, as people usually go online for shopping and entertainment at that time (OPA 2003a).

Customer Acquisition through Daypart Targeting: Budweiser

Let's look at an online campaign for Budweiser that aimed to create new customers for the popular brand (Porres 2003). (See Figure 2.2.) Budweiser targeted affluent, at-work male professionals and, keeping lifestyle firmly in mind, brewed a daypart strategy. Understanding daytime daypart characteristics, Anheuser Busch tapped CBS MarketWatch, a news and information site that, like its content category, overindexes for its target group. The ads were served on Friday afternoons (near the end of the daytime daypart) when guys are thinking of packing up and relaxing with a beer or two.

FIGURE 2.2 Budweiser advertising on CBS MarketWatch filled the glass in this rich media skyscraper ad on Friday afternoons for two years running.

Source: Joseph Jaffe, "Targeting by Immediacy," iMedia Connection, March 3, 2003.

Budweiser used sophisticated and compelling rich media ads. One showed a transparent Budweiser bottle rolling across the screen that then ushered the viewer to the Budweiser site. A second ad really nailed the brand attributes of "fresh, clear, crisp" by showing an animated Budweiser bottle (in a banner) filling up a glass (skyscraper ad) below it.

Daypart Targeting to Generate Demand: Columbia TriStar *Hollow Man*

"Think you're alone? Think again." That haunting tagline from science fiction movie *Hollow Man* resonates even today, more than five years after its theatrical debut. For the DVD release, Columbia TriStar Home Entertainment faced a challenging marketing situation: The film fell short at the box office, so Columbia TriStar was under pressure to generate compensating revenue from DVD and video sales. Compounding matters, the home releases occurred after the holiday sales period and competitive films, including the popular *Gladiator*, crowded the field.

Columbia TriStar and media buying agency Universal McCann joined for a campaign designed to stimulate *Hollow Man* sales among its target market: young, tech-savvy, entertainment-oriented men likely to purchase DVDs and videos.

Their goals: reach as many likely buyers as quickly as possible, raise awareness, and stimulate purchase intention. To do that, Universal McCann adapted a tried-and-true television technique to the online venue, the roadblock. (Roadblocks stop consumers in their tracks by showing viewers one ad at roughly the same time across a number of outlets. Even when viewers click their remotes to see what else is on another channel, exposure occurs there as well, and advertisers thereby increase the likelihood that their target audience sees the ad.)

Keenly understanding internet daypart audiences and their customers' likely buying behavior, the *Hollow Man* campaign bought media on top portals, entertainment properties, and sci-fi sites during the lunch hour and prime time on one Friday, when decisions for the weekend are often made.

The approach worked. According to Universal McCann, "several of [parent company] Sony's online vendors reported huge sales spikes, including one vendor that reported a 25 percent sales increase during the time the campaign was live." "In addition, the DVD debuted in the number one position for sales and remained in the Top-Twenty Chart for three months" (Jaffe 2003a).

KFC Popcorn Chicken: Daypart Targeting to Support New Product Rollout

Satisfied with the test market results for Popcorn Chicken, KFC decided to promote a national rollout. How do you get people at work to try your product, a new product, when they're hungry and looking to go out? KFC decided the best approach was to promote Popcorn Chicken with a free trial offer coupon and make an event of it by limiting the promotion to just one day. (See Figure 2.3.)

KFC delivered ads to the at-work audience during lunch hours, 11 A.M. to 2 P.M., rolling the campaign across each time zone. Ads appeared in banners and rectangles on "top web sites" and on MSN

FIGURE 2.3 The KFC Popcorn Chicken ad targeted to the at-work audience during the daytime daypart. The promotion rolled across time zones to match lunch hours across the United States.

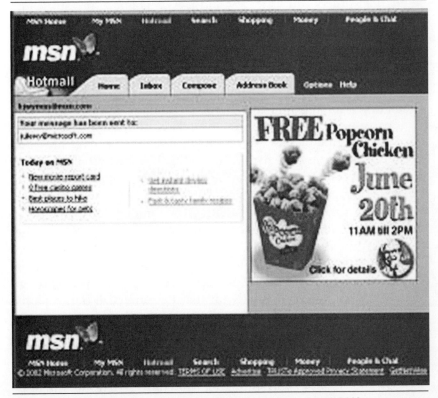

Source: Joseph Jaffe, "Targeting by Immediacy," iMedia Connection, March 3, 2003.

properties like MSN Messenger, Hotmail, and Calendar sections to extend reach. A click on the ad transferred viewers to the KFC site, where they could print the coupon and learn more about the product through branding messages. KFC's appetite for results was satisfied: Over the 12-hour period the promotion ran, 120 million impressions were served; 345,000 clicks were recorded on the home page (a record then); and, when it came to sales, "the Internet accounted for 2.6 tracked awareness and decision-to-purchase for the free sample promotion" (Jaffe 2003b).

Affinity Targeting

We all know there are numbers of sites for any particular interest, whether it's cars, planes, celebrities, social networking, independent films, music, soccer, or stamp collecting. When someone likes one site better than others in a category and feels a connection with it—an affinity—does it matter? Yes it does, and in ways important to targeting advertising, according to the Online Publishers Association Audience Affinity Study (OPA 2002a).

OPA, with research partners comScore Networks and Millward Brown IntelliQuest (MBIQ), studied the webwide behavior of a sample recruited from comScore's opt-in panel. These people gave comScore their explicit permission to track their every click. Millward Brown IntelliQuest surveyed attitudes toward websites and web advertising, and predisposition to buy branded products. From the responses MBIQ created an "Affinity Index" comprised of three correlated measures: site visitors' "likelihood to recommend" a particular site, their "satisfaction with [its] content," and whether a site was bookmarked by users and placed in the "favorites" section of their browsers.

MBIQ also created an affinity gauge with high, medium, and low levels. The key finding: Websites attract loyal visitors. Fifty-one percent of visitors displayed high affinity for the sites on which they took the survey. Forty percent exhibited medium affinity. And the low-affinity group? Just 9%.

High-affinity visitors distinguish themselves in a variety of important ways.

They spend more time at the site. One-third spend more than 60 minutes per month. That's not a self-reported figure; it's based on actual measured usage.

They're more favorable to the sites. On all attitudinal statements, there is a clear pattern of increasing favorability from low affinity to high affinity. Especially, high-affinity visitors are more likely to view sites as high in quality, relevance, content freshness, and features, and informative for researching purchases. Moreover, they perceive the sites as less cluttered.

They're more favorable to advertising. High-affinity visitors agree that what are advertised are relevant, respected, quality products and services. (See Figure 2.4.) They're interested, and therefore more likely to notice and read ads and to agree that "ads interfere less." According to an OPA study (2003c), they demonstrate greater aided and unaided brand awareness as well as message association. All of these factors finally result in greater purchase/behavior intent,

FIGURE 2.4 Consumers are more likely to view advertising positively on sites they feel positively about.

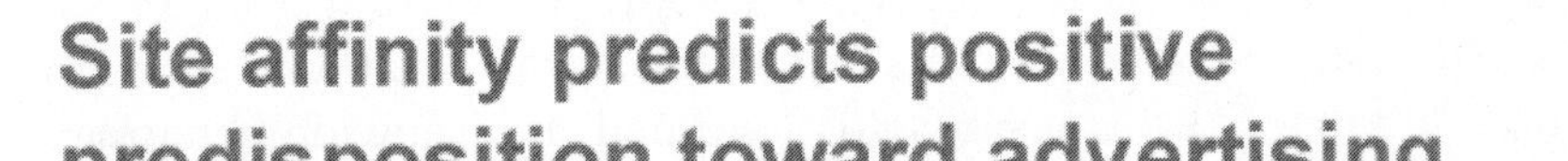

Site affinity predicts positive predisposition toward advertising

ATTITUDES TOWARD ADVERTISING ON SITE	AFFINITY (Top two box agreement)		
	Low (%)	Medium (%)	High (%)
High-quality products/services advertised	36	66	82
Ads interfere less	31	59	75
More respected brands	25	53	69
Brands are more relevant	22	48	68
Read the ads	30	49	63
Notice the ads	25	42	55
More ads than other sites*	41	43	40

*The only statement without significant differences among the three cells.

Source: Online Publishers Association, "The Impact of Audience Affinity on Advertising Performance," 2003.

and lend support to the findings we discussed earlier on the importance of relevance and website reputation.

Affinity Targeting to Acquire Customers: *Queer as Folk*

Showtime Networks Inc.'s *Queer as Folk* depicted the lives of a group of gay men and women living in Pittsburgh who "are focused on their relationships, careers, loves, and ambitions." This very character-rich show ran for five seasons (Queer as Folk 2006).

After the first season, Showtime knew it had good buzz and potential for a breakthrough show. Jordan Berman, Showtime's online marketing manager, looked to build buzz among the program's core gay audience by advertising on sites showing a strong affinity for the show. Plugging *Queer as Folk* into a search engine, Berman located hundreds of sites created by the show's fans that focused on the program, its individual actors, the show's music, and every other aspect. Update: Program affinity is enduring. Repeating the search while writing returned pages upon pages of results.

Showtime created a campaign that added a bit of anticipation and an event quality to the second season premiere. It used a countdown ticker showing the time remaining to the exact date, day, hour, and minute of the program's airing. (See Figure 2.5.) It performed a branding function, too. When clicked, it sent viewers to the show's site, where they could learn more about the show, order products, use message boards, buy ring tones, and enter sweepstakes entries for a Subaru car. Showtime arranged to have the ticker incorporated into 650 of the fan sites, some well known, some obscure, until the premiere. Showtime also used an extensive offline campaign to build audience among the broader population.

Buzz created by the campaign resulted in the most heavily watched episode in Showtime's 25-year history. More than one million people saw the countdown ticker. On direct response measures, 10,000 clicked on the ticker and 58,000 entered the sweepstakes (Jaffe 2003b).

Affinity Targeting for Customer Retention: Pepperidge Farm Milano Moments

Pepperidge Farm looked to deepen relationships with its core customers for the Milano brand (Jaffe 2003b). The brand already had a

FIGURE 2.5 The *Queer as Folk* countdown campaign used affinity targeting to successfully market the program.

Source: Joseph Jaffe, "The Potential of Affinity Marketing," iMedia Connection, March 24, 2003.

community-based site, but Pepperidge Farm's strategy was to go deeper, providing customers with the opportunity to engage with the brand and share with one another. They created a "Milano Moments" minisite with "sweepstakes, quizzes, screen savers, a weekly email, a viral component, as well as an invitation to women (among other activities) to share their private Milano indulgences with each other."

Researched by Dynamic Logic for this campaign, the results speak strongly. The measure of future sales, purchase intent, increased 29%. For comparison, Dynamic Logic MarketNorms average banner impacts range from 1% to 5% lift on all measures.

A powerful targeting tool, affinity marketing differs from some other targeting approaches in its requirements for propriety and trust. Showtime's Jordan Berman (quoted in Jaffe 2003b), advises marketers:

> There's a responsibility factor that comes into play when a brand reaches out to an affinity group. The interactivity of the Web requires brands to maintain a dialogue with consumers, especially when the brand has extended a line of communication. It takes time and energy to maintain that dialogue.

Purchase-Based Category Targeting

Purchase-based targeting is one of the newer targeting approaches made possible by online tracking of consumer behavior and integrating that information with related data. Purchase-based targeting serves ads to web surfers whose online personas suggest that they are in a brand's target market. This targeting approach begins with a careful study of a brand's segments and then identifies characteristic qualities they exhibit. Then, marketers look for a distinctive fingerprint of online behaviors that predict that characteristic. Marketers might want to target the heavy half of category buyers or brand-loyal consumers, for example. "Heavy shaving gel users," ACNielsen researchers explain, "spend a great deal of time at sports sites, online auction sites, and automotive sites, but spend very little time at bulletin board sites. Low-carb product users spend more time at health and wellness sites" (Khandelwal et al. 2004).

Purchase-based targeting is claimed to be more efficient than random targeting, by about 70% with less waste. But does this additional precision really matter? To find out, ACNielsen's Manjima Khandelwal and colleagues tested the branding and sales impacts of purchase-based targeted advertising for a newly launched brand extension for a personal care product.

Purchase-Based Targeting for Branding and Sales: Personal Care Product

Just how do brands find the fingerprints that predict which consumers are in the target group? For a new personal care product, that was accomplished by merging two databases, one of online user behavior, the second from customer purchase data. In this case, Yahoo!'s database was overlaid with ACNielsen's opt-in panel called HomeScan to spot matches. Finding about 1,000 matches, the research team mined for behavior patterns they could use for targeting.

The brand's introductory media plan called for online and television advertising for two months, which presents the opportunity to learn not only which branding measures increased, but also the relative performance of purchase-based targeting online versus on TV. The researchers created exposed and matched control groups, with the exposed groups seeing brand ads and the control groups an unrelated ad. Branding results showed that web and TV advertising, by themselves, worked equally well, lifting awareness, familiarity, and purchase intent about the same 25% over the control group. But combining web and TV advertising doubled the lift to about 50%. Purchase-targeted online buys were as effective as TV for branding, but how about sales?

Virtually all consumer packaged goods are sold through offline retailers. Gauging sales impacts and relating them to advertising exposure requires creating a control panel comparable to the exposed group and accounting for all influences on purchases like coupons or promotions. The researchers tracked panel purchases one purchase cycle after the introductory advertising ran its course. Advertising lifted sales volume by 25% (the same rate as the branding improvements).

Purchase-based targeting appears to be promising for its relevance and effectiveness. We need to keep in mind that it demands resources. Unlike some of the other targeting technologies, which can select or omit consumers with check boxes or standard business rules, this one is tailored like a bespoke suit. In order to execute great campaigns, brands need high-quality data and analysts to profile their customers, find their unique characteristics, and then identify repeatable online behaviors for targeting. That's a lot to ask for and may not be appropriate for every brand. For the right brand and right set of marketing objectives, purchase-based targeting may be the right way to go.

Key Considerations in Online Targeting

Know the Data You Use to Make Targeting Decisions

The best targeting strategy means little if the underlying data are weak. A number of factors may compromise data integrity. Gaps exist due to limited information, as we mentioned regarding geotargeting. Accurate tracking usage for individuals can be hard to collect when computer sharing occurs in homes, at work, or in public spaces like internet cafes and libraries. How can click-stream analysis differentiate children from their parents or siblings, or users from roommates, co-workers, or other library patrons? Who's the user? Adware and spyware protection programs routinely remove tracking cookies, and pop-up blockers are included in browsers and search company toolbars. Reach and frequency projections from syndicated research and actual campaign delivery vary from one to another (Cohen 2003).

The online data industry knows about these issues and diligently works to resolve them. DoubleClick, for example, commissioned studies by three media research companies to develop and share methodologies for improving postcampaign reports on target demographics (Bruner and Koegel 2005). Advertisers learned to be eternally vigilant about offline media research and demand quality and accountability. The same needs to be true for online research. The quality of your online targeting and marketing depends on it.

Looking beyond data collection and data integrity, the new targeting capabilities available make it possible to overdefine your market. It's possible, for example, to serve your ad only to people who have been to your site three times during the early news hours who clicked on it. In most cases, you wouldn't do that (would you?), but we want to make the point that emphasis on too much precision can be a risk. You may be advertising to your most responsive customers, but they may represent only a small slice of your customer base. Because ad networks often charge premiums for such precision, those relatively few customers or prospects will be expensive to reach and may not generate sufficient revenue to achieve business goals.

Winning Plays

- A primary benefit of online advertising is the ability to locate *precise* groups of consumers who are current customers or attractive prospects for your brand. Often successful targeting strategies are those that combine several classic methods of selecting a profitable audience. It might be geographic markets combined with purchase patterns for a regional retailer; or it could be a demographic segment such as male office workers and the lunchtime daypart for a fast-food chain.

- Targeting strategies must support your marketing objective. We've seen various targeting approaches work toward achieving branding goals, prompting direct response actions, and stimulating offline sales. These targeting approaches tied to key objectives included customer acquisition (*Hollow Man*), new product introduction (KFC Popcorn Chicken), increasing favorability and purchase intention (Budweiser), and customer retention (Pepperidge Farm Milano).

- Each targeting approach provides marketers with different consumer lenses. Demographic targeting defines customers in terms of personal characteristics (their age, gender, and income) and therefore is best for broad usage categories. Contextual targeting looks for shoppers with interest in a category or subject matter related to your brand. Behavioral targeting describes online usage patterns of potential buyers. Daypart targeting is life- and work-style oriented. Geographic targeting overlays customer location data onto products and services categories and is particularly valuable for local business objectives. Affinity targeting reaches people where they congregate around shared interests. And purchase-based targeting looks to predict your best prospects based on their online behaviors.

- The most popular way to target with online advertising is to select a "good fit" content site (or microsite) that matches the subject of your product or service, such as a site on fishing and your desire to sell rods and tackle, and ones with good reputations from your consumers' perspective. This targeting strategy has demonstrated that not only does it find interested and motivated customers, but the engagement in the content of the site, or its halo effect, enhances the engagement in the specific brand advertising.

- A much newer targeting approach, unique to the internet, is based on tracking internet site behavior, via a cookie, of an attractive customer and placing your ad in a highly visited site by that customer (which may have content unrelated to the product/

service category). For example, a prospective car buyer may often visit a weather site. Thus, the weather site offers an excellent targeting opportunity to reach that prospective car buyer. The engagement in the specific ad often occurs because it is the only car ad on the site and benefits from the surprise.

- Success in generating growth via targeting involves linking the targeting approach to the overall marketing goal. Simply selecting an interesting targeting approach without linking to the marketing goal will lower the chances of sales success. Daypart and behavioral targeting, for example, are good for expanding brand awareness when that is your primary marketing goal. If your goal is to generate good-quality leads for the brand, contextual and demographic or category usage profile combinations often work best. And if your goal is to remarket to customers, behavioral targeting is a good candidate. We would like to stress that these are not hard-and-fast rules, but serve as examples for matching targeting strategy to marketing objectives. Marketers should find the best fit for their brands.

The key is that the more information you have on customers or potential customers, the more innovative, cost-effective, and successful your targeting strategies can be.

CHAPTER 3

Online Advertising Reach and Frequency Concepts

"How many ads should I show my prospects to achieve the effect I want?" For over a half-century advertisers have asked this question and researchers have studied it. You can appreciate the interest—how many people you reach and the number of times you expose your ad to them costs money. Underexpose your ad and you risk underperformance. Overexpose an ad and you may be overpaying for performance. Effectiveness does not improve directly as the number of exposures increases. According to a common industry rule of thumb, most brand objectives reach diminishing returns somewhere between 4 and 10 exposures to an individual. For direct response measures, recent thinking places frequency at lower levels.

Planning online advertising campaigns that achieve impression delivery in ranges brands specify requires marketers to adroitly balance target market reach and frequency of message. Doing so is one of the fundamental practices in advertising, both online and offline. In this chapter, we focus on the strategic aspects of online reach and frequency.

While new thoughts on reach and frequency are under way, the practical reality is that reach and frequency concepts and planning practices are firmly ingrained in online advertising today.

Online Reach and Frequency Measures

Here is a list defining commonly used concepts and terms that will help you navigate through this chapter and the literature in general (comScore 2003).

Percent reach The percentage of individuals who visited a particular website among the total number of individuals using the web during a given time period.

Planned impressions The number of impressions in the media buy for the particular site during a given time period. This is reported at the total site level.

Target impressions The number of impressions in the media buy served to a particular target audience at that site. This number is derived from the total pages viewed at the site by the target audience as a percentage of total pages viewable at the site.

Percent planned/target impressions Number that shows the "demo conversion factor" for each entity (i.e., the factor used to convert planned impressions to target impressions).

Frequency The number of ads the average person could be exposed to in a given time period.

Unique visitors (UVs) delivered The number of people in the target audience who will have the opportunity to see an ad at least once.

Percent reach delivered The percentage of the target audience who will have the opportunity to see the online advertisement at least once.

Average frequency The number of ads the average person in the target audience is exposed to in a given time period.

Strategies for Managing Online Reach and Frequency

Websites' abilities to reach consumer audiences vary. Some, like MSN or Yahoo! email sites, generate high reach quickly, while others with a narrower, more specialized focus, like Bicycling.com, may reach a sizable audience of interest to certain advertisers (of bikes and gear, for example), but take longer to reach all of them. Reasons why they vary have to do with consumer behavior, consumer interest, website content, and website popularity.

DoubleClick, a major web advertising infrastructure company, serves ads and provides media professionals with tools to manage most aspects of online advertising—ad targeting, ad serving, and monitoring and analyzing campaigns. In a joint study with online audience measurement firm comScore Media Metrix (both firms are profiled in the Appendix on measurement), Lynn Bolger and Marie Pauline Mörn analyzed their audience data to explain website reach from a number of angles: light versus heavy internet users; the composition of website visitors; and usage patterns (the time of day or day of the week when visitors frequent a website or the portions of a site that see more traffic than others). These different lenses on online audience reach have valuable implications for media planning and strategy (Bolger and Mörn 2004). (When it comes to online advertising, our interest is in regular users of the internet and viable prospects in our category who can purchase our brand. The best way to think of reach is to focus on internet users, who are about 70% of the total population).

Build Reach by Balancing Heavy and Light Website Users

Bolger and Mörn selected "page views" for their measure of internet consumption. Looking first at viewership, they categorized internet users into three groups by the number of days they spent online per month: heavy users (more than 19 days, 39%), medium users (11 to 19 days, 25%), and light users (under 11 days, 36%). They found viewership correlates with page viewing. Heavy users accounted for 73 percent of all page views, while light users tallied just 6 percent.

This disparity presents an advertising challenge most marketers face, which is to "reach effectively that third of the audience generating only 6% of all pages, while avoiding having heavy users consume ad impressions at disproportionately high frequencies" (Bruner and Gluck 2006). The graph in Figure 3.1 illustrates this challenge quite well. After about four exposures reach drops and ad impressions climb: Fewer people are seeing more ads more often.

Another way of visualizing this issue of heavy viewers dominating page views and advertising impressions is by looking at a specific site. Using a standard approach that divides the audience into five equal groups (a quintile analysis), Steve Coffey and Mainak Mazumdar (2002) looked at the site traffic (page requests) each fifth viewed ("consumed" in media jargon). (See Figure 3.2.) Forty percent of the

FIGURE 3.1   Heavy internet users account for a disproportionate number of advertising impressions. Reaching lighter users requires astutely managing reach and frequency.

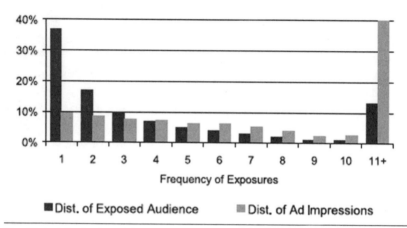

Online Ad Campaign Frequency Distribution by Audience and Impressions

Note: Typical distribution of frequency, DoubleClick client.

Source: Rick Bruner and Marissa Gluck, "Best Practices for Optimizing Web Advertising Effectiveness," DoubleClick, 2006.

site's visitors claimed 95% of the pages and, by extension, 95% of the ads. The remaining 60% viewed only 5% of the pages and the ads. Without balancing light and heavy viewers, the potential to waste advertising is very present and real.

Bolger and Mörn, however, make a practical, nuanced observation: "Light internet users are heavy users on certain sites" (2004). Usage isn't monolithic, which makes sense. Most people do what they enjoy or are interested in most often, and other things, like looking up a recipe for a dinner party, when they can or need to do so.

The key implication: To increase reach against lighter users, spread the media buy across several properties. Don't put all your eggs in one basket site. Back in 2002, the research firm then known as Jupiter Media Metrix demonstrated that an ad campaign of four million impressions could reach an audience at least a third larger when spread evenly over three sites as opposed to concentrating the same-sized buy on a single site (comScore 2002a).

FIGURE 3.2 A small number of unique visitors often account for the bulk of the traffic on a single site or section of a site. In this case the heaviest 20% of visitors account for 86% of the pages and ads served. For this reason, advertisers usually reach their consumers across several sites.

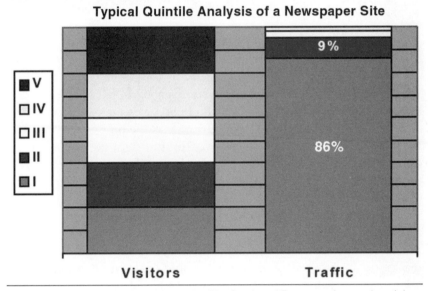

Source: Steve Coffey and Mainak Mazumdar, "The Reach and Frequency Approach to Advertising Planning on the Internet," ESOMAR Week of Conferences, 2002.

Buying ad space on sites is both art and science, as most experienced media planners know. Space buys can take on all sorts of variations—continuous, pulsed, daypart, demographic, psychographic, roadblocks, or usage based, to name a few. One promising strategy that can guide buying is to identify sites that attract light internet users where they're likely to be heavier viewers who represent a significant number of prospects for your brand.

We can find those sites by indexing page view percentage over audience percentage. On MSN Money, for example, light users comprise 39% of the total audience but 75% of all page views, an index of 199. Calculating this index for other popular sites indicates that CNN.com home page (132), MSN WomenCentral (166), Autobytel.com (152), and Epicurious.com (127) show themselves to be attractive sites for reaching lighter users who consume a disproportionate number of pages and ads (Bolger and Mörn 2004).

Keep in mind that not all competing sites in a category can

substitute for one another vis-à-vis lighter users. Although the focus may be similar, each site has its unique personality that influences consumer behavior and site use. Given the dynamics of online advertising, sites can be leaders and followers, hot or cold, and can switch places quickly. Continually monitoring the light user index is good practice.

Build Reach by Selecting Websites That Concentrate Brand Target Audiences

Deftly balancing the lighter and heavier usage groups is one consideration in building effective reach. Matching a website's audience characteristics to those of your target customer is the best way to improve the probability of an ad being viewed by the right person. Websites differ. The large portals draw broadly from all parts of the internet population, while more specialized sites draw narrower segments or concentrate exclusively on one or two segments.

Advertisers wishing to reach sports, movie, and gaming enthusiasts would more likely find their principal target of males aged 18 to 34 on sites whose content attracts and aggregates them. That group makes up 25 percent or more of the audience on sites like ESPN, eBay Motors, Yahoo! Sports, WindowsMedia, Musicmatch.com, and IMDB.com.

Similarly, high-income households (yearly household income above $100,000) are overrepresented on personal finance sites and news sites (CBS MarketWatch, CNN.com home page, NYTimes.com home page), as you might expect. But they also are overrepresented on sports and entertainment sites (SI.com, About Health and Fitness, and E!Online). Look for all the types of sites that attract a brand's customers; don't be lulled into thinking that targeted reach limits the variety of sites to advertise on.

Using Targeted Reach and Frequency for Branding: Florida Department of Citrus

Orange juice is big business in Florida; the industry generates about $9 billion through growing and processing fruit and selling finished products. The Florida Department of Citrus (FDOC) keeps that industry healthy through a variety of initiatives, one main one being to increase consumer demand for orange juice. We're concerned with their "best start under the sun" campaign targeted to mothers with kids at home.

Here's how the FDOC explained its goals: "We want moms to understand that we can identify with the challenges they face in getting the family up and moving each morning," said Michelle Chandler, deputy director of marketing and public relations for the FDOC. "We're reminding moms that a glass of delicious Florida orange juice is an easy way to help get the whole family off to the best start under the sun" (quoted in Richards Group 2006).

As part of a national $20 million campaign, the FDOC earmarked some budget for an online rich media campaign that had branding objectives as well as a usability one—to make the experience complete and not send recipients to a different website.

FDOC agency The Richards Group selected Eyeblaster, a rich media solutions vendor, to create the ads and add interactivity to them that offered additional information like orange juice factoids, recipes, and such (we cover this more fully in Chapter 5 on display advertising). The media buy was placed on sites with concentrations of the campaign's target audience, mothers 25 to 44 with school-age children at home. That included sites such as those of American Greetings, *Better Homes and Gardens*, iVillage, *Ladies' Home Journal*, and Parents.com. Planners set the advertising frequency at four-plus exposures for a five-month flight.

The campaign's rich media ad units included page takeovers and floating ads that simulated pouring juice into a glass and other eye-catching visuals. And it was kept user-friendly; pop-ups providing facts or other elements were easily dismissed with a close button (Eyeblaster 2002; see Figure 3.3).

Gauging branding success came from a Dynamic Logic study (we review Dynamic Logic's research approach in the Appendix on measurement), and real-time data on consumer interactions came from ad network DoubleClick and from Eyeblaster. The campaign generated a click-through rate of nearly 12% overall, with some sites ranging as high as 19%. That click-through performance implied branding success. Dynamic Logic's branding research demonstrated significant increases in message association, brand favorability, and purchase intent, which exceeded its online advertising norms by nearly 80%. These impressive results demonstrate that selecting websites based on audience composition enabled the FDOC to reach the

FIGURE 3.3   The Florida Department of Citrus served ads across a variety of sites with concentrations of its target market and used compelling rich media ads to dramatize benefits. The campaign resulted in significant branding improvements.

Source: Eyeblaster, "Florida Orange Juice, the Best Start under the Sun: Case Study," presented at iMedia Summit, May 2002.

right audience on sites with the right message and with engaging advertising enhanced with rich media.

As we have seen, audience composition is an important factor when reaching target consumers. The next question we can ask is: Can we enhance our understanding of a site's audience and its composition for a particular brand and use that knowledge to target and reach consumers better? Media researcher Erwin Ephron makes a compelling point that is applicable to our question. Writing about television programs, he argues that demography alone provides insight into audience composition, but not much about the program's ability to select and concentrate people exhibiting a particular interest, such as golfing or movie-going (Ephron 2005). For that, he describes a method for calculating added value for a specific television program. Using data from MRI, a source that measures both television ratings and people's activities, he indexes the program user rating among, say, male 18-to-34-year-old golfers compared to all males aged 18 to 34. An index greater than 100 indicates selectivity of the target group. Higher numbers mean greater concentrations. By comparing programs in this way, Ephron contends, we can learn which programs attract target customers better than others and therefore have greater value to a specific advertiser.

Although Ephron's focus was on television programs and using specific data sets, the concept of indexing for target audience selectivity is very transferable to online advertising and can add dimension to the light user index we described earlier. Advances being made in online audience research, like panel data, and the expansion of media covered in usage studies mean that these types of indexes can be computed and used to guide media planning and buying. They can factor into answering the thorny questions advertisers face like "Is the premium charged for this property going to help us reach our target more effectively?"

Pay Attention to Website Traffic Patterns to Build Reach

Websites don't attract visitors evenly throughout the day. Website visitors arrive at different times of the day or on different days, apparently when the users have time and inclination. Businesspeople start and end their day with news. You might expect the *Wall Street Journal* audience to spike at the beginning and end of the workday, and you would be right. Thinking about going to the movies? The Yahoo! Movies audience climbs on weekends during the early evening as people look for reviews, screen times, and tickets. New baby? Caregivers turn to AOL Parenting on Sundays.

Because of different traffic patterns, sites build audiences at different rates, some more quickly or more slowly than others. Audiences for website services (such as web-based email) and portals scale very quickly because of their relevance, name brand recognition, and content variety. Roughly 80% of the monthly accumulated audience to those sites, such as AOL, Yahoo!, and MSN, had already visited by the seventh day of the month. However, even within the sites audiences build at different rates—not every section has the same appeal.

Yahoo! News takes just four days to garner 40% of its monthly audience. Yet Yahoo! Health takes more than twice as long, nine days, to reach that level (DoubleClick 2004).

More specialized sites, such as real estate, automotive, and health sites, build audience more slowly. WebMD, Yahoo! Health, About Health and Fitness, RealAge.com, and iVillage Health all take about 23 days to reach 80% penetration. However, not all sites, even those with similar content, build audience at the same rate. Minor differences in content, creative approach, and user experience can affect build rates. AutoByTel, for example, takes 15 days to reach half its audience, but eBay Motors needs just eight days or about half the time.

Should marketers go for those sites that build quickly? Bolger and Mörn advise against that, and take a more balanced approach: "It's important to point out that a site's build rate is not the only measure that should be considered when evaluating performance and formulating best practices for attaining reach. Rather, it should be taken into account when formulating schedules for a campaign: In general, to maximize reach, slower building sites require longer runs, while a short, heavy blast on sites with steep build curves is sufficient to reach the majority of users" (Bolger and Mörn 2004, 6).

Expand Total Brand Reach by Combining Online Placements with Traditional Mass Media

Does adding online advertising to the current media plan extend reach? Now that we've seen how reach can be built online, let's look at the more common real-world situation where online advertising is combined with offline media to build total brand reach. Most advertiser media plans combine two or more media types (television, radio, newspaper, online, outdoor, etc.) and specify one or more vehicles (TV or radio show, particular magazine, newspaper, or online site, for example) or times of day in order to reach customers and prospects.

DoubleClick (2003) examined the impact on reach by reallocating the media mix. It worked with Nielsen//NetRatings panel-based data and IMS analytic tools to model actual and then alternative media plans for several Kraft Foods packaged goods (Oscar Mayer Lunchables, Philadelphia Cream Cheese, and Planters Peanuts);

American Airlines; and Subaru. The simulations performed were grounded in marketing reality. DoubleClick worked directly with Kraft, served by the FCB ad agency (formerly Foote, Cone & Belding) and with American Airlines, which had hired Temerlin McClain, the agency of record for the other brands.

What did the study look at exactly? A number of marketing and media factors: target market, original media mix, and the composition of the online audience (people who accessed the web in the prior 30 days) and the offline components of the target market.

- Target markets were defined for each brand. Some of them were very specific. In the American Airlines case it was business and leisure travelers aged 25 to 54 with incomes at $60,000 or above. Subaru targeted adults with the same age and income demographic. For Oscar Mayer Lunchables it was mothers aged 25 to 54. Others, like Philadelphia Cream Cheese, were broadly defined and sought women in general aged 25 to 54.

- Original media mixes included national or spot television, and one or more buys in newspapers, magazines, cable TV, and online properties, but not necessarily all. The online component of the original mixes ranged from none to 5%.

- The online portion of the target markets ranged from 57% (Planters) to 70% (Subaru) to 83% (American Airlines, Philadelphia Cream Cheese, and Oscar Mayer Lunchables).

Owing to the high proportions of online users and their lighter levels of TV watching, the simulations reallocated dollars away from television and boosted the online spending share by 7% and 15%. What did they find?

- Shifting dollars to online media from television increased incremental reach in all cases except one, Philadelphia Cream Cheese, with the largest gains coming at the 15% level. (The reason for the absence of improvement in Philly may be that the target market, women 25–54, was defined too broadly and the websites not selective enough against them). Targets for the other cases were more finely qualified or younger enthusiasts.

In all cases, online advertising increased reach by exposing ads to the lighter television viewers.

Experience with Frequency of Online Advertising

Could you run just one ad and get business results? Yes, according to a trio of experimental studies that used identical methodologies, measurements, and reporting approach (Briggs et al. 2001; Nielsen Consult 2001a,b). Fielded in three countries (Australia, New Zealand, and Hong Kong), a total of 45 online ads for 26 brands across the automobile, financial services, consumer packaged goods, computers, and consumer retail categories were researched. Online internet users were randomly assigned to one of two groups—one saw the test ad, while the other saw a control ad. Surveys gathered responses on brand measures—awareness, recall, brand perception, and intent to buy—before and after exposure. The findings revealed improvements on all measures, and, depending on the brand studied, some significant differences in brand perception were seen. These were intriguing results, but as Rex Briggs, who authored all studies, notes:

> By measuring just one impression, we simplify the measurement challenge and allow for easy direct comparison of the performance of each advertisement. However, by measuring a single ad impression, our results may understate the cumulative value of an online campaign that successfully builds frequency.

Let us look now at what happens when we increase frequency beyond a single exposure online. Years of online research show that frequency effects generally follow a curve. The most dramatic effects occur early; then, the rate of improvement slows and declines at higher levels of exposure.

We can see the impacts of different levels of exposure frequency by taking a look at results from a study on the repeated use of banner ads to brand a technology company and product (Broussard 2000). Unfortunately, the data are proprietary, so we can't name names.

This major company acquired and retained customers through a number of media and channels. Online advertising was used for branding. Simple but attractively designed banner ads displayed the company's product and message. Clicking on banners sent consumers to a corporate site where additional information was available; the site did not include e-commerce or direct sales offers.

Participants were recruited from two sites known to have high concentrations of the company's target market among their visitors. Each person completed an online branding survey following exposure. Data on awareness, purchase intent, and brand attributes were captured for the company and the product. Cookies written in the browser captured frequency—the number of times the banner was delivered to the browser. Testing first established baseline values of branding levels preexposure; then data were collected in two subsequent waves at two weeks and five weeks.

Positive impacts on branding resulted. For the company and product, awareness and product knowledge rose significantly. Purchase intent increased for the product.

Study participants saw between 1 and 40 ads. The total lift, expressed as a percentage of change, in awareness was near 90%. But how did it grow? It turns out that by the eighth exposure, 80% of the lift was achieved. A bigger eye-opener is that the largest gains occurred from the first to second exposure (45%). From the second to the third exposure the lift reached 60%. This finding also demonstrates why it is critically important for brands to reach their target audiences broadly with a reasonable number of exposures, rather than reaching a relatively narrow target audience many numbers of times.

Is there a magic frequency number? Little research exists on the subject, and results vary according to the product and campaign objectives. According to the DoubleClick study, for example, the optimal frequency for most campaigns is around four to seven ad exposures, and, much beyond that, results hit a point of diminishing returns for both brand and direct response objectives (DoubleClick 2006a).

Getting a fix on optimal frequency, and balancing that frequency with target consumer reach, is critical because without it some parts of online media plans may overdeliver heavy users who could easily see your ad without acting. Minimization of that waste and increase of the frequency against lighter users, who may respond, contributes to good planning, buying, and effectiveness.

Interplay of Reach and Site Visiting

Now that we have established the basics of online reach and frequency and brought forward a number of strategic approaches for building reach and thinking about frequency, we are ready to tackle a couple of advanced topics. The first we address concerns where a person is reached on a website, and the second looks at the issue of when consumers respond to online ads.

When people visit a website—like WSJ.com or ESPN.com, say— they normally land on a home page, click to another page, then another page, and so on until they leave. We can think of each succeeding page visited as depth; after three clicks, people are four pages deep into the site.

Ad network Tribal Fusion (Goodman 2006) homed in on action-oriented behaviors—banner click rates and conversion rates, which they ordered by page depth. Analyzing 2.6 billion impressions over 600 campaigns that ran over 750 sites in their network, they found that click-through rates were highest in the first few pages. When click-through rates were indexed to the first page exposure, the rate dropped to 60% for the second page. By the fifth page click-through rates declined to 50%, and then they steadily tailed away. The conversion rate trend is less predictive. It showed a dip from the first page to the third page, but instead of a steady decline pages 4 through 13 stayed at the third-page level and then dropped. It may be that consumers prefer to see more information before taking a commitment step like converting for many products and services.

Does when people click affect return on impressions? A different Tribal Fusion study looked at this question for a major educational publisher that sought to generate new leads. Using a media plan that bought lower-cost impressions across high-reach media, the findings were in line with other statistical analysis. Earlier pages delivered the best click-through rates, and most of the clicks, 91%, occurred by the fifth page. Cost per lead was shown to be more cost-effective (below the level the advertiser wanted to pay) for the first handful of pages.

Earlier exposures to display ads work better than later exposures do and can move people toward action. But does that action have to be immediate? Here the answer may surprise you. It's no. Web agency Avenue A ran banners for a travel site client and looked at the click-through rates. Among the people exposed to the ads, 80% of conversions (in this case website registrations) resulted from people who *did not* click on an ad. Avenue A dubbed these "awareness conversions." People saw the banner ads, noted the site, then later plugged the URL into their browser and registered (Goodman 2006).

Click-through and conversion rates are proxies for awareness or interest that promotes branding. Even though the rates drop off after a few exposures, this research tells us that an ad reaching a consumer early is more likely to be effective and also gives us insight into the immediate and delayed branding impacts of banner ads. When you put yourself in the consumers' position, the results make sense: If we're interested and have time, we click. If we notice something of interest but are too busy to click immediately, we'll make a note to visit later when we have the time. But does that work?

Continental Airlines: Measuring Indirect Effects

Many campaigns are multichannel, usually mixing online advertising into some combination of media. With consumers being exposed through multiple channels that send traffic to websites, how can we gauge online advertising's performance?

With client Continental Airlines, DoubleClick (2004b) ran a test using exposed and control groups. The exposed group was shown ads for an advertised fare, while the control group was shown Red Cross public service ads. To avoid variances due to differences in advertising weight, impression levels and frequencies were standardized.

Deploying a track-back capability, DoubleClick identified people who were exposed to the Continental ad or Red Cross ad, did not click, but later went to the website to purchase the advertised fare. By comparing the two groups, they could determine the effects of exposure to Continental's online advertising. In this case, the exposed test group bought two-thirds of the tickets, clearly demonstrating the impact of online advertising. Online ads are effective even when consumers do not take direct action on them at the time of exposure, like clicking through to brand websites. Reaching consumers online with the right frequency levels can lead to sales. It's very important to look beyond the immediate conversion effects like click-throughs and also consider the delayed effects of advertising on consumer purchasing. This is a topic we explore more fully in Chapter 7, "Online Shopping and Buying."

Determining exposure frequency, like reach, should be steered by the understanding of your branding and behavior goals and what it takes to achieve them, all the while balanced by your knowledge of what you're willing to pay for results. Reaching the right people the right number of times with the right combination of media contributes to advertising effectiveness. Keep in mind, too, that not all ad impressions are equal. Online ads that appear early are noticed and acted upon more quickly, and may have longer-term branding impact. Don't pin your campaign evaluations entirely on immediate performance, like click-throughs. Take a balanced approach instead and bring additional resources into play that help gauge success, like tracking customers overall as in the Continental Airlines case, or tying consumers' online or offline behaviors to the conversion outcomes your brand seeks after reaching them and exposing them to your advertising.

Winning Plays

The smart way to use online advertising to achieve broad reach for your brand is to use a combination of online and offline advertising. Research has shown the combination to be superior to either one used alone. The advertising planning skill needed for success in building adequate reach for the brand is the ability to create the best mix or balance of online and offline advertising to achieve your goals. That skill needs to be sharp because traditional and online advertising is not an either/or proposition. Blending media will only increase as marketers shift budgets to exploit the benefits of different media for achieving their advertising goals. Most marketers test their way to winning combinations.

- While television is still considered the most "mass" of media, it does have a concentrated audience of heavy viewers. The same is true for the internet. The key is that in many cases they are different groups of people. Thus, to optimize your total reach, a balanced combination of online and offline, especially TV, is critical.
- There are many situations when online advertising alone may achieve your reach goals, but offline may still be needed to drive a certain number of prospects online to the location where brand advertising appears on your or other websites.
- The principles that apply for gaining reach within any single medium apply to the internet channel. Usually a mix of formats (banners, billboards, text, rich media) and a variety of portals or sites with high concentrations of your best prospects can quickly achieve your reach goals.

- More important to ultimate success, however, is the quality of the idea. A weak idea can achieve a level of reach equal to a strong idea, but the highly motivating idea will create significantly more sales. Thus, before investing time and resources in planning for reach, focus on getting an engaging, motivating idea. Often the idea can influence the selection of certain sites in a campaign as well as be a multiplier for building awareness.

- Finally, remember that the nature and capabilities of online services and advertising are constantly changing and evolving, not only on the internet, but through emerging channels like mobile communications and immersive experiences in massively multiplayer games, such as the extraordinarly popular Second Life. Traditional reach and frequency measures are being supplemented with newer engagement and brand interaction metrics now being studied, developed, and applied. Successful online marketers will be those who embrace online advertising with concepts and metrics that emerge organically from online advertising, and reduce their dependence on ill-fitting reach and frequency measures from an earlier age.

CHAPTER 4

Winning Strategies in Online Advertising

A casual observer of online advertising would probably conclude that it is a tactical medium with banners, pop-ups, promotional email, and brief text search ads. Our analysis of many success stories and research studies, however, has concluded that without a clear strategy (usually linked to business strategy), online advertising has weak outcomes.

Every major success story started with clear business objectives, which were tied clearly to marketing strategy that included online advertising, and used a relevant mix of online and offline advertising. Even in cases where online advertising was the primary medium, a clearly defined strategy was the primary driver of success.

This chapter elaborates on the key strategic objectives for which online advertising is well suited to deliver positive results. These span the full spectrum of business goals: lead generation, customer acquisition, branding, sales, and growth strategies (brand extensions, new product introductions), and customer loyalty.

We selected marketing strategies that use online advertising creatively. Each strategy is supported by real, in-market cases ably demonstrating the business value of that strategy to the marketer.

Generate Leads and Acquire Customers

We begin with one of the most widely employed strategies for online advertising—generating leads or building lists of prospects. Sometimes the execution is straightforward, but the best stories we encountered had a creative insight that enhanced the advertising's overall effectiveness. Our cases, the HGTV Dream Home Giveaway and a recruitment campaign for the U.S. Air Force, demonstrate new ways to acquire customers by leveraging capabilities that are unique to online advertising.

HGTV Dream Home Giveaway: Partnering for Qualified Leads

Who can resist a gorgeous home built with the finest materials, featuring great rooms and outside spaces, spectacular views, and state-of-the-art kitchens dripping with amenities, all for free just by entering a sweepstakes form? That's HGTV's Dream Home Giveaway, the biggest online sweepstakes around—36 million entries in 2006. (See Figure 4.1.)

A Scripps property, HGTV promotes the Dream Home Giveaway across Scripps' collection of old and new media—cable channels,

FIGURE 4.1   HGTV Dream Home Giveaway entrants are encouraged to tour the home, providing branding opportunities for sponsors from the outset.

The 2007 HGTV Dream Home Tour

The 2007 HGTV Dream Home is open! Take a tour of the Winter Park, Colorado, home and get decorating tips and ideas for YOUR home.

Source: HGTV.com.

magazines, websites, and email newsletters; runs display ads in affinity sections on MSN, AOL, and Yahoo!; and airs TV specials. The aim: drive traffic to the HGTV.com registration page.

HGTV partners with about 15 advertisers, spanning the range of building materials, home products, interior decorating products, household appliances, and household furnishings and fixtures companies, which sponsor the Dream Home. The registration page features a sponsor roll with display ads and links that drive visitor traffic to the sponsor sites. Being so tightly integrated with the sweepstakes provides advertisers with interested visitors from the get-go.

For many advertisers, that quality pool might be sufficient. But HGTV.com came up with two innovations that help advertisers attract even more qualified prospects.

First, they offered visitors 360-degree virtual tours of the Dream Home. With mouse in hand and an inquisitive nature, visitors traipsed around or stopped to inspect items that caught their fancy—windows, floors, lighting, or refrigerators, for example. Clickable hot spots added to the images provided details and links to sponsor sites. Viewers absorbed that information, spending about four minutes on sponsored content and consuming three million sponsored pages during the sweepstakes (2004 data). The upshot: Not only are consumers interested generally, they also educate themselves and further qualify their interest in sponsors' products.

Does this strategic initiative generate attractive leads? Listen to sponsor Lumber Liquidator's president Tom Sullivan: "The traffic to our website and stores skyrockets when people start virtually walking through the Dream Home and clicking on our flooring products. It performs better than any other aspect of our marketing and advertising" (Newcomb 2005a).

Tracking every click of registered users made the second innovation possible: HGTV.com partnered with behavioral targeting vendor TACODA Audience Networks, Inc. Analyzing the 36 million entries, they reduced it to six million unique visitors. They then profiled each visitor by their brand interactions and rolled them up into about 200 different segments. That allowed HGTV.com's advertisers to reach broadly defined or highly targeted prospects with precision advertising (Anfuso 2005). HGTV.com's database will only become richer over time as behavioral tracking continues with each successive year of the Dream Home Giveaway.

Focus on Life Events: U.S. Air Force, WhatAmIGonnaDoNext.com

Young men and women don't always know what they want to do careerwise. It's not uncommon. Some may have tried jobs that didn't work out, some are unaware of the variety of jobs out there, some may not have thought about a career at all, and some may lack the necessary educational background.

The U.S. Air Force, like all service branches, recruits constantly to meet staffing levels. With interactive agency GSD&M, the Air Force developed a lead-generation strategy designed to tap into high school seniors who were searching for opportunities. The online campaign, "What Am I Gonna Do Next?" sought to help by educating about careers in the Air Force. (See Figure 4.2.)

With graphics partner Transistor Studios, the team developed a very creative microsite centered around the question "What am I gonna do with my life?" Animations and navigation were especially engaging, abandoning a graphics-rich, page-based, top-gun-as-hero approach for a sketchy, exploratory, nonlinear feel. (See Figure 4.3.) Contentwise the site contrasted often unrealistic dream jobs, like vice

FIGURE 4.2 When clicked on, the images lead prospects to explorations of different careers, contrasting unrealistic dream jobs with Air Force alternatives and providing suggestions appropriate to recent graduates.

Source: www.whatamigonnado.com.

FIGURE 4.3 The campaign's exploratory, nonlinear approach continues as prospects spend more time with the site. This highly creative campaign succeeded in generating recruitment inquiries at a rate of roughly 100 per week.

Source: www.whatamigonnado.com.

president of Mountain Operations at a ski resort, with Air Force alternatives through images and just a few words. It was very tongue-in-cheek and pretty cool; it made its points well.

One year after launch, the site had generated over 5,000 leads for the Air Force.

Generate Excitement and Word of Mouth: Chili's Grill "Margarita Madness/Art of the Margarita" and MySpace/Cinco de Mayo

Margaritas are a bit like martinis—mixed by the book for years, now morphed into tens, if not hundreds, of subtle or bold flavored variations. Margarita-making today requires flair and artistry. For the legions who drink them, few cocktails come close to matching their implied promise of fun and good times, Southwestern food, and unwinding after a long day. But no one has a lock on the magic recipe, and it's certainly not hard to find a place serving them. Casual restaurants like Chili's Grill & Bar draw customers on trendy menu items and drinks like margaritas. Their marketing challenge: increase awareness of Chili's margarita expertise and variety to stimulate trial and restaurant visits among their target customers.

Chili's interactive agency, GSD&M, utilized the online campaign "The Art of the Margarita," which included banner ads, a specially built microsite, and in-store merchandising. (See Figure 4.4.) The core of the campaign focused on activities that allowed for self-expression and brand participation, such as the margarita drawing contest on the microsite, where the winner received a trip to Mexico to learn about tequila.

Featuring an art contest, Chili's microsite replicated an art gallery with studio space and exhibit halls (www.ChilisMargaritaMadness .com). Rendered in rich media, the microsite reflected the experience of walking from one place to the next. Smooth transitions (wipes) avoided the jumpy quality that sometimes occurs with linked pages. In the studio, Chili's furnished artists with an array of templates and drawing and painting tools capable of composing quite complex artistic images. Visitors could view artists' works and vote on them, or take in Chili's margarita gallery, "coaster art" wing, or cinema. The margarita gallery hung pictures of Chili's 12 drinks on the wall, each

FIGURE 4.4 Chili's "Art of the Margarita" campaign.

Source: www.ChilisMargaritaMadness.com/home.php.

accompanied by captions listing their ingredients (accomplishing some co-branding as well). We found the "coaster art" section amusing. These remixes of iconic masterpieces placed margaritas into well-known canvases of Magritte, Warhol, Lichtenstein, Van Gogh, and others. Taking advantage of every integration opportunity, the paintings were incorporated into some cheeky, laugh-inducing short films. Finally, a "send to a friend" feature added a word-of-mouth component. To our eyes, this microsite is one heck of a branding experience.

Additionally, Chili's reached its savvy and marketing-aware consumers through a MySpace profile, allowing "friends" to discuss Chili's food and vote on favorite photos and margaritas. Chili's entry into the MySpace community was received well, with over 200,000 visits, and because of the immediate relationship that it was able to foster with this new audience Chili's has maintained its commitment to the Chili's online community.

Chili's "art" campaign appears to integrate with the company's overall marketing strategy, not an add-on to grab a hot part of the market. After reviewing Chili's site, microsite, and MySpace pages, we made two observations that led us to that conclusion. First, "The Art of the Margarita" meshes with a broader consumer trend: empowerment through choice and individual selection. As we write, Chili's "Triple Dipper Challenge" lets customers choose any three of nine items, each with different sauces. Second, Chili's home page features integrate closely with the themes of self-expression and doing good. There's Jonah, a Chili's waiter and musician, embodying the creativity and coolness of Chili's and its customers. Chilis.com visitors can click to hear his song "Tip Yo Waiter" or click to his personal MySpace page where more information about Jonah's music, interests, and friends resides. Chili's goes further, adding a cause marketing element to the mix, through its "Create a Pepper" program benefiting childhood cancer center St. Jude Children's Research Hospital.

As we go to press, we don't have sales data, but GSD&M shared visitor data with us. The microsite generated more than 11,000 submissions and generated more than 250,000 visits to its gallery. On average, visitors spend about 5 to 14 minutes on the site, depending on the interactions they choose to have with the brand. Considering that each picture is about a margarita and incorporates Chili's imagery, especially the chili pepper, "gallery patrons" are actively processing and evaluating the brand and its interpretations.

Word of mouth is searchable, especially in the blogosphere. It didn't take us long to find evidence for word of mouth working. One blogger we came across posted her artwork, then exhorted readers to vote for it and provided the link, along with the helpful comment that readers could create their own artwork, too (The Healthy Mom 2006).

MySpace results also are impressive for what is essentially a sponsorship strategy without explicit branding. GSD&M reports over 200,000 visits and about 10 comments per day to MySpace/ Cinco de Mayo.

Generate Brand Preference to Stimulate Sales

When marketing strategies have a branding component—such as raising awareness, enhancing knowledge of the brand, or increasing purchase intention, for example—online advertising alone, or in combination with traditional media, can be very effective. In the series of cases to follow, we take you through examples where marketers achieved branding goals using predominately online campaigns, and several that used mass media/new media combinations. In these latter cases, the crucial matter of budget allocation comes into play, which provides us with insights into one of the thorniest questions marketers grapple with today.

Engage the Core Audience: Sony Pictures Entertainment/Columbia Pictures, "The Da Vinci Code Web Quest"

Nearly 60% of moviegoers learn or hear of a new movie three to four weeks before release. That gives friends and family plenty of time to make plans to see a movie, which they do by talking with one another in person, on the phone, by email, or by texting (AOL and Nielsen 2005). This being a social experience, individuals with more knowledge may influence the decision of which movie to see.

Studio film marketers typically advertise across the variety of offline and online media, with online the place to turn usually for more information like showtimes and theaters (Google 2006c). For most Hollywood pictures, industry economics dictate boffo opening weekends, so generating buzz in the few weeks prior to opening is critical. Great weekends stimulate further interest and ticket sales.

The Da Vinci Code, the phenomenal best-selling book (over 40 million copies translated into 40 languages), is enjoyed by readers with penchants for piecing together clues and solving puzzles. In fact, it's common for copies of the book to be left behind on French Eurostar trains by readers visiting sites mentioned in the book, such as Saint-Sulpice church in Saint-Germain-des-Pres (ParisInfo 2006).

Columbia Pictures sought to generate advance word of mouth among these passionate readers by creating a worldwide contest, *"The Da Vinci Code* Web Quest," with Google that required entrants to complete 24 daily puzzles to qualify for a grand prize of trips to key locations in the book—London, New York, Rome, and Paris. (See Figure 4.5.) As an effort with Google, search was an important tool in researching answers. (As a side note, Google promoted the branded contest on its home page, the first time the company had ever given

FIGURE 4.5 *The Da Vinci Code* movie's online promotion engaged the book's core puzzle-solving readers for several weeks prior to the movie's release through an ingenious search-oriented "advergame." The online portion of the prelaunch campaign raised awareness and interest in the film and generated advance ticket sales, which helped to ensure a successful opening.

an advertiser any space at all on it. As we will see, the partnership worked well, suggesting the merits of online co-branding for specific brands in particular instances.)

If we take search-generated traffic to Sony's site, advance ticket sales, and opening weekend sales as proxies for campaign effectiveness, this promotion was a winner. After the contest's first three weeks, 30% of Sony's *Da Vinci Code* traffic came from consumers searching through Google. By comparison, in the week prior to the promotion's launch, Google accounted for only 3% of traffic to Sony's website. During the promotion period, Google outperformed competing search engines by 30 to 1. Buzz is great, but does it put fannies in the seats? Yes. Online ticket vendor Fandango reported that *Da Vinci Code* tickets were the hottest sellers of the week beginning May 7, 2006, almost two weeks before the movie's release on May 19, 2006 (Gupta 2006b). The movie's opening weekend grossed about $78 million, accounting for a bit more than a third of all tickets sold and half of its U.S. box office through its first three months of release (Box Office Mojo 2006).

Advergames: An Emerging Option

Advertising games, so-called advergames, involve consumers with branded entertainment that contains advertising. The advertising adds realistic touches to scenes, as when a gamer drives by a billboard advertising Mountain Dew. Advergames may use branded characters as actors or be based on brand storylines. Advergames aim to create, reinforce, or build on brand preference and sales. As you probably know, these games can range from simple games (e.g., catch the fish, drive the car) to sophisticated massively multiplayer games such as World of Warcraft and Second Life, or result from tie-ins between companies, such as the partnership between Burger King and Microsoft's Xbox. When used, advergames are typically components of advertising plans, designed to reach and engage core brand users or prospects. Advergames are used in almost all consumer categories. The *Da Vinci Code* case provides an excellent example of their branding value when part of a larger campaign. Advergames are growing in importance; new games and tie-ins appear daily.

Co-create a Brand Story: Audi of America, "Art of the H3ist"

Audi of America sought to generate awareness and purchase interest in a new car model, the A3, a premium compact hatchback. The auto press was skeptical of luxury carmakers offering "downscale" models. Audi's campaign, "Art of the H3ist," sought to overturn that experience and conventional wisdom by positioning the car as a premium model (McKinney-Silver 2005).

In particular Audi wanted to go after a younger, highly affluent male buyer with a profile higher than the A4 model in order to avoid the "cheap Audi" tag and reach an intelligent and independent consumer. They found a tech-savvy, web-addicted, active, and mobile segment detached from traditional communications. Conventional message and advergame strategies wouldn't be bold enough for them. Audi and their agency, McKinney-Silver, sought to immerse prospects in an alternate reality, one they could participate in and one that would drive interest and purchase intention for the Audi A3.

McKinney-Silver's team created the fictional "Art of the H3ist" game, a thriller running over 90 days. The aim: Find an A3 model that contained a decryption key that would expose detailed plans for the world's largest art theft. (See Figure 4.6.) The story, created by Hollywood screenwriters, was very rich and complex, with all sorts of plot twists, murder attempts, and vivid characters. It can't be described here with justice. A very good recap is provided in Leavitt (2005a).

Audi and McKinney-Silver created their alternate reality in real time using practically every communications channel—a family of web-based microsites for the characters; TV ads; radio spots; small space ads in magazines giving clues (*Wired*, *The New Yorker*); billboards; and wild postings to live events (e.g., New York International Auto Show, American Film Institute film parties, E3 Expo). Email, videos, blogs, chats, direct mail, puzzles, photos, and scanned images surrounded and engaged the A3 prospect.

This campaign worked. More than 500,000 people participated on "an ongoing basis," spending from 4 to 10 minutes at each of the story sites. Moreover, *BusinessWeek* and the *Wall Street Journal* wrote features, amplifying interest in the campaign and extending its reach to readers unaware of the H3ist.

FIGURE 4.6   Audi's "Art of the H3ist" campaign presented a taut, suspenseful story promoting high levels of consumer engagement over three months. The campaign generated more than 10,000 leads and over 4,000 test-drives among younger, affluent male buyers.

Source: McKinney-Silver Agency (www.mckinney-silver.com/A3_H3ist/).

The objective of attracting those younger, male, affluent buyers was achieved based on the profile of active participants. Audi microsites drove traffic to Audi's main site by over 40% during the three months the H3ist campaign ran. That traffic led to over 16,000 "indicator actions," more than 10,000 leads, and 4,000 test-drives (McKinney-Silver 2005).

Educate Future Customers to Build Long-Term Brand Preference: Toyota Scion

Youth marketing experts like Alloy Media and Marketing's Matthew Diamond see a trend toward targeting teenagers before they can actually purchase a brand. "It's early branding. You're establishing that brand presence and positive association, since important buying decisions are forthcoming" (quoted in Bosman 2006a). Staples and Office Depot have programs in place grooming high school juniors and seniors for their college purchases and later career shopping behavior.

Scion buyers are different. They're younger, unconventional, and most have no prior Toyota purchase history that colors their perceptions. The Scion buyer is the un-Toyota car owner—excited, edgy, and experimental, standing in sharp contrast to the Camry buyer who, at 51 (median age), favors other qualities like safety, comfort, and reliability. "A lot of what we do," Scion's national marketing communications manager, Deborah Senior, says, "is based on the mind-set rather than the age of the specific group." As Toyota builds the Scion brand, it needs to create future customers by investing in the next generation coming up of car owners.

Toyota created "Club Scion" on Whyville, a gamelike virtual world peopled with 8- to 15-year-olds, the next generation of adults and potential Scion customers. Registered users, called citizens, participate in government, have jobs, visit health centers, sun at beaches, take in museums, use airports, shop at flea markets and malls, and eat in food courts. Citizens create and play through avatars who go about living, learning, communicating, working, earning virtual money ("clams"), buying cars, driving, and voting. The site is supported by sponsors: Whyville's museum is underwritten by the John Paul Getty Trust and its nutrition center by the University of Texas Health Science Center at San Antonio; NASA underwrites science education.

As a media property, Whyville appeals. As we write, the site has 1.8 million citizens; the base is growing by 60,000 each month. About two million registered visitors log in monthly, spending more than three hours per month. Whyville works closely with each sponsor, specializing in "custom integrated games and activities that empower the audience to actively experience your message, product, or brand" (Whyville 2006).

Club Scion's interactive world enables kids to do the things adults do—buy or finance cars; ride around and pick up their friends; configure and customize their engines, wheels, or bodies (there's even a custom decal shop); and vote on the coolest ones. (See Figure 4.7.) That personalization dovetails with the individualism and "my way" mentality young Millennials are known for.

FIGURE 4.7 Whyville allows tweens and teens to configure and purchase virtual Scions. Clicking the purchase button presents Whyvillians with buying and financing options.

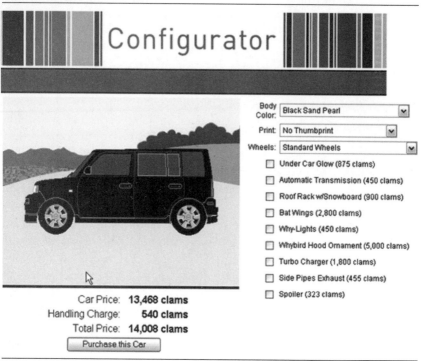

Car Price: **13,468 clams**
Handling Charge: **540 clams**
Total Price: **14,008 clams**

Purchase this Car

Source: Whyville.com screen shot.

While Club Scion appears to be just a game going on within a safe social networking site (parental approval is required and there's a strict code of conduct enforced with penalties), a ton of brand learning is going on. "Ten days into the campaign," the *New York Times* reported, "visitors to the site had used the word 'Scion' in online chats more than 78,000 times; hundreds of virtual Scions were purchased, using 'clams,' . . . and the community meeting place 'Club Scion' was visited 33,741 times." From May to July 2006, drivers bought and built virtual cars in the low 1,000s and gave 140,000 rides to their pals (Bosman 2006a; Rodgers 2006).

Club Scion bears resemblances to the real world in other ways. Priced at 14,000 clams, the cost citizens pay is in the neighborhood of Scion xBs in the showroom. Because it takes a long time to earn that basket of clams, citizens complained that only a few could afford to purchase the xB. Scion responded by offering a financing program (sponsored by Toyota Finance) that enabled more citizens to purchase cars while giving object lessons on credit scores, sales contracts, down payments, interest rates, leasing, and payment plans.

Generate Interest in a New Brand Line Extension: Dove Nutrium Bar

Dove's advertising campaign for its Nutrium bar allocated the $10 million media budget across television (75%), print (23%), and online (2%). Dove Nutrium's study explored specifically how media work to impact four measures: unaided brand awareness, aided awareness, brand performance image, and purchase intent. After taking baseline measures and comparing consumers exposed to advertising, analysis showed that TV and magazines individually had a larger effect on average scores than online advertising. When online was added to print and TV in combination, the lift was even higher. The campaign was considered a success, but could they do better?

Dove asked the follow-up question: If we keep the budget the same but give online advertising a bigger share of spending, could we get better performance? They decreased spending on TV and print to increase the online share to 15 percent. They found that raising the online share improved all brand metrics by 8% and purchase intention by a hefty 14%.

Why did the bigger online proportion work? Essentially, the budget reallocation enabled Dove Nutrium to reach the same number of TV viewers and print readers but lower the exposure frequency (a desirable outcome because effectiveness drops after the first few exposures), while simultaneously increasing reach dramatically among the online target audience, women aged 25 to 49, and exposing them to Nutrium ads more frequently than had been done with the original plan (Briggs 2004; MSN, IAB, ARF 2002; Nail 2002).

If we look at this performance through a different lens, that of cost per point of improvement, we see another compelling picture. Average brand metrics exhibited a 25% lift over the original plan at a cost 28% less per impact point. The new plan was not only more effective, but also made more efficient use of the budget.

Generate Brand Sales with Increased Online Spending: New Ford F-150

The Ford F-150, the best-selling truck in the United States, was completely revamped for the 2004 model year, and its introduction was a major event for the corporation. Creatively Ford leveraged its heritage "Built Ford Tough" while telling the market that this was not a merely refreshed vehicle but a worthy successor: "[the truck that's] earned the right to be called the next F-150."

Ford's media plan called for English- and Spanish-language television (90% of the budget) and radio, magazine, outdoor, and direct-mail ads. The online component (2.5% of the budget) used several approaches. Display advertising on specialized leading car-related sites using leaderboards, rectangles, and skyscrapers reached prospective buyers assumed to be in the market. For two days, one month apart, Ford used page takeovers on heavily visited areas on portal sites, especially home pages and email pages. A small portion of the online campaign went to search engine marketing. (See Figure 4.8.)

The first step in the research was to create a sample of buyers and relate their advertising exposure to their purchases.

With opt-in panel researcher comScore, Marketing Evolution created a sample of 360,000 individuals exposed to the Ford ads. Ford provided about three months of retail sales data, more than 30,000 buyers, who were then merged with the panel. Researchers were able to identify who bought and who didn't, and then correlate their media exposure to ads on different sites and their online habits, such as search, with the purchases.

Mining the converged database, Marketing Evolution identified 128 buyers in the comScore panel, and then analyzed them further by breaking them into two groups: viewers exposed to the brand's online advertising or viewers who saw the control ad. Their analysis showed that buyers exposed to the all-new Ford F-150 ads bought 20% more than those control group buyers. Online advertising directly contributed to an incremental 6% sales increase.

Demonstrating the sales power of online advertising, coupled with insight into the relative branding cost and performance by

FIGURE 4.8 Sample ad from Ford F-150 online campaign. Online advertising's cost, relative to its performance, exceeded that of TV and magazines. Sales data would later show that online advertising overperformed in its contributions to sales.

Return-on-Marketing-Objectives Analysis		
Brand Metric: Purchase Consideration (top 2)	Impact	Relative Cost Index
TV	6.1	1104
Magazine	6.1	456
Roadblock	3.8	100
Online	6.2	135

Definitions: Impact = Point gain over baseline is calculated by measuring the postbranding level and subtracting the precampaign level. Costs per person impacted indexed against campaign as a whole. **Index** = Relative cost-efficiency (cost per impact) based on campaign as a whole.
Source: Rex Briggs et al., "Integrated Multi-Channel Communication Strategies: Evaluating the Return on Marketing Objectives—The Case of the 2004 Ford F-150 Launch," Marketing Evolution, 2005.

medium, provided the team with the basis for reallocating spending. The recommendation? Increase the online share from under 3% to 6% of budget (about $3.6 million). Shifting dollars from TV toward online outlets and magazines would increase sales another 5% or 25,000 trucks, resulting in $625 million additional revenue. In other words, "same budget, different allocation, better results" (Briggs et al. 2005).

The cases we just reviewed, in categories as disparate as movies, packaged goods, and trucks, reveal the potential for online advertising alone or in conjunction with traditional media. These cases illustrate elements associated with branding and sales performance.

First, the online portion defined target markets precisely, and then reached and engaged core customers or prospects in ways traditional advertising can not—advergames, co-creating brand meanings, and participation in unique events, such as the *Da Vinci Code* puzzles, the Audi H3ist, or the simulated world of Whyville. It's important to point out that these programs involved consumers on a more or less continuous basis over periods of weeks and months, a level of involvement just not practical with conventional media.

Second, the campaigns involved a web of interrelationships among brand advertising, brand microsites, and the main sites for brands. Converged communications systems unify and reinforce brand messaging and enable consumers to access brand resources as their needs and interests dictate.

Third, the campaigns emphasized relevant consumer benefits and presented them in interesting, compelling, creative ways.

Fourth, upping online advertising's share of the budget enabled advertisers to reach the right consumer with the right message an appropriate number of times by using multiple sites to balance audience reach and better control exposure frequency.

Last, leaders like Scion positioned themselves for future sales, spending time and money on future consumers through long-term, carefully thought out engagement strategies. These types of campaigns are capable of creating brand preference very early on and before the time when consumers enter the market, building a competitive advantage for Scion and a hurdle for competitors.

Brand Growth, Rewards, and Loyalty

Leverage Integrated Multichannel Communications to Launch a Line Extension: Tylenol Eight-Hour Relief

To grow, pain relief brands rely heavily on brand extensions that meet the needs of new segments. As baby boomers seek to stay young by working out and doing strenuous exercise, Tylenol saw a need for a longer-lasting pain reliever for muscular soreness related to so-called active pains from exercise and sports. The company formulated Tylenol 8 Hour.

Tylenol's consumer insight revealed that men took pain relievers to treat their aches and pains after sports workouts. That might have been enough right there, but not all guys are that physical and their need for pain relief would be occasional at best. Looking to develop a strong niche market, Tylenol instead focused on a mind-set, the "weekend warriors" who like to play hard and exercise vigorously, those for whom "not playing is not an option." These warriors like the simplicity of "one and done" to cope with the lingering effects of achy muscles and mild tweaks, unlike, say, parents who carefully monitor their children's dosing and don't want them to take any more than needed to deal with an acute situation. Sounds great, right? Now the question is: How do you carve out a messaging strategy that speaks directly to the weekend warrior and doesn't get lost in general advertising against the larger demographic? Attitude targets are terrific, but if your brand can't address them through media channels, there's little point to defining them.

Tylenol 8 Hour aimed to create excitement and an engaging brand experience just for the weekend warrior. In addition to introductory advertising, the brand created the Sore Winner Challenge, a series of contests, fun activities, and games in a half-dozen cities. Winners went on to represent their city in the national Sore Winner contest. (See Figure 4.9.)

Tylenol 8 Hour earmarked a portion of the budget for a multichannel campaign with the sports giant ESPN (ESPN.com 2004). Integrating all ESPN properties—cable, magazine, radio, website, and online ads, including rich media (ESPN Motion)—Tylenol

FIGURE 4.9 Utilizing ESPN properties in a multichannel campaign, Tylenol 8 Hour reached its "weekend warrior" conceptual target and built the foundation for a successful launch of this brand extension, as shown by the branding results.

Tylenol 8 Hour Branding Results		
	Control (pre-wave)	ESPN Media
Aided Brand Awareness	48.9%	83.1%
Ad Awareness	20.6%	63.4%
Brand Favorability	27.2%	56.8%
Purchase Intent	39.5%	60.5%
Message Association	3.6%	37.4%
Sponsorship Association	4.6%	47.7%

Source: ESPN.com, "Tylenol 8 Hour: A Cross-Media Advertising Case Study," October 2004.

created an enveloping brand environment. Deepening the connection to competitive sports online, the brand furnished warriors with their own Sore Winner Training Room, which freely dispensed advice on training, equipment, and clothing so that men could perform at their best.

With research partner Dynamic Logic, Tylenol 8 Hour examined the cumulative impact of ESPN messages on brand awareness and interest. Comparing people exposed to at least one ad on each ESPN property—TV, magazine, radio, and online—to the prelaunch group, the study showed dramatic effects across all measures of online engagement. Most important, a majority of the warriors learned about the brand (awareness up 33%), developed positive attitudes (brand favorability up 30%), and were moved to considering trial (purchase intent up 20%).

Engage Consumers in Launching a New Product: Holiday Inn Express "Guest Bathroom Experience"

Marketers introducing new products can use online advertising effectively as part of their multichannel communication effort. This example shows one way online advertising is used to engage consumers in a new brand experience offered by Holiday Inn Express.

Budget-oriented road warriors want "clean, well-lighted places" (sorry, Hemingway) with satisfying showers. Above all, they want showers with sufficient water pressure (their number one complaint), then the comforts of home—large, soft, absorbent towels; comfortable rugs underfoot; and a little more room in the bath (Harris Interactive and reported in Hotel Online 2005).

Reading their own internal customer satisfaction research, Holiday Inn Express marketers learned that a satisfying shower weighed heavily in a positive score and decision to stay. They discovered, too, that their shower experience fell short for their guests. They redressed the situation, ordering bathroom retrofits for all their North American hotels.

Holiday Inn Express's strategy was to create the "Simply Smart Guest Bathroom Experience." Holiday Inn spent 30,000 hours to get the products right. Express designed a proprietary, branded "Stay Smart Showerhead" with Kohler, the highly regarded maker of bathroom fixtures. (See Figure 4.10.) The showerhead solved the water

FIGURE 4.10 Holiday Inn Express learned that the quality of a shower influences guest decisions to stay. This ad involves consumers in understanding the benefits of the Guest Bathroom Experience showerhead. Rich media allows consumers to view the showerhead, change the water stream, take a personality quiz to determine the right setting, purchase the showerhead, or pass the news along by "telling a friend."

Source: Holiday Inn Express website.

pressure complaint and offered the three most popular spray settings, which they dubbed "relaxing," "reviving," and "invigorating." Those names place the focus on consumer benefits in ways that settings like stream, pulse, or jet just can't do. Guests responded so well to the showerhead's qualities that they purchased (and continue to buy) thousands of them through Holiday Inn Express' online catalog—at $80 each.

Holiday Inn Express featured the Guest Bathroom Experience primarily on its website. Guests learned about the shower curtains and rods that increased space, all-cotton towels, and specially formulated amenities along with the hero product showerhead. We especially liked the "setting finder," a lighthearted personality quiz culminating with assessments and recommended shower settings. One of your authors took it and found the results to be uncannily accurate, pegging his personality and advising, "You'll flourish under the Relaxing setting with its wide spray." Wouldn't you stay there?

Express agency Fallon Worldwide built the web showerhead experience under the overall brand campaign of "Stay Smart" to introduce the new showerhead. As stated in their Effie Award brief, "By playing off the expression, 'You do your best thinking in the shower,' Express was were able to align the showerhead as proof of the overall 'Stay Smart' brand promise" (Fallon Worldwide 2006).

In order to efficiently target the online effort, Fallon found that travelers watch cable news, weather, and sports before work. At work, they switch to the internet for more news, sports, and weather. Relaxing at night after work, their tastes run to popular shows like *SportsCenter*, *The Daily Show with Jon Stewart*, and the History Channel.

Given this pattern, Express' media plan priorities to reach guests and prospects gave television the highest priority, with online media second. Some online travel sites drove traffic to the Holiday Inn Express website through their affiliate marketing relationships.

On the key revenue measures, the campaign performed admirably. Occupancy increased 1.5% percent to 75% percent from July 2004 to July 2005 (the campaign started in November 2004). Their financial metric, revenue per available room, increased 8.2% percent over the 12 months, with two percentage points of that gain directly attributable to the Simply Smart Guest Bathroom Experience. Due to this performance, the brand made its systemwide investment back in about six months.

Stimulate Trial through Online Coupons and Sampling: KFC and Tide Coldwater

Over the decades, couponing and sampling have proven their value in stimulating product trial and sales. Today's online couponing provides marketers with new abilities to distribute those valuable offers to more targeted audiences.

Tide Coldwater's sampling campaign contributed to that new

product's success—over one million samples were claimed in the first 90 days. Tide also used online sampling successfully for earlier brand extensions such as Tide with a touch of Downy. KFC's Popcorn Chicken effort smartly delivered online coupons to office workers near lunchtime, targeting them with a time-limited daypart offer. Email promotion offers, like KFC's target offers to specific customer segments at just the right time. Online advertising, like radio, has this time-driven flexibility for strategic promotions of new products and the ability to create trial.

Online couponing and sampling go well beyond the spray tactics typical of offline sampling programs, by leveraging the unique qualities of online media. For example, marketers applying business rules to visitors sent to their brands' sites by search engines can serve offers to consumers meeting specific criteria, or can apply rules relating to their on-site search and browsing. Similarly, email rules can be developed for opt-in list members and for friends, families, or associates whom recipients forward them on to.

Take note that online coupons are evolving. While many online coupons are strictly promotional, acting as their offline counterparts do by giving a purchase discount or a complimentary offer, online coupons are morphing into branding media. Today's coupons display personalized ads, play video, allow consumers to request information and view it, serve as email and text messaging hubs, and let consumers make appointments and reservations.

Provide Rewards That Promote Product Usage: Virgin Mobile USA

What could be more appealing to young mobile phone users than free minutes, earned in exchange for a few moments of their attention? That's the premise behind Virgin Mobile USA's recent "SugarMama" service, summed up by its "earn airtime in your spare time" tagline. (See Figure 4.11.)

Virgin's service works by engaging its 14-to-24-year-old core customer with advertising and surveys from SugarMama partners. Charter brands included preeminent national youth brands like Microsoft Xbox and Mountain Dew, and high-profile public education programs like the American Legacy Foundation's anti-smoking truth® campaign. Participants opting-in furnish demographic information, which permits very precise targeting; they watch and interact with

FIGURE 4.11 Consumers participating in the SugarMama program have personal account pages. From these pages consumers can view their account details, learn more about the program, or participate, all within Virgin's branding environment.

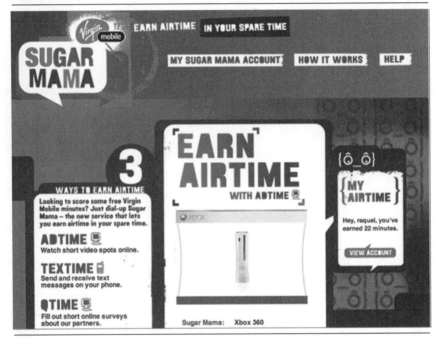

ads online at their computers, through SMS text messages on their handsets, or take short surveys over either. SugarMama awards minutes for the type and duration of the transaction.

Ultramercial LLC provides ad serving, back-end program management, and a customer-facing website where SugarMama members manage their accounts. Virgin caps minutes earned per day to five and 75 for any month.

SugarMama is especially interesting because the service never aimed to be a general advertising program and was designed specifically for—and with—Virgin's teen and twenty-something customers. Research among Virgin's 2,000 "Insiders" revealed that they didn't want their phones spammed, but were interested in being able to choose advertisers and brands to interact with and say something to, and a "minute for a minute" was the right formula. Or, in the words of Virgin Mobile USA chief marketing officer Howard Handler, "It's about advertising with the control and access in the hands of the customer" (quoted in Kaye 2006).

In just eight days after launch, 56,000 people signed up and acquired 685,000 minutes. Testifying to the appeal of earning free minutes, Ultramercial CEO Dana Jones told us that "the minutes are used very quickly" (2006, personal communication). They've become a great way for customers to manage their plans' minutes, extend them, and control their costs (Virgin Mobile's plans are all pay as you go)—a major consideration for young people especially. And for advertisers there's a potential branding boost: Consumers spend about double the time, 90 seconds, with SugarMama ads than they do with the typical Ultramercial.

Brands like Xbox see the potential in SugarMama for branding and consumer insight. Chris De Cesar, Xbox's director of marketing, is on record as saying, "We're always seeking opportunities to learn from our customers how we can deliver the best gaming experiences possible on Xbox 360. SugarMama . . . provides us with a new way to drive consumer awareness yet gain valuable insight from our customers that helps us continually deliver new breakthroughs in gaming entertainment."

SugarMama exemplifies the emerging interest in what we call "explicit exchange-based" online advertising, made possible through a crystal-clear understanding of mutual benefits and enabled by new advertising channels.

Apart from SugarMama, we know of experiments under way testing reward strategies for a variety of applications, including one trading music downloads for compliance with a health care regimen. Given the anticipated growth of premium content and "pay per (fill in the blank)," we expect marketers will step up experiments and develop rewards-based programs that reach very targeted customer segments, especially the highly valued but hard-to-reach groups.

Create Emotional Engagement to Promote Loyalty: Purina Pet Care

Many consumers have passions—for travel, Harleys, the Boston Red Sox, or pets, to name several examples. Marketers whose brand users exhibit passion can help evoke or sustain loyalty by creating experiences that respect and value those feelings, as this example from Purina shows.

Visit Purina's site today and you'll discover an emotionally rich destination focused on the deep bonds between pet owners and their (animal) family members. Going well beyond dispensing their first-rate product and pet care knowledge, Purina has woven community features into the site like photo sharing, podcasts for on-the-go advice, wallpaper, ring tones, and opt-in newsletters. Home page topics headlined "preventative training," "traveling with your dog," "emergency first-aid tips," or "caring for your older cat" resemble popular articles on parenting or caregiver sites.

It wasn't always thus. Back in 2002 the marketing team knew owners, veterinarians, breeders, and nutritionists visited their sites. They set out with the assistance of opt-in panel research firm comScore.

Purina and comScore looked to answer several questions. Do Purina purchasers use the Purina website? Does banner advertising influence purchase intention for its brands? ComScore combined a grocery buyer database with its panel, finding 50,000 individuals who met Purina's targeting criteria. (See Figure 4.12.)

FIGURE 4.12 ComScore tracked the delivery of banner ads to a select group of Purina's customers and prospects in order to determine the ads' effectiveness. Exposure increased purchase intention for Purina One.

Source: Joseph Jaffe, "Beyond a Website," iMedia Connection, April 14, 2003.

Purina learned that, yes, brand buyers went to Purina.com, and did so more often than average internet users (comScore 2002; Saunders 2002).

To gauge online advertising's effects, researchers assigned dog or puppy owners to an exposed or control group. For the exposed group, Purina banner ads appeared on sites they visited, while the control group saw other ads. Purina banner ads raised awareness and recall of Purina. Getting closer to purchase, data for the Purina One brand showed dog owners exposed to the advertising were more likely to "definitely or probably" consider buying the brand by double digits over the control group (comScore 2002). These findings led Purina's Michael Moore, worldwide interactive marketing director, to conclude: "This data reinforces the impact of online advertising and Purina websites improving the emotional engagement in building [loyalty for] our brands" (quoted in Saunders 2002).

The Power of Convenience—Simplify Reordering to Build Repurchase: HoneyBaked Ham

Retailers seek repeat business from loyal customers, and consumers typically want hassle-free, "set it and forget it" convenience. Replenishment programs, when they're appropriate for a brand's customers, move brands toward recurring revenue models that generate sales and boost profits at lower costs.

HoneyBaked Ham, that welcome centerpiece for holiday tables, offers gift services for its home and business customers. Holiday time is huge, of course, but how does a marketer maximize those sales, especially from existing customers?

It's probably safe to assume that most customers keep accurate records of their gift expenses for income tax reporting purposes, but far fewer keep handy lists of gift recipients. Chances are that when gift season comes around, gift givers remember some of the previous recipients, but not all.

HoneyBaked decided to give their customers push-button convenience. Their two-step strategy, executed via email, did the following:

1. Created and delivered personalized emails to each of the prior year's corporate customers containing their gift recipients' names and order details (accomplished through dynamic content and integrating with customer order databases).

2. Enabled recipients to click a link within the email to repeat and place the order.

HoneyBaked Ham's email service provider reports that this effort "was the most successful holiday campaign in the company's history. The campaign's 6.5 conversion rate led to sales that were 15 times the prior year's, with average order values 50% higher" (Silverpop 2006a).

In one tailored online communication, the company increased consumer convenience, while building more value in the relationship. Consumers saved time by avoiding the need for researching their gift list. HoneyBaked kept valuable customers, while reaping the business benefits of incremental revenue acquired at a low cost, shortening time to order, and blocking potential customer defections, which might have occurred if customers waited until the last minute.

This just-in-time strategy should appeal to marketers of all sizes and types whose customers need to replenish just about any product or repeat a service.

Build a Loyal Community of Brand Customers: NewEgg.com

"Email began as an acquisition channel but has since emerged as a critical and highly productive channel for customer retention and loyalty marketing." Why? Apart from expecting to receive order confirmations and shipping notices, consumers are receptive to follow-on offers, are interested in discounts or special offers for frequently ordered products, open to joining membership rewards programs, and want to know the location of bricks-and-mortar outlets (DoubleClick 2005d). Any company can send periodic emails and newsletters, or drop online coupons, but engaging customers, prompting ongoing purchases and creating a customer listening loop requires strategy, not an ad hoc program.

Email is at the core of retention and loyalty programs, but new developments, primarily driven by CRM systems and integrated data, are updating and reenergizing them. Examples: couponless promotions targeted to individual customers, invitation-only clubs based on interests and preferences, and personalized websites that deliver customized messages while a customer is shopping (Loyalty Lab 2006). These developments are moving loyalty and retention to an ongoing real-time, relationship-driven activity and expanding programs for all types of marketers, such as supermarkets (Jewel-Osco), florists (1-800

Flowers), jewelers (Platinum Rewards program for independent jewelers), and Broadway theaters (Nederlander).

Rapidly growing e-tailer NewEgg.com sells computer components, systems, games, electronics, and other high-tech items to younger do-it-yourself IT, web development, and computer enthusiasts. Known for competitive prices, superior customer service, and high customer satisfaction, the company sought to strengthen ties with their uber-savvy customers.

The company first concentrated on its website to attract more direct traffic. They improved navigation, made certain features like customer product reviews more visible, added content, encouraged manufacturers to contribute their own, and improved checkout and some other features like wish lists, which are very important to their customers. Additionally, they optimized the site for better search engine indexing and easier finding.

With the website humming, NewEgg looked to reduce the acquisition fees it paid to search sites, tech sites, or comparison shopping engines. With vendor Loyalty Lab, it started an email-based retention program in order to market directly to its 500,000 opt-in subscribers (and counting). NewEgg sends two emails a week to subscribers. One adopts a newsletter format that usually introduces a new state-of-the-art product, like a new video chip set, along with best sellers and special offers. The second one features promotions and deals.

An "insiders" e-tailer, NewEgg depends on pass-along. Word of mouth is extremely important for product reviews, purchase influence, wish list sending, and community approval. NewEgg knows its wired customers will forward the emails (and wish lists) when they see fit. Said Stuart Wallack, NewEgg's marketing director: "We're a private company and haven't had a lot of money to do mass marketing, and yet we've grown tremendously. We've relied on that viral word-of-mouth component, and I'd like to find out how we can further enhance that" (quoted in Quinton 2006a).

NewEgg cares deeply about list quality and takes care to build and manage it properly. Doing so minimizes churn, brings on more qualified names, and ensures relevance. The firm departs a bit from other email marketers in list building. Like many marketers, it offers a sweepstakes for collecting names. Unlike most marketers, the sweepstakes is not offered on the home page, but is included in the emails. This shields the promotion from the legions of sweepstakes participants who have no interest in the sponsoring company.

NewEgg is looking to improve its email retention program by adding more personalization and consumer controls over message frequency.

In early 2006 NewEgg built on its retention program, adding a loyalty initiative based off of its branded charge card. NewEgg created a "Preferred Account Member" group. As we write, program features match customers' needs and overcome common purchase hurdles. Members receive time-limited cash-back offers, zero interest and rush processing, a dedicated line of credit, periodic personalized discounts and promotions (tied to CRM data), express checkout, zero fraud liability, and online tools to manage the account. Adding value to the customer relationship through this program, NewEgg appears to have the insight to build substantial customer loyalty and blunt attacks on its loyal customer base from competitors.

The retention email program is working. In an average month, the newsletter "creates a click-through rate of more than 20%, which in turn generates sales conversions that average between 7% and 10%," according to NewEgg's marketing director, Howard Tong. He credits this success, in part, to copy that identifies with the needs, interests, and styles of subscribers: "It's very important to write in a language that our customers understand. By knowing how younger gamers and tech-savvy IT and computer workers converse, we can educate them in ways that convert more sales" (quoted in Brohan 2006b).

Preliminary data on the card suggests the loyalty program will be successful. When the card was introduced in late 2005 (without a loyalty program attached), basket sizes increased to between $700 and $800, up from the average $300. Promotional offers related to the card were carried over to the Preferred Member loyalty program. NewEgg said the Preferred Member purchases will account for 10% of 2006 sales (Internet Retailer 2005d). Overall 2006 sales are expected to climb from $1.3 billion to $1.6 billion (Internet Retailer 2006a; LA Business Journal 2006).

Especially interesting is NewEgg's achievement in organizing and sustaining a community of interest, where relationships among customers, NewEgg, and its suppliers are grounded in customers' experiences, values, and preferences. Retention and loyalty emerge from within the community and its shared meanings; they're not behaviors brands can impose for any real length of time.

CHAPTER 5

Display Advertising Online

WHAT TO CHOOSE?

What types of ads work online? What's the most typical size? Can we just tweak our current print or TV ads and use them online? Here we're going to review what we know about the executional and message factors that get display ads noticed and contribute to their effectiveness.

Standard Online Advertising Formats

Every medium has its ad standards, like the 30-second spot in television or one-quarter page ad in print. Because the web started as a page-based medium, online advertising originated by dividing the page into defined units that serve as containers for display advertising. These started small, as clickable text buttons and banners, and then expanded into a variety of shapes and sizes. Technology advances in ad creation and ad serving, coupled with widespread broadband penetration, are beginning to fill these containers with everything from clickable print ads and graphics pictures that push advertising to richly interactive brand experiences that pull consumers in, engage them, and prompt them to take actions marketers desire. Some are reaching levels of sophistication so high that consumers need not leave the site they are visiting to have their activity interrupted by a side trip to a brand's website.

The Interactive Advertising Bureau (IAB) recognized that standard ad sizes were needed to initially develop the market and, with industry consultation, created a set of specifications. Those specs were formalized as voluntary guidelines. Now widely adopted, they serve their purpose, bringing consistency to ad specifications, ad buying,

81

and ad serving while leaving creative executions wide open and virtually unlimited. Biannually reviewed, the guidelines are revisited and refined, ensuring their freshness and fit with advertising practices.

Ad Sizes

The IAB defines three ad categories: rectangles and pop-ups, banners and buttons, and skyscrapers. Like print media, online ads are sold in different shapes and sizes. They are called interactive marketing units or IMUs. The Standards section of the IAB website (www.iab.net) provides the most up-to-date guidelines and examples.

What are the most common sizes advertisers use? Four sizes accounted for over half the ads in 2006. According to Nielsen's study of roughly 92,000 unique ads during one week in March 2006, the leaderboard (20%) is number one, followed by the medium rectangle (13%), full banner (10%), and wide skyscraper (10%). (See Figure 5.1.)

The remainder, including the standard skyscraper, rectangle, large and small buttons, square button, and nonstandard sizes, each came in between 4% and 5%. Other (undefined), a relatively large group (17%), rounds out the size list, indicating there is still a significant amount of custom, nonstandard sizes employed.

That advertising units are measured in height and width gives them characteristics common to print advertising in newspapers, magazines, or out-of-home media. Given this practice, it is easy to lapse into printlike habits of thought, which is to consider the units as space to be filled and used primarily for static push advertising ("Oh, we just need a one-sixth page ad here"). We urge marketers and their creative partners to find great ways to engage consumers by reaching out and bringing them in *through* the box. See the "Rich Media Advertising on Broadband" section later in the chapter for evidence and inspiration.

Are consumers aware of different ad types, and do they like some better than others? Yes, according to research firm Dynamic Logic's "AdReaction 3" study (2004). Recruiting web users through the standard web intercept approach, the researchers looked at nine different types of ad formats—banners, rectangles, skyscrapers, ads with audio or video, pop-ups and pop-unders, "pop-ins" (ads that appear between pages, also called interstitials), and out-of-frame ads (having animations that move over and around the page).

The most positive formats preferred by consumers are the least intrusive ad formats, which have a well-defined place on the screen or

FIGURE 5.1 The standard leaderboard, medium rectangle, full banner, and wide skyscraper are the four most commonly used interactive marketing units (IMUs) by online advertisers.

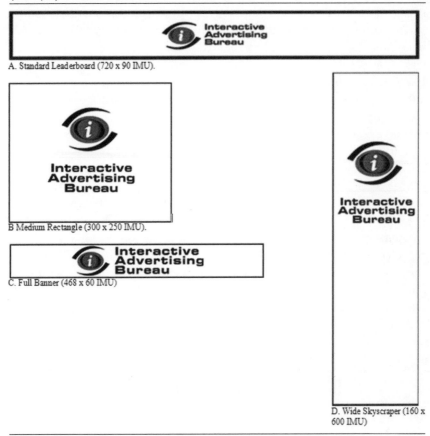

A. Standard Leaderboard (720 x 90 IMU).

B Medium Rectangle (300 x 250 IMU).

C. Full Banner (468 x 60 IMU)

D. Wide Skyscraper (160 x 600 IMU)

that provide transitions. Banners, skyscrapers, and pop-ins had the highest combined positive scores (very positive and somewhat positive), around 20%. Factoring in "neutral" gives us a range of roughly 40% to 60%.

The least positive? The more intrusive ad formats—out-of-frame ads, pop-under ads, and pop-up ads. Between 85% and 90% gave these ads the lowest marks, with the lowest of all given to pop-ups.

Is it a surprise that the better-liked formats are those most commonly used by advertisers? At this point in the evolution of internet advertising, we think not. Both consumers and advertisers have experience with these formats and are learning more about them daily. When ad formats, like pop-up ads, cause consumer frustration, advertisers get the message and change their practices. Does it mean the lesser-liked formats are not useful for advertising? Not necessarily. Even the pop-up, maligned for its unwelcome in-your-face visits and effort required to close the window, might be a powerful communicator for the right occasion, with a tight target audience and a compelling execution. Orbitz, for example, claims that its pop-under ads, which feature interactive games that change frequently, are very effective in driving people toward that travel site. In 2003, Mark Rattin, the creative director at Orbitz's agency, Otherwise, told eMarketer about the efficacy of a campaign: "We do have quantifiable data, and what we've seen is that the more games we introduce and the higher frequency with which we are able to change these games out, the more consistently we're able to drive very, very high levels of traffic to the site. We get double what the industry average is on a pop-under click-through, from a percentage standpoint" (Bruner and Gluck 2005, 13). Creative execution counts.

Creative Factors That Influence Display Advertising Effectiveness

Which creative elements communicate the message and work to engage the consumer? Several studies of this question explored branding impacts (awareness, knowledge, persuasion) across a variety of aggregated campaigns or case studies. Their results showed that, yes, creative factors affect branding measures. No surprise there. But which ones do?

Uncluttered banners raise brand awareness and recall. Large logos, or repeated logos, clarify the message and offering. Large banners clarify the message, too. They and the presence of a human face increase consumer desire to learn more about the advertised product or service. Online, a clear, visible, rapidly comprehended message with human interest works (Nielsen//NetRatings 2006a).

What factors make consumers sit up and take an interest in online ads, and are they similar to those for branding?

CNET Networks looked into this question They sought and entered into a partnership with venerable copy-testing firm Starch to adapt Starch's industry-standard print readership technique for the web. CNET Networks sponsored studies across three of its properties, each having a different audience: CNET, a consumer-oriented technology site; GameSpot, an online gaming site; and ZDNet, a technology site oriented to IT professionals (CNET Networks 2006).

Overall, the study included about 17,000 participants and analyzed more than 200 ads of different ad types, messaging, and creative elements. Visitors to the websites were randomly intercepted and shown ads on mock pages of the site they were visiting, and were then asked a series of questions relating to Starch measures—Noted (stopping power), Associated (can link ad to brand), Likability (of the ad), and One of the Best Ads for a product or service.

The study highlights and supports the branding results and, as we'll see, provides additional guidance to develop ads that get attention, communicate, and engage the audience.

Key findings of the CNET Networks studies include best practices for developing ads that get attention, communicate, and engage their audience.

CNET Networks' research demonstrates that the strongest ads get attention with powerful images, color, and contrast. Their guidelines:

- *Use powerful images.* Big, expansive photography gets ads noticed. Emphasizing contrast between the foreground and background, especially a black background, gives ads a three-dimensional effect and visual drama. Bright, eye-catching colors such as red, blue, golden yellow, and green generate impact. And models who look straight at the viewer resulted in higher Noted scores.

- *Keep it simple.* The "most remarkable" ads, the study reported, "are often the most simple executions with a clear focal point." Cluttered ads didn't hold viewers' attention, nor did ads that distracted with shaking, flashing, and related animation gimmicks. Creative elements need to work together, not at cross-purposes.

And visual balance counts. Ads with elements that were cut off, slanted, or askew in some way got lower scores.

Prominent logos, clear ad flow, and ad formats matched to the jobs they need to do are associated with communicating the ad's message effectively. Specifically:

- *Follow the flow.* Online the eye is drawn to motion or animation first, and then turns toward the copy. Make certain that the ad takes advantage of this pattern. When motion and text compete for attention, the motion tends to win.

- *Understand and leverage the unique strength of each ad unit.* Not all are equal or interchangeable; each has specific strengths. The IAB standard medium rectangle worked best for visually rich graphics and motion, giving the advertiser the ability to present complete images. The leaderboard makes its point quickly, capably communicating product image, benefits, features, and price. The most successful skyscraper ads take full advantage of the vertical format to communicate, revealing the message as a user scrolls. Commenting on this finding, CNET Networks' Kim Black adds that "it is useful for the brand logo and benefit statement to appear at the top of the ad unit, or at both the bottom and the top." That gives advertisers the means to repeat and reinforce brand messaging and increases opportunities for consumers to read them.

Recent eye-tracking research conducted by Jakob Nielsen produced revealing "heat maps showing how and where consumers pay attention to ads" (Nielsen 2006b). The researcher recorded how 232 users looked at thousands of web pages. Think of weather maps that show colored bands of temperature or infrared photos, and you get the idea. Eye-tracking visualizations show that users often read web pages in an F-shaped pattern—two horizontal stripes followed by a vertical stripe—and that their main reading behavior is fairly consistent across different sites and tasks. Take a look at three different scenarios in Figure 5.2. From left to right, users are reading an "About Us" page on a corporate website, a product page on an e-commerce site, and a search results page. The F pattern shows

FIGURE 5.2 This heat map of reading attention on three different types of web pages shows that readers scan rather than read, concentrating on the tops and lefts of pages. The most important words are the first few on a line.

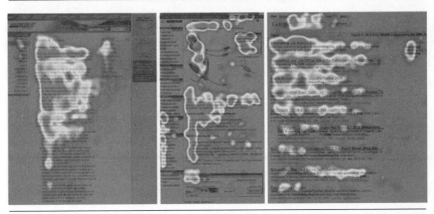

Source: Jakob Nielsen, "F-Shaped Pattern for Reading Web Content," Jakob Nielsen's Alertbox, April 17, 2006.

that readers don't read; they scan for words that interest them, with the most important ones being the first few words on the page. The key implication: Marketers and their copywriters need to understand how consumers read their ads or pages and the words that resonate most soundly, and apply that knowledge when creating ads. We explore the importance of scanning again in Chapter 6, on the search market.

Rich Media Advertising on Broadband

Macromedia Flash, Java, dynamic HTML (dHTML), animation, and streaming media have taken internet ads from just words and pictures on a page to exciting, engaging, and cinematic motion. These technologies, dubbed "rich media," are making the internet more like Times Square, TV, and games. Why? Consumers are better able to experience rich media due to broadband adoption. Ad networks have made the ads more affordable by reducing premiums for rich ads. And new capabilities by the ad-serving industry have reduced the complexity of running, tracking, and reporting ads (Dynamic Logic 2004).

Rich media ads also come in many shapes, sizes, and feature implementations. To simplify these, DoubleClick researchers describe most rich media executions by the following standard formats (Bruner and Gluck 2005, 5):

- *In-page:* standard IAB ad unit shapes that may include advanced rich media functionality, such as embedded games, animation, video, registration forms, or interactive marketing brochures, and that may allow for larger file sizes through polite download technology.

- *Expandable:* similar to in-page units, but they expand in size when a user moves the mouse over the ad or clicks to interact with it. Some publishers are experimenting with ads that automatically expand when the page loads, then retract after a small delay. These ads are sometimes called push-downs or server-initiated expandables.

- *Floating:* ads that appear as a layer on top of the user's current page; these are typically free-form ads that can move across the page in a variety of shapes and sizes and may resolve into an in-page ad on the same page or a smaller floating reminder ad unit that continues to float above the page.

- *Pop-ups:* ads that launch a new smaller browser window that appears above the open page.

- *Transitionals:* also known as between-page ads or interstitials, these ads appear between one page and another as a user clicks through a site.

Rich media ads claimed over 40% of all ad impressions served by DoubleClick in 2004 (Romeo et al. 2004).

With creative elements like animation, sight and sound, and visual interest, are rich media ads just the latest flavor of eye candy, or do rich media ads get more consumer attention? Rich media provider Eyeblaster tracks the interaction rate (the percentage of people who interact with an ad) and click-through rates of all ads running through its platform. Over all its formats in 2005 the interaction rate averaged 5.5% and the click-through rate was 1.7%, far exceeding the standard banner rates, which were 0.25% for each score. Rich media get people interested in the ads. But does that interest translate into effective advertising?

In order to determine the impact of rich media, and its quality, on branding, Latzman and Ryan (2003) researched over 800 campaigns with more than 880,000 respondents in Dynamic Logic's MarketNorms database. They analyzed awareness, association, persuasion, and a composite by comparing an exposed group to a control group. (See Figure 5.3.) For their analysis, they included only campaigns with one exposure so that each campaign was comparable. Most of the products studied appeared to be relatively known; the baseline measure of awareness among the unexposed group was nearly 50%.

Their results showed that a single rich media exposure lifted all brand measures an average of 3% over the composite baseline score (39%), with the greatest gains for awareness and association, each at 5%, followed by persuasion at 2%. Subsequent DoubleClick analyses of MarketNorms data continued to show an advantage for rich media (Bruner and Gluck 2005).

FIGURE 5.3 A single rich media exposure is capable of raising branding scores over nonrich media advertising.

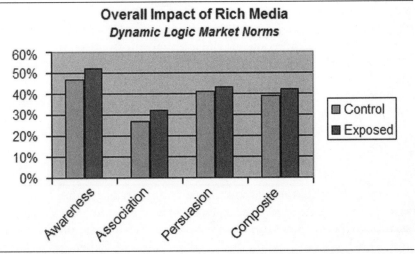

Source: Adapted from DoubleClick, "Rich Media: What? Where? Why?," 2003.

Use Rich Media Interactivity to Build New Brand Interest: Scion

Advances in rich media technology move creative units from different kinds of banner treatments or animations to truly interactive ads that place consumers in control, allowing them to personalize and tailor ads to their interests, request information, or send messages directly from within the ad. Adding interactivity generally promotes branding, especially message association, in a number of industries, particularly entertainment, CPG, electronics, and automotive (Bruner and Gluck 2005). Toyota's Scion brand shows us how.

Scion's online campaign uses a single rich media unit to advertise its three models, xA, xB, and tC. To get things rolling, one ad asks users to choose their personality type within the unit, which then refreshes with information about a corresponding Scion model. But that's not all. A results panel appears providing up-to-the-minute content. And from within the ad unit itself, prospects can watch product videos, configure cars, locate dealers, or instant message a friend. That's a lot of potential branding power for one ad (the campaign launched while we were writing and we did not have any performance data available). Creating these types of ads requires that marketers think through the many different interaction scenarios and accommodate them in order to provide consumers with an optimal, relevant, personalized brand experience.

Back-end systems track the questions asked, the information delivered, and the actions taken. Having that information on hand enables Scion and its partner, InterPolls, to optimize the campaign by changing out low-performing questions for higher-performing ones. Each ad is not only a message but a test that feeds back to improve the overall campaign (MBP 2006; Newcomb 2006a).

Online Video Advertising

Thanks to broadband, watching video online is becoming a routine activity for most internet users. Over 50% of internet users watch at least once a month, a bit more than 25% watch at least once a week, and a hard core 5% watch daily (OPA 2005). We expect consumers will watch more as video becomes available and video sharing expands.

What are people watching? AccuStream iMedia Research tells us that the music is the most popular streaming video content category, followed by news, internet TV, sports, entertainment, and movies (Palumbo 2006). (See Figure 5.4.)

As we write, video advertising is sizzling, going from a rarity to a staple offering from consumer-oriented online networks, such as AOL, and downloadable as podcasts from iTunes and related services, as well as being obtainable from user-generated video sharing sites like YouTube, from television network websites, and from emerging B2B networks like ScribeMedia.

Video advertising started with preroll and postroll advertising. The latest advance is embedding video in rich media units. Embedded ads offer several advantages over preroll ads: namely, their placements are more flexible, they don't require separate players that need to be launched before play begins, they are more easily tracked, and they don't have inventory issues. Embedded videos have the edge in popularity with advertisers, taking nearly 60% of

FIGURE 5.4   Music and news are two of the most popular streaming media viewed by consumers.

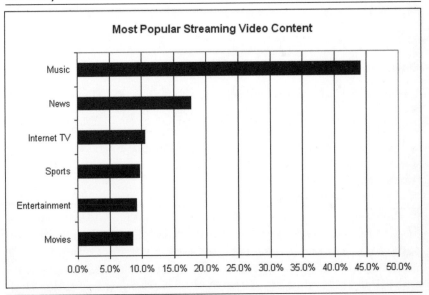

Source: AccuStream iMedia Research, reported in Palumbo 2006.

the roughly $320 million ad spend for streamed videos in 2005. We don't mean to imply that embedded videos are superior; the value of each video ad type depends on the brand, its customers, and the marketing objectives sought.

Online video outperforms the familiar static forms of online advertising on branding measures, achieving larger results faster. Dynamic Logic compared the impact of one exposure of a video ad to multiple exposures of conventional online units (leaderboards and skyscrapers) on brand awareness. Results showed a 10% increase for the group exposed to video after one exposure. Skyscraper ads took six exposures to rise 8%, and leaderboard ads took 10 exposures to increase brand awareness 6%. Message association, brand favorability, and purchase intent also increased (Maddox 2005). Video gets people's attention.

To determine how video impacts branding, Dynamic Logic studied 108 different online video ads across a number of product categories and surveyed 125,000 consumers. Top-performing ads lifted brand awareness as high as 38%, while poor performers barely registered a gain. The best ads shared a number of characteristics: The brand was central to the creative elements, the interactive power of the web was used to offer links to more brand information, and the online ads related to their offline campaign counterparts. Among the poor performers, consumers weren't sure what brand was being advertised (Klaassen 2007).

Online Video for Branding: AT&T, Buick, and BMW

While online video for brand advertising is hot, it is also very recent. But the experiences of three major advertisers provide us with clues to effectiveness and changes in practice as they not only adapt to the online environment but create new advertising forms that take advantage of online advertising's uniqueness or combine with traditional media.

Following the merger of AT&T and SBC, the new firm decided to rebrand the company under the AT&T name. The campaign, a $200 million effort, sought to reposition AT&T from a telecom company to a leading provider of networking and communications services. With a budget that big, a hefty amount went to television and print, and a slice to online media. Working with vendor Digitaledge, which used rich media vendor Unicast's video commercial, the campaign created online video ads with side-by-side interactivity as in the Scion ads. People viewing the ads could request additional product information, register for a newsletter, or read case studies.

"The results have been fantastic," Digitaledge's partner and group director Jay Krihak said. "We saw a significant lift with all [branding] metrics" (quoted in Maddox 2005). Although he demurred from reporting the actual results, he mentioned increases in brand awareness, message association, and purchase intent.

Savvy marketers are using video in bold and subtle ways, breaking free of a half-century of convention. BMW Films, perhaps the boldest of all, hired famous directors to create a series, "The Hire." They completely replaced the brand's TV advertising for a time. Staying in the automotive category, Buick's "Tiger Trap" (starring Tiger Woods and surprised public course golfers) introduced the Rainier through a skillful blending of online and offline elements that created an entertaining, reality-type campaign. Both automakers generated very positive results in branding and sales.

Games: An Emerging Online Advertising Medium

Gaming is enormously popular. Just witness the excitement when a new console comes to market or a new entry in a game franchise is released. The Mario titles, for example, have sold more than 193 million units. Pokemon comes in at 155 million. And Madden's NFL has sold over 56 million (Wikipedia 2007).

More than 40% of Internet users play online games. Publishing high-quality online games is already a big content business. Within games, brand placement is forecast to grow from a $75 million market in the United States in 2007 to about $1 billion by 2010. This shift in allocation reflects the trend toward increased online spending generally under way and a determination to target and reach consumers with relevant advertising.

Marketers need to be aware that online gamers are not stereo-typically young and male. Age is distributed more widely than most assume; fully 35% of game players are under the age of 18 and 19% over the age of 50. And, according to the Entertainment Software Association, 43% of game players today are female. Women typically favor different types of games than men, with preferences for parlor games, quizzes, and intellectual puzzles rather than first-person shooters, sports, or car racing (Gluck and Sinnreich 2006).

Gamers are accepting of—and receptive to—in-game advertising. Nearly 40% of heavy gamers agree that games appear more realistic when actual brands are embedded in games. And half of these heavy gamers agree that in-game brand advertising will be in most of the games in the future (comScore Media Metrix Game Metrix, reported in Wharton 2007).

Advertisers such as mass merchant Kohl's, chip maker AMD, and food products company Sara Lee have sponsored games tied in to the movie *Flushed Away*. It would be a stretch to call them pioneers. Of 77 branded food websites studied by the Kaiser Family Foundation, three of four offered advergames, and some sites offered as many as 60. Advergames are not just for kids. M&Ms' "50 Dark Movies Hidden in a Painting" presents players with a series of riddles that are answered by the characters in the painting. Marketers also combine advergames with search to deepen and extend brand exposure and interactions (Wharton 2007).

Games have been available on mobile devices for some time, originally as premium paid services. Free games, from companies like GameJump, use an ad-supported model to help gamers control their bills and furnish marketers with another way to target consumers and expose them to advertising. Zagat, ModTone, and GPShopper are three early adopters (Gupta 2007).

In-game advertising also appears in so-called massively multi-player online role-playing games (MMORPG), such as World of Warcraft or Star Wars Galaxies. These games, usually fantasy-oriented, enable players to control fictional characters who are organized into groups (guilds or clans) and have economies, systems of character development, and persistence (worlds continue to run continuously). Consumers register as players and typically pay a membership fee. Popular globally, memberships exceed over 15 million worldwide, with World of Warcraft the leader at 8 million. Games may involve thousands of consumers at any time who may work together to battle enemies or accomplish some other goal (Wikipedia 2007).

Linden Labs' Second Life typifies a new genre of noncombat MMORPG games. Second Life has received online marketing attention from major brands and mainstream media. This popular game, with 2.3 million registered members as of January 2007, allows players to socialize, but it is known most for its economy. Players make, sell, or buy products, or develop real estate with Linden dollars, which are convertible to U.S. currency. Remarkably, the most entrepreneurial Second Lifers earn real income. The most notable one, Anshe Chung, has earned over a million hard dollars from her online real estate development. Fashion designers, automotive designers, tattooists, architects, and wedding planners, among others, have set up shop. B2B opportunities are also available. Brands as diverse as Circuit City, American Apparel, Wells Fargo, Sony BMG Entertainment, Nike, Sun Microsystems, Toyota, and Starwood Hotels have set up shop to test and experiment (BusinessWeek 2006a). It is too early for results, but this blog posting from American Apparel's "Raz Schionning" (2006) expresses brand marketers' motivations for exploring such games as a new marketing and advertising medium:

Why did we do it and what do we hope to achieve? On a personal level I see Second Life as a budding example of the evolution of the web experience. The potential is amazing and very compelling. The constant expansion and participation is energizing. Our store in Second Life is an experiment in how we may establish relationships with our customers in this evolving medium. To speak like a marketing person for a moment . . . I see a strong overlap between SL [Second Life] users and AA [American Apparel] consumers. They are sophisticated, educated, have money to spend, and fall into our target age range. So it makes sense to investigate how we can speak to this community . . . Not unlike the way we approach any potential audience in order to grow our business.

Guidelines for Creating In-Game Advertising

Marissa Gluck and Aram Sinnreich

- Don't allow product placement in video games to diminish game-play quality.
- Do provide opportunities to promote action. Look beyond branding— video games are interactive, and in-game marketing should be as well.
- Don't rely on traditional creative and media models. The immersive environment of video games allows marketers to unleash their creative genius.
- Do know your audience.
- Don't be afraid of self-deprecation. Gamers tend to be sophisticated, savvy, and somewhat cynical, with a uniquely interactive and critical relationship to the content. Gamers are more likely to enjoy a brand presence in their games when the campaign is ironic and self-aware,
- Do use Easter eggs. These are hidden features buried inside the code of interactive entertainment. They have become a way for programmers to reward engaged and enthusiastic audiences.
- Don't ignore audio.
- Do be sensitive to privacy and regulatory issues.
- Don't imitate.

(Gluck and Sinnreich 2006)

Pay Attention to Online Advertising Clutter

A survey by Burst! (2002) found that web users generally accept advertising on a web page. However, their findings also show that for a large majority (63%) there is low tolerance for more than two units; one-third of web users said they could tolerate a single advertisement per web page, and another 30% of respondents said they could tolerate two ads per page.

More than one in three (36%) respondents said they would immediately leave a site if it appeared cluttered with advertising. This finding is nearly identical for men and women, and for all income segments analyzed. Teens (13–17) are more likely than other age segments to abandon a site perceived as cluttered.

Message effectiveness on a cluttered site will deteriorate. Nearly 70% of respondents who remain on a site they perceive to be cluttered said they pay less attention to the ads. One of the most resounding findings from this survey, however, is the negative impact advertising clutter can have on consumers' perception of advertisers' products and services. It found that 58% of respondents said they had a less favorable opinion of an advertiser's product or service when it appeared in advertising on a web page they perceived as cluttered.

Eye-tracking research adds further support for a less cluttered page. Research firm MarketingSherpa's eye-tracking study on retail suggests that attention to an individual ad is higher when there are fewer ads on the page, and lower when there are more ads on the page (MarketingSherpa 2006a). But where do people look? Recalling Jakob Nielsen's F-shaped reading pattern, consumers can eliminate entire blocks of the screen, usually sections with ads in them. Obviously, learning how consumers look at the pages your ads will appear on can guide decisions regarding placement and the ads' effectiveness.

Online's evolution and the changes it is bringing in advertising technology fundamentally alter the way people are exposed to ads and interact with brand advertising. Innovative research techniques coming to market, inspired by changes in media, consumer behavior, and society, furnish new capabilities to explore these questions and interpret the answers in new ways that are valuable to creating effective advertising. For example, online copy-testing that combines eye-tracking or attention-tracking to show the focus and flow of ad perception, and using so-called predictive markets for concept testing are just two of the growing number of new-wave approaches available today that may help optimize creative effectiveness (Maddox 2005).

The rapid expansion of sites, content, and competitor actions online means that performance can change abruptly. Monitoring performance is simplified by online advertising's accountability but, unless it's coupled with a quick strike capability to counter downturns or maximize upturns, the data are just numbers, not guides to action. Build the ability to adapt into the creative process.

That online advertising innovation happens daily is both challenging and exciting, with changes constant for advertisers and consumers. New ad types, streaming formats, immersive experiences, consumer control, community, and mobility stoke the creative fires.

The challenges of transitioning from mass media models are real. But as Marshall McLuhan argued, every new technology first assumes the character of the previous one before eventually creating its own forms, content, and experience. Discover, invent, and explore new ways to exploit the new creative capabilities that communicate your brand and engage the customer.

Winning Plays

- Online advertising has two unique characteristics—flexibility and real-time feedback—that permit advertisers to experiment inexpensively and quickly with different appeals and formats. Successful brands use online advertising in a "learn as I do" marketplace—a continuous quality improvement mind-set.

- Ad types, ad sizes, and the use of rich media video, games, and other new creative forms impact branding and advertising effectiveness. Research from a variety of perspectives suggests guidelines. Use them and test your ad's creative elements in a variety of formats, sizes, and online environments to determine the optimum type, size, and mix that will achieve your advertising goals.

- The world of online advertising is changing and evolving faster than any other advertising platform. It is critical therefore to try out and test the effectiveness of emerging approaches. Some are emerging, like streaming media, online games, and handset advertising, due to technological advances in broadband (approaching 100 million subscribers) and wireless. Other new approaches are emerging from innovative concepts, consumer insights, and interactivity.

- The most popular text format today for online advertising is the leaderboard, which is comparable to a 30-second radio or TV spot or a single-page print ad. Popularity, however, does not always mean effectiveness. The majority of research and learning indicates that dramatizing a relevant benefit is more effective than any single format. Figuring out the "what's in it for me?" from the vantage point of the customer is the best predictor of success. Additionally, think beyond pushing advertising through the ad unit box, and start thinking about interactive ways to pull consumers in and engage them to promote brand involvement and underscore brand benefits.

- Creativity is critical. Colorful, engaging executions with eye-catching headlines or interactive capabilities will be needed more and more as clutter increases and as brand advertising becomes more interwoven with content. Think through and bring about those concepts and capabilities that brand consumers want, enjoy, and value.

CHAPTER 6

The Connection of Online Search and Advertising

"Online search," Ken Cassar of Nielsen//NetRatings claims, "is the primary tool most people rely on to do everyday research" (Nielsen//Net Ratings 2006b). Indeed. U.S searches nearly doubled from December 2004 to November 2006, rising from 3.3 billion to 6.2 billion searches across 60 measured search engines (Nielsen//NetRatings 2006a).

Beyond "everyday research," more than 90% of people find or launch websites through search (Spiderhelp 2006), even when they know the URL. At one public school we know, the teachers' lounge directory lists the school website as "Google Our School Name." Typing in a few keywords or phrases, browsing a results page, and clicking on a link saves time and is more accurate. Because search engines index websites, results pages often contain links to different sections or individual listings within them, like product pages, making it easier and faster for searchers to go where they want and get the information that answers particular questions. For others requiring learning, research, and evaluating information, searching is more like a journey.

As we write, some online advertising commentators point out that while the number of searches is growing, search's growth rate is slowing. But that's expected: After such explosive growth, percentage gains become smaller as bases get larger. For search engines, though, the battles shift to percentage of share, new products, revenue growth, and profitability. Can we say search is a maturing market? Yes. A mature market? Hardly.

Search is a big business for advertising. In this chapter we first review consumer search—the number of searchers, the popularity of search as an online activity, what people search for, and how they search and read results, all of which influence search advertising buying strategy. After establishing the consumer side of search, we turn to search engine marketing, which is not one but a family of techniques. We explain them and then illustrate the ways search engine marketing strategies are used to accomplish a wide range of online advertising objectives.

Portrait of the Online Searcher

Just about everybody who goes online does it. More than any other online activity, search reflects people's far-ranging interests and motivations guided by who they are, where they live, their interests, and events in the world at large. Search is not an end in itself. It works through ads and listings, provides gateways to websites large and small, social to technical, pop to highbrow, mass to class that are not merely sites, but destinations and immersions.

The most popular activity online, Pew (2005) research tells us, is email for 77% of the consumers they surveyed. Like bringing in the postal mail, most people check their in-boxes daily. The second most popular internet activity? Looking for stuff with search engines, at 63%. Expanding online offerings makes search ever more necessary. After search, getting news ranks third at 46%, and then activities become quite specialized. Doing job-related research, instant messaging, and online banking range from 29% down to 18%. Visiting chat rooms, making online travel reservations, reading blogs, and participating in online auctions bring up the rear at 8% or less. Search aggregates audience, and is a chief reason why search is of such interest to online marketers as a primary way to reach consumers online.

Searchers comprise 80% of the total online population and 51% of the U.S. population (Pew 2005). Their numbers will grow—eMarketer (2006h) forecasts the searcher population climbing to 166 million in 2010, 85% of all online users and 56% of the U.S. population. Along with the number of searchers, the frequency of searches will grow as well as search engines expand to be the primary interface between online users and the internet and as people use search more and more for navigational purposes (Hotchkiss 2006).

The power of search is for buying advertising targeted to a context, interest, or category.

The Internet & American Life Project studies conducted by Pew

Trusts in conjunction with comScore Media Metrix track a panel of internet users. They find that over 60% of all adult web surfers, about 60 million, use search engines on any given day (Pew 2005), and they conduct an average of two searches per day (Fallows 2005). You probably know from your own experience that some people, about 25%, type into the search box several times throughout the day (eMarketer 2006h). They're checking stocks, doing business research, grabbing sports scores, dropping in at MySpace, checking movie listings, or looking for some cool product to buy. Advertising opportunities abound—connecting intent with content.

Although hundreds of search engines exist, about 44% of searchers use just one engine, about 48% use up to three engines, and only about 7% use more than three. Differences exist among these groups. According to Fallows (2005), the number of searches people launch and their search confidence increase with the number of engines used. "More engaged" searchers often match their search questions to individual engines and evaluate information by cross-checking different results and sources. "Less engaged" searchers typically search for less important information and appear content to take the results they're given at face value.

Google skews slightly more toward men (53%). Yahoo! splits evenly. Women outnumber men on MSN Search, Ask.com, and AOL Search by margins ranging from 6% to 18% (Advertising Age 2006). Keep in mind that these splits may not apply to the entire site. Audience profiles for specific sections, such as technology or health, often differ. For targeting and media buying, make certain that search engines' user profiles match your customer profiles.

Most folks who search every day use broadband connections: cable, DSL, office networks, satellite, or mobile web-enabled handsets, like pocket PCs, BlackBerrys, or Apple iPhones. High speed contributes to searching in a big way. People with broadband at work or at home are about equally likely, 57% and 54% respectively, to look stuff up with search engines each day. But the "killer searchers," nearly 80% of these searchers, take advantage of broadband at work *and* at home.

While search is the second most popular activity online, people spend far less time with search than they do with other internet activities, accounting for a shade under 5% of their total online time in the fourth quarter of 2005 (eMarketer 2006h). Search advertising spend, which we detail a bit later, commands currently about half of all online ad spend. Why would advertisers allocate so much money to an activity where people spend such little time?

When you think about it, spending much less time on search sites makes sense. Like fast-food meals, people look to "grab and go." Contrast that with email, which is more of a sit-down meal. Reading and writing take considerably more time. How much of a difference? Pew's research (2005) shows in general people spend 24 minutes on email but only 3.5 minutes with search engines on any given day. An Enquiro et al. study (2005) found that people spend, on average, only 6.4 seconds on an entire search results page before clicking through to another page.

Consumers Search for Personally Relevant Information

Search interests are as diverse as online searchers. Just as many of us read the *Wall Street Journal*, *BusinessWeek*, the *New Yorker*, and *USA Today*, we're just as likely to indulge our pleasures, follow sports, or shop through catalogs. It's the same for search. In fact, a majority (55%) of searchers strike a work/life balance; half their searching is "important to them" and half is "trivial" (Fallows 2005). Searchers like having fun and doing their business, just as we all do offline.

People search widely—any topic is fair game—but most searches in a typical day or week relate to pop culture (music, movies, TV, celebrities, games); seasonal activities; holiday; or current events. The big search engines list popular keyword searches, providing keyholes through which marketers and general users can glimpse searchers' myriad interests. On June 18, 2006, Yahoo! Buzz Index listed World Cup, U.S. Open, Britney Spears, Shakira, WWE, Paris Hilton, FIFA, Angelina Jolie, RuneScape, and Lindsay Lohan as the 10 most popular search terms. Six months later, on January 16, 2007, Britney and Lindsay had stayed but the others had been displaced by other hot celebrities (e.g., Fergie, Beyonce, Victoria Beckham) or more timely sports (e.g., NFL) (Yahoo! Buzz Index 2006, 2007). AskIQ, Google Zeitgeist, AOL Hot Searches, Lycos 50, and MSN Search Insider are some of the many lenses advertisers use for insight into searcher trends.

Going beyond individual terms, search engine marketer iProspect examined the popularity of search categories (respondents could answer more than once). Their research identified travel and health as the most popular search categories. More than half of search activities related to news and information services, and just about half concerned entertainment-oriented websites or activities.

People fire up search engines in order to learn more about the panoply of events occurring in the world at large in greater depth. Researching its log files, Google (2005a) demonstrates the strong relationship between the two. A few examples: Intel's press release for Viiv, a new processor, caused a 15,000% spike in searches that day. Search volumes often persist more than a day or two. The strike at Heathrow Airport and British Airways caused searches from non-UK locations to peak 3,900% above average and then decrease, but stay at higher than normal levels for over two weeks as travelers followed the news.

Search Is a Journey

Because consumers search for personally relevant information, searchers usually have a high level of interest in what they are searching for, yet they also want to find and act on the best results quickly. Consumers have evolved strategies for achieving these goals, which influence search marketing.

Searchers share one trait in common: They spend very little time with search engine results—we mentioned earlier that consumers spend only 6.4 seconds on average on an entire search results page (Enquiro et al. 2005). That being the case, how do searchers process pages?

When you sit down to perform a search, take note of why you're searching and what you do to find satisfactory answers to your questions. Most likely, you're motivated, hot on the trail of something, and looking to find out, get an answer, and possibly make a decision. Gord Hotchkiss told us in an interview, "Consumer intent plays an important role in search behavior. People actively look for knowledge, products, or services and are receptive to new information." The high levels of intention and interaction, Hotchkiss pointed out, distinguish search engine advertising from offline forms and some online types where readers, viewers, or listeners passively receive advertising and later may take an action (Hotchkiss 2006).

How do motivated consumers search? Searchers use a type of trial and error that researcher Marcia Bates calls "berrypicking." That's very unlike searching in the preinternet days when limited, carefully planned and constructed searches yielded one set of results that included copied pages from reference books and/or restricted electronic databases like Dialog or Lexis/Nexis. Going around the berry patch, distinguishing ripe fruit from green, then picking and collecting some more accurately describes today's searcher behavior.

In berrypicking:

- Typical search queries evolve; they are not static.
- Searchers commonly gather information in bits and pieces instead of in one grand best retrieved set.
- Searchers use a wide variety of search techniques.
- Searchers use a wide variety of sources.

Search, in the berrypicking view, is a series of successive approximations based on testing, feedback, and learning; it's not making a beeline. Search engine marketing authority Shari Thurow (2006) explains that other search behaviors—querying and refining terms, scanning results, expanding terms, browsing, pogo-sticking from results to website and back, foraging for new materials, and ultimately reading—all relate to berrypicking and describe how people find the most relevant links.

Berrypicking searchers gauge the credibility of different sources in their work. They assess ad and natural listing positions (higher is better), look for similarity of the natural listings to the paid listings (closer is better), and assess the perceived authority of the information (more is better). As we'll see later in the chapter, relevancy drives clicks and conversions.

Paid Search Advertising Spending

Paid search dominates marketer spending on online advertising. In 2005, the most recent year for which complete data is available, search attracted $5.1 billion, or 41%, of the total $12.5 billion spent on internet advertising (IAB 2006b). Display advertising, the next highest category at $2.4 billion, claimed just a 19% share of dollars. Revenue for the first half of 2006 shows a consistent spending allocation picture, but at a higher spending level.

Will search remain online advertising's King Kong? eMarketer (2006g) believes so, projecting search reaching $11.3 billion, just under 40% of the $29 billion total for all online spending in 2010.

Measurement, low entry barriers, e-commerce, and the ability of search engines to aggregate lots of prospects for targeting contribute and justify the growth of search spending.

Search advertising is open to companies of all sizes, not just the deep-pocketed (eMarketer 2006h). It doesn't cost much to pay to play. The ante for major search engines can be as low as $5. As companies become more knowledgeable about search, analysts expect local search (geographically restricted search) dollars to flow in.

Paid search advertising offers measurability and control historically unavailable offline, which offers the promise of greater accountability to the marketing function. Server log analysis reveals every detail of searching, the keywords used, the ads and results displayed, the clicks made, and the actions taken. Advertisers see their results second by second. *BusinessWeek* (2006) asserts: "[Computers'] knack for numbers has helped turn the internet into an advertising sensation. No medium before has been able to provide advertisers with such detailed information on how many people see an ad—and how many respond to it with a click." Beyond measurement, search marketing growth is joined by a number of additional drivers, namely:

- *More search terms.* Searchers use more words in their search queries (OneStat 2005). Advertisers, as a result, purchase more keywords.
- *E-commerce.* Where there's e-commerce, there's search and search advertising to support it. Forrester projects U.S. e-commerce sales to nearly double, reaching $329 billion in 2010 from $175 billion in 2005. That means more brands and more places to buy them must be found.
- *Customer aggregation.* A handful of search engines reach most online searchers.
- *Targeting.* Search engines offer multiple ways to target customers. To the traditional keyword targeting, search engines offer geographic targeting capabilities that localize ads. New daypart, demographic, and behavioral targeting capabilities are available.
- *Niche sites.* Sports, travel, and finance sites, for example, concentrate desirable customers into well-stocked "trout ponds," granting advertisers fly-fishing precision.

Keyword tracking firm OneStat (2005) shows searchers pumping more words into the search box. As the trend of navigational search becomes more popular, the length of the search phrase is becoming longer. One-word searches, like typing "stereo," "diabetes," or "car" into an engine, number just one in five searches. Longer phrases rule. Three of five people search on two- or three-word phrases like "home theater systems," "Angelina Jolie," "fuel-efficient cars," or "wardrobe malfunction" (the second most used search phrase of all time). More extended phrases, four words or more, account for the remaining searches. Advertisers purchase additional keywords to keep up.

DoubleClick reports that while the numbers of words are rising, the growth rate of campaign keywords may be slowing. Comparing the fourth quarter of 2005 with the third quarter, keywords increased only 8%. Why keyword growth slowed wasn't explained, but it may be a function of the law of large numbers (as the base increases, percentage gains become smaller), or that through developments in analytics and search engine professionalism advertisers better spot and remove poor performers, need fewer words because they have adjusted to searchers' use of short search phrases, or want to concentrate more on high performers.

Keyword Pricing

Keyword prices are market driven, resulting from supply and demand, competitor bidding, and user clicks. Are prices rising or falling? The answer, like so much in this transactional, auction-based world, is "It depends." It depends on methodology: which keywords are tracked (not all services track the same types); their rank in the lists of sponsored links on different search engines; keyword performance; industry activity; seasonality; and time periods analyzed. No matter the method used, all agree that holiday shopping—Christmas and Mother's Day ("online flowers" rose 67%), for example—causes price spikes as retail advertisers aim to capture that business.

Search Engine Marketing Techniques

Search engine marketers use several established strategies to reach their brand marketing goals. Search marketers divide their techniques into paid search advertising and organic search engine optimization, or SEO (SEMPO 2005).

Paid advertising comprises three types, paid search ads, contextually targeted search ads, and paid inclusion.

1. *Paid search ads.* The Search Engine Marketing Professional Organization (SEMPO) defines these ads as "Text ads targeted to keyword search results on search engines, through programs such as Google AdWords and Yahoo! Search's Precision Match, also sometimes referred to as paid placement, pay-per-click (PPC) advertising, and cost-per-click (CPC) advertising." Paid search ad advertisers bid on keywords whose prices, in part, govern the appearance of the ad on a search results page and its position. When consumers type in "Caribbean beach vacation," ads keyed to those words typically appear on the right side of a search results page or across the top, above other listings.

2. *Contextually targeted search ads.* These ads, SEMPO writes, are "targeted to the subject of writings on web pages, such as news articles and blogs, using programs such as Google's AdSense and Yahoo! Search's Content Match programs." You've seen them on pages you read. Quite often, web publishers group the ads under headings, such as "Ads by Google." Additionally, search engines may assemble specific sites, usually vertical, specialty, or niche sites from their "long tail" into a mininetwork in order to target specific types of visitors for advertised brands. Here, too, advertisers' keyword bidding influences appearance and position.

3. *Paid inclusion.* SEMPO describes the practice of paying a fee (fee structures vary) to search engines and similar types of sites (e.g., directories, shopping comparison sites) so that a given website or its web pages may be included in the service's directory, although not necessarily in exchange for a particular position in search listings. Paid inclusion listings can, and often are, optimized so that they appear in favorable positions in the natural results. Advertisers assign keywords to paid inclusion listings so that their appearance is triggered by the search terms. Note, paid inclusion doesn't guarantee a listing, only inclusion in the index. At the time of writing, Yahoo! is the only major search engine offering paid inclusion, along with a number of secondary engines.

Organic search engine optimization is the practice of improving how well a site or page gets listed in search engines and placed in the results for particular search topics. Organic search engine optimization uses a range of techniques, which we describe later in the chapter.

If you've searched, you're familiar with text ads. These appear on results pages, often on the right side, but sometimes above and below the organic listings themselves, and set off from them with headings. "Ads by Google," "Sponsor Results" on Yahoo!, "Sponsored Sites" on MSN, or "Sponsored Results" on Ask.com are examples.

Paid Placement Campaign Elements

Pay-per-click advertising campaigns are straightforward in principle, but their underlying strategies are often quite sophisticated. Paid placement campaigns typically include these steps: (1) target customers through keyword selections, (2) create the ad, (3) set bid price and budget to achieve marketing objectives, (4) evaluate, and (5) optimize in the future. We cover the first three areas now, and then turn our attention toward search engine optimization and paid inclusion. Following those discussions, we turn to the last element because it applies generally to all forms of search engine marketing.

In search engine advertising, ads are primarily targeted by keywords, and may be secondarily targeted by geography, daypart, demography, or behavior.

Prior to creating ads, advertisers select and assign keywords, or combinations called keyphrases, to their product or service. Ads appear when customers type terms into a search engine that match keywords advertisers purchase. Type in "riding lawn mower" and you'll get ads for riding lawn mowers and related products, such as replacement parts, with links to website landing pages, which may be home pages, catalog pages, or other relevant linking destinations, where prospects engage with your brand experience.

What makes a good keyword? Gord Hotchkiss, CEO of search engine marketer Enquiro, stresses the value of words consumers use. "A big issue today," he told us in an interview, "is getting corporations to pick great keywords. There's a disconnect between product marketers who are trying to uniquely describe themselves and the words consumers use. It's especially bad in B2B and high-tech. Corporate marketing departments want to control search, but it's the consumer that controls it. Marketers need to understand that at a fundamental level, then leverage the consumer language" (Hotchkiss 2006).

As a practical matter, keywords need to overcome poor typing. Advertisers add plural words, "fat-finger" typos, and common misspellings in order to capture variations that make ads visible and boost traffic from clicks. Just how important are misspellings? Take Netflix. "Netflicks," "net flix," "netflex," and similar misspellings numbered half of the top 14 search terms driving traffic to its site (Hitwise 2006b).

"Search marketing budgets can be justified," eMarketer analyst David Hallerman (2006) says, "when marketers can trace the path between link and return on investment." That means finding great keywords. He reviewed a study ranking various keyword-finding techniques by their ROI. Nearly 4,000 search engine marketers, affiliate marketers, and merchants assigned "great ROI," "medium ROI," and "low ROI" to them.

The best keyword-locating methods data mined site visitor search terms and clicks. Roughly 60% agreed that detecting customer language paid off handsomely. Analyzing log files to spot keywords and frequently used words that were associated with high conversion rates found them. The roll call of techniques with a middling ROI, cited from 50% to 60%, appear removed from the customer: client customer service or sales staff feedback, negative matching, client marketer feedback, scraping or analyzing competitor websites, and tools search engines furnish. The worst-performing technique, focus groups, signed in at 44%. Yet it had a split personality. An equal number considered focus groups a great ROI method. The difference may be due to the quality of the focus group research for eliciting powerful terms, interpretation of ROI, or other factors like product category.

Once found, keywords can be made to work as hard as possible for marketers when they control the type of matching rules their keywords will follow and choose wisely among generic and brand terms.

Consider Unilever's Dove soap. Hitwise research (2006b) shows us that broad matches alone would decrease relevancy for what is a common term. Ads would appear in response to searches for poet Rita Dove, the book *Lonesome Dove*, candy maker Dove Chocolates, and many others. "By adding negative keywords to the broad match," Hitwise concludes, "Unilever is able to control when its Dove ads appear," resulting in qualify traffic, more relevant clicks, and more efficient use of the search budget. Combining keyword matching approaches expands or narrows target definitions and influences the type of traffic generated to your site.

Should you bid on your own brand keywords in addition to generic and competitor terms? Reviewing data from a campaign for the Westin St. Francis Hotel, furnished to Did-it's Kevin Lee (2004a) by Westin's agency Digital Marketing Works LLC, Lee concluded that brand terms dramatically outperformed nonbranded terms for impression-to-click and click-to-booking conversions. Where allowed, advertisers buy their brand and competitor brand keywords. The tactic is to drive traffic to your site with the competitor keyword. Westin's brand keywords pulled better and outperformed on relative ROI.

Smart keyword selection enables marketers to increase reach at a reasonable cost and effectively target. One way of accomplishing that, IBM's Hunt and Moran (2005) suggest, is to use descriptive, low-volume keywords that play a secondary, supporting role. Keyphrases like "business transformation" for IBM, "grass stain" for Tide, or "clear cellular" for a mobile provider do the trick. These related terms target and reach the audience that may be aware of the finer points of your messaging.

A second keyword finding approach recommends using keywords from related activities, such as sponsored events, spokespersons, TV shows, movies, games, actors, or characters (Hunt and Moran 2005; Lee 2004a). Lee calls these promotion sponsorship keywords, or PSKs. In many cases, he says, their cost-per-click is reasonable and in line with average cost-per-click prices.

Promotion sponsorship keywords reinforce the association between the character, personality, property, or event and your targeted customers. These PSKs multiply the brand's visibility and extend your audience reach. Assume you're Coca-Cola for a second. If you bought "American Idol," "Simon Cowell," "Carrie Underwood," or "Taylor Hicks," your brand would appear whenever consumers stuffed the search box with those keywords. You don't have to be a major advertiser to benefit, however. Local banks, car dealers, YMCAs, restaurants, and myriad local businesses usually sponsor charity, community, or local business events. The same principle applies.

The following case illustrates the value well-chosen keywords have on brand performance.

Use Carefully Chosen Keywords to Build an Online Business: Angler's Vice

Online fly-fishing retailer Angler's Vice launched in 2004 to provide enthusiasts with quality equipment and products at reasonable prices. Catering to savvy fishermen, the store sought to build traffic and sales through search engine marketing (details for this case come from Yahoo! Buzz Index 2006).

Initially Angler's Vice started, as many companies do, with a relatively modest list of about 50 keywords. If you know a little about fly-fishing, you know that the hobby is filled with all types of arcane names for flies, fly-tying materials, or rod parts, for example. Working with Yahoo! Search Marketing, the team expanded the list to over 450 keywords, leveraging low-volume but highly targeting keywords like "dubbing fly-tying material" or "green butt skunk." Using a combination of specialized generic and brand keywords enabled Angler's Vice to "pay less for clicks, but reach very highly qualified prospects; those who were further along in the buying cycle." The Angler's Vice team also scrutinized the firm's bidding strategy in order to understand which ad position worked best for conversions. (We treat this point in greater depth a bit later in the chapter.)

Angler's online strategy started the company toward meeting its goals. Its ads appeared alongside those of more established competitors, giving it visibility and raising awareness. Although we do not have specific results, Angler's Vice reports increased qualified site visits and sales.

Having selected keywords, it is time to put them to work in the text ads themselves. Text ads contain a title and a body. But is one element more important than the other? To answer this question Marketing Experiments.com (2005) created two test sites, one for an internet marketing services site, the other for a specialty pet store. The researchers studied the differences in click-through rate generated by five different pay-per-click ads that varied and combined "good" or "poor" titles and "well-written" or "poorly written" body copy.

"Good title" copy used search keyword insertion. This technique customizes the title by placing the keywords searchers use in the title. "Poor title" copy used a static headline. "Well-written" body copy aptly described the product or service; "poorly written" body copy was vague or dull. So that they attributed differences to the five different ads, the researchers held other variables, like ad rank, constant.

Ads ran for four days; the pet and business services campaigns generated about 800 clicks. Which performed better? Ads with good titles outpulled those with poor titles by about 50%. "The impact on CTR [click-through rate] with a poorly written body copy was slight," MarketingExperiments.com concludes, "but the effect of poorly written title copy was quite significant, which leads us to the conclusion that most potential customers focus on the title rather than on the body or on the ad copy as a whole." Great user-centric keywords and location are extremely important.

Seven Tips for Optimizing Pay-per-Click Copy

MarketingExperiments.com

1. Heading or title is the most important element of your PPC ad copy. The more potential customers relate to your heading, the more likely they will be to click on your ad.
2. Use relevant keywords in the title.
3. List prices in the title if they are the lowest or near the lowest.
4. "Free" add-on offers work well in the ad title.
5. Make sure the display URL is the shortest possible URL. Display URLs are basically free brand exposure for your domain name. Even when no one clicks on your ads, you are still receiving exposure.
6. Create a sense of urgency in your ads if it can be done without hype. Rather than using words like "amazing" or "unbelievable," try "limited-time offer" or "available for overnight shipping."
7. When space is available, always add a credibility indicator. Examples of these include "30-day money-back guarantee" or "five-star rated merchant."

(MarketingExperiments.com 2005)

Consumers' experience does not end with seeing the ad. After communication, paid ads' second purpose is persuading consumers to visit brand websites by clicking on them. The postclick experience is crucial in online marketing because it either provides consumers with the beginnings of a quality brand experience or it does not. Astute marketers see the text ad and landing page as a unit, and give as much attention to landing pages as they do to the text ads themselves.

"ROI," Google (2006b) tells advertisers "usually improves if your landing page directly relates to your ad and immediately presents a conversion opportunity—whether that means signing up for a newsletter, downloading a software demo, or buying a product." Landing pages can be tested and optimized for the conversion of interest. Because landing pages contain numerous regions, graphical elements (product pictures, diagrams, buttons, etc.), and offers, performing split tests or conducting multivariate studies (where several variables are manipulated) can improve conversion performance, as we'll see in the following case.

Optimize Landing Pages to Increase Sales: Dale & Thomas

Dale & Thomas, the gourmet popcorn company founded by Detroit Pistons great Isiah Thomas, looked to increase sales during the holiday season by optimizing its landing page. With its vendor, Optimost (2006), they tested seven web page variables: main layout area, order area headline, order area image, order area button, popcorn flavors imagery, free shipping area, and mailing list sign-up area. And within these, they tested a variety of different copy elements: six different headlines, six order area images, four flavors images, and so forth. With 1.9 million combinations possible, Optimost took a sample for live testing.

Compared to the control page, website sales increased over 13% within a month. Multivariate testing shed light on factors driving performance. Page element positioning was important: Flipping the position of two images from left to right at the top of the page contributed. The design and choice of images made impacts. One test, for example, comparing pictures of the popcorn chef and pictures of the scrumptious popcorn showed that the product images worked better. Last, copy generally did not influence results, but, Optimost notes, further testing may reveal better phrases.

Manage Ad Rank to Impact Website Traffic

The higher your ad appears in a list of paid search ads, the better its performance (Brooks 2005a; DoubleClick 2006b; Enquiro et al. 2005). Atlas Institute's Nico Brooks looked at ads in different ranks and their ability to generate click-throughs that send visitors to websites. Analyzing millions of impressions and thousands of keywords across a variety of industries in different positions, Atlas discovered that clicks steadily declined as keywords moved lower on the list.

How much lower? Brooks created a measure called click potential, which shows the expected drop in the number of clicks by ad position. He calculated data for Google and Overture (now Yahoo! Search Marketing). Over the first three places in Google, click potential starts at 100% for the top rank, then goes down to 60% and 48% for the second and third positions. By the fifth position, we're down to 35%, and by the tenth slot we bottom out at 14%. Overture exhibited a similar directional trend.

Let's use an example to demonstrate the point. Say you operate Scootin' Scooters, a motor scooter reseller. Your click-through rate is 7% for the key phrase "motor scooter," and prospects conduct 1,000 searches on that phrase per month. That's 70 prospects directed to your store. Now assume, as many search marketers do, that belonging in the top-three ad group is sufficient. We know that the click-through rate for third position is 48%. Doing the math (taking 48% of 70), we lower our expected traffic level to 34 visitors. Ad rank matters.

Now that we've established the impact of rank on traffic, let's explore the impact of rank on conversions, which many consider the most important consumer action. Atlas' Brooks (2005b) conducted a second study, focusing on "primary conversions"; these were mostly sales but also included lead acquisitions, account sign-ups, and requests for information like those ever-popular white papers. This time Brooks studied 42 million clicks and over 408,000 keywords, looking for differences as keywords moved up and down on Google and Overture. To place everything on an even basis, Atlas developed a metric, conversion potential, that "combines the effects of traffic volume and conversion rate by rank." Brooks based all changes off the first rank to see any decay trends. The key finding: Conversion rates drop as search ad position drops.

Appeals of Natural Listings: Organic Search Engine Optimization

Search engine marketers value natural, or organic, listings (the words are interchangeable) for four reasons: (1) lower cost compared to pay-per-click, (2) higher click-through rates, (3) consumers use organic listings to judge paid listings, and (4) organic listings outconvert paid ones.

Lower Cost Compared to Pay-per-Click

Combining organic and paid search can generate advertising cost efficiencies.

Organic listings resulting from search engine optimization are essentially free, meaning there's no cost-per-click (CPC) charged. The additional traffic generated from natural listings effectively lowers the CPC cost of paid search ads. That's a budget stretcher and potential campaign productivity booster, as this study from MarketingExperiments.com (2004) shows. They examined the additional contribution an organic search engine optimization effort made to an existing pay-per-click campaign; five search engines were used. Sponsored listings drew 90,516 clicks for a total cost of $7,358, at an average click cost of $.81. The organic campaign generated an additional 39,160 clicks at no charge, a gain of 43%, and overall reduced the per-click cost of the campaign by almost 30%, down to $.57 per click.

Higher Click Rates Generate Additional Traffic

People click more often on natural listings. Search engine marketer iProspect (Marckini 2004) and partners studied where the users of four search engines—Google, Yahoo!, AOL, and MSN—clicked. Researchers showed individuals sample results pages for a "used car" search, and instructed them to click on the most relevant result. Consumers clicked text ads and organic listings, but in a 60/40 split favored organic listings. The organic listings champ? Google at 72%, followed by Yahoo! at 60%. Over on AOL, organic clicks and sponsored clicks were evenly divided. MSN deviated from the pattern—only 29% clicked on organic listings. The key strategic point here: Consumers click on natural listings and paid listings, but display preferences for organic.

Consumers value natural listings more highly than paid ones and see them as more relevant initially (Jansen 2005). Searchers start out being skeptical toward paid ads and personally vet them by berrypicking among result listings and text ads. They perform their own cross-checks, evaluating sponsored listings in the context of the natural, organic listings, all the while gauging advertiser credibility and relevance.

Using Search Engine Optimization to Raise Brand Awareness: Specialty Software Company

For advertisers of any size, high positions in the organic results or having a mass of results in the search page potentially builds awareness. Take one company we know, kept anonymous for competitive reasons, that grows its software business online through an in-house search engine optimization program. The company uses very targeted keywords, fresh content, benefits-oriented copy, extensive and often updated white paper collections, downloadable full-working demos, regular product updates, and a spider-friendly website. Users typing their category, product name, or specific task they need to perform into a search engine see the company's listings in the organic results only. Its listings are often first, but typically appear at least within the first five listings above the fold and bracketed by well-known competitors. Through its program, this highly reputable but lesser-known firm generates brand awareness and drives traffic to its site, where prospects learn more about the product through deeper content and deeper engagement, and then can make a purchase.

As the specialty software example portrays, search engine optimization is a family of techniques that aim to have search engines index your pages and assign them a high relevance score. The higher the relevance score, the higher they appear in the listings.

Best Practices for Organic Search Engine Optimization

Search engine optimizers tweak factors that search engine spiders (automated collection tools) capture and the search engines eventually use in their relevance computations. Website structure, keywords, text on pages, hidden text in web page (HTML) tags, and linking patterns feed the search spider beast (Boswell 2006; Position Research 2002).

Optimizing Organic Search

- Choose the right keywords and phrases that are well-targeted and offer significant traffic potential.
- Focus individual pages on specific keywords.
- For sites that sell products or services, include a few lines of copy at the top of each offer page.
- Title tags should be keyword rich, with the most important at the beginning.
- Give your pages relevant names.
- Submit your site to DMOZ.org and as many specialized directories as you can find. This creates relevant inbound links and helps spiders find your site.
- Encourage reciprocal linking.

(MarketingExperiments.com 2006)

Listing Position Influences Performance

Searchers scan and skim search results pages, favoring the top positions and lending them an advantage. In a 2005 Enquiro eye-tracking study, 82% of fixation points for searchers were the top organic results and top sponsors ads. These two top positions also took up 78% of readers' first scanning activity and 56% of first click activity as well (Enquiro et al. 2005). Based on these results and on our discussion of ad rank and performance for paid ads, we can reasonably assume that more highly positioned organic ads get more clicks. Even if not clicked, ads at or near the top may work in additional ways: as ad impressions generating branding awareness, and as the evaluation standard when searchers assess relevance and credibility of pay-per-click ads.

Paid Inclusion

Paid inclusion ensures that specific listings are included in search engine indexes. Advertisers pay search engines to index named URLs and they purchase keywords that trigger display in natural search result listings. When searchers type keywords into the search box, advertiser listings may appear in organic results, but there's no guarantee of the top positions. Most often, paid inclusion is used to extend audience reach and generate leads.

Search engines build their indexes by spidering or crawling websites and including pages they deem relevant. It can take time for your pages to appear in the search engine listings, and the pages that do appear may be hit-or-miss. Some pages, such as those assembled from databases, escape indexing because they are constructed "on the fly" and appear on demand in response to specific search queries.

Paid inclusion programs overcome these problems. Annual fee directories, per-URL listings, and XML feeds are three of the most popular types. Such programs allow webmasters to specify the pages indexed by the search engines. Search engines regularly respider the designated pages and include them in the index quickly. As we write, fees run between 15 cents and 40 cents per listing, rendering them cost-effective in relation to pay-per-click ads. When advertisers submit thousands of URLs, pricing may shift to a cost-per-thousand model.

Paid Inclusion Generates Traffic Volume and Conversions

Paid inclusion listings capably drive significant qualified traffic volumes at substantially lower prices than pay-per-click advertising. Performance varies by vertical. ICrossing's Marckini (2004) presents several cases illustrating these points, but here's one. For a B2B industrial e-commerce site, the prices of five targeted keywords ranged from $0.65 to $3.51. Paid inclusion listings cost 25 cents, generating savings ranging from 40 cents to $3.26 per click. Traffic generated by the organic listings increased 4,000% and computed ROI positive. Marckini points out that even when cost-per-click and paid inclusion fees are about the same, it often makes sense to use paid inclusion, so long as the effort generates acceptable ROI. Over time, the pay-per-click rates may increase and the traffic generated from paid inclusion listings can work to lower overall cost (a similar point to the one we made earlier on SEO results reducing the per-click cost of paid search ads). When ROI is positive, Marckini says, "investing in PI increases the overall volume of qualified visitors and conversion[s] at sites."

Measuring Search Engine Marketing Campaigns

There is a need for better measurement and measurement practices. Within those firms that do measure, only 28% of them circulate reports (Eisenberg and Novo 2002). Even in e-commerce, where one expects paid text ad ROI to be diligently and closely managed by green eyeshade types, the metrics picture is equally dim. Jupiter analyst Nate Elliot believes that pay-per-click costs and trends toward campaign complexity underscore the need for better use of metrics by marketers for campaign evaluation and smarter bidding. "In that environment," he says, "it is even more important they become sophisticated" (quoted in Morrissey 2004).

Our discussion of metrics is organized into three parts: (1) advertising performance, where we review the pulling power of text ads and listing; (2) the application of survey and website metrics to gauge branding; and (3) business measures.

Advertising Performance

- Keywords are analyzed for their abilities to generate traffic and website conversions.
- Rankings refer to positions for organic search listings or search text ad position. Not all advertisers seek the top rank, but want to appear within a targeted range. Advertisers focus on managing rank for their best-performing keywords.
- Click-throughs count the number of times consumers click on text ads or organic links that drive traffic to brand websites

during the campaign or within a defined period of time. Click-throughs have become less important over time as marketers shifted from seeing success as click-generated site traffic to understanding and analyzing consumer actions.

- Traffic measures the number of site visitors within a period of time. Raw numbers are not that insightful. Traffic becomes meaningful when site visitors are qualified in some way by the brand's advertising or on-site behavior for a conversion action.

- Site visiting metrics of greatest interest serve as proxies for consumer interest in the brand, including time spent on-site and the percentage of returning visitors.

- Conversions measure the number of desired actions consumers take at the website. These can range from site registration all the way to sales, support, and relationship activities. As one of the two most common measures of performance, conversions are arguably the most important because they capture specific behavior of interest to the brand and factor most directly in brand marketing results.

Branding

- *Survey-based research studies.* As search's job expands from direct response to branding, we naturally want to know about search's branding impacts like brand image, preference, and meaning. Can sponsored text ads lift traditional branding metrics: brand awareness, familiarity, and brand image associations?

     The Interactive Advertising Bureau and Nielsen//NetRatings found the answer to be a pretty strong "yes" (Nielsen//NetRatings 2004). Their study, a controlled experimental design with over 10,500 participants, exposed people to test (brand) ads or control (public service) ads as sponsored links on search results pages or as contextual listings on content pages. Tested ads came from leading brands in a variety of industries: health, auto, beverage, electronics, retail, and finance. Participants evaluated ads based on their ranking in the search engine results or by their position on the content pages. Nielsen collected data via online survey. Respondents did not know they participated in a study on advertising, which eliminated bias that might creep in from a person's decision to participate. The study demonstrated that "sponsored text advertising in the search environment works for an array of branding objectives," especially for brand awareness.

Business Measures

These gauge the brand's ability to meet business objectives and perform on criteria essential to success; they fall into two categories:

- *Direct costs.* These often include return on investment metrics. The most common ones are cost-per-lead, cost-per-acquisition, cost-per-sale (or transaction), campaign revenue generated, and campaign profitability. Related measures are defined in the Glossary.
- *Brand specific.* After cost measures, metrics typically become specific to brand objectives. These can include subscriber renewals or cancellations for publishers, lead-to-close ratios for e-commerce or B2B sites, or changes in cost factors that result from moving a business process to the web or improving an existing one.

Strategies for Effective Paid Placement Advertising

Use Paid Inclusion to Increase Visibility and Conversions: Radisson Hotels

Paid inclusion campaigns can work well for marketers whose prices change often and that have sizable inventories, like catalogs or hotel chains, as this case for Radisson illustrates.

In early 2002, Radisson Hotels, a Carlson Hotels brand, realized that it needed a search boost: its many pages, buried in subdomains and in "deep property-specific content," were generally left unindexed by search engine spiders. Radisson's search engine marketing firm, TrafficLeader, remedied this situation. They created trusted feeds from Radisson's entire database and supplied them to its search partners, Yahoo!, Alta Vista, Looksmart, InfoSpace, Lycos, Mamma, Excite, and Dogpile.

The program increased traffic and conversions. Traffic to Radisson's site started at 7,000 users per month in 2002 and had risen to over 125,000 per month about two years later. Radisson's paid inclusion program increased their visibility and provided consumers with up-to-date information on rates and availability, a relevance booster. Conversion rates, the company reports, "have been excellent," but they did not provide hard numbers.

Increase Leads: Compass-Guard Security Systems

What happens when you have a website and it's not generating leads? This common problem often stems from a poor-quality website and the absence of a search engine marketing campaign. Compass Security Services, a watch guard and patrol agency, provides this case study (Ramos 2005).

The Compass-Guard website "did not present a professional appearance, nor capture leads; therefore, minor updates alone would not be enough." The company retained a search marketing firm that took a two-staged approach. In the first, they designed a new corporate image, including logo, and wrote a dozen pages of new copy, with each one having strong call-to-action statements. (See Figure 6.1.) Compass-Guard relaunched the site and implemented a new pay-per-click campaign to jump-start results. In the second stage, the company sought to optimize results in organic listings by writing and integrating 15 more pages into the site.

Compass-Guard tracked results over a six-month period, establishing a baseline in February 2005 and concluding in August. Site visits, a traffic measure, "were significantly higher . . . and page views were 79.4% higher overall. The 'call to action' text performed well with 278 visitors clicking on the 'Contact Us' page." The pay-per-click conversion rate rose from 0.6% to 9.5%. "They went from almost zero leads to dozens of leads per week. These figures include job seekers and agencies looking to contract Compass-Guard for private security."

Build Traffic through Paid Placement: National Instruments

Computer instruments maker National Instruments sells more than 950 highly technical items in over 90 countries. "Broad and diversi-

FIGURE 6.1   Redesigned Compass-Guard security systems home page.

fied" describes the customer base. No single customer accounts for more than 3% of sales, no industry accounts for more than 10% of sales, and sales are split almost evenly between the Americas and Europe/Asia. National Instruments historically published a print catalog that, exceeding 900 pages, not only cost a lot of money to produce but became outdated fairly quickly.

The company sought to distribute information more rapidly and more accurately to its prospects, primarily scientists and engineers. Learning that potential customers relied on the internet for product research, the company redesigned its website, making it very content rich, and used search engine optimization in order to increase the appearance of product links in the organic listings. (See Figure 6.2.) Learning also that the bulk of visitors originated through Google search, National Instruments initiated a paid listings campaign, purchasing keywords related to the company's products and customers.

FIGURE 6.2   For a search on "Labview," National Instruments' organic listings attained a high position through its search engine optimization program.

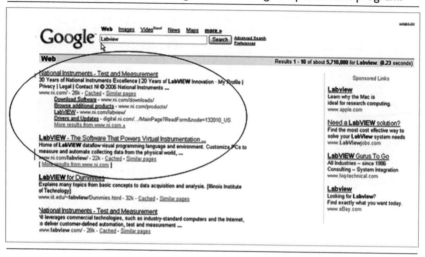

At the outset, National Instruments identified measures for success, which were site visits and page views, and which were later used as inputs for lead generation and online revenue sales forecasts. National Instruments partner Google (2006d) reports a successful campaign: Site visits from Google to the website increased 60% year-over-year by quarter; site visits from the paid placement campaign rose 108% year-over-year by quarter, and cost-per-click for paid placement grew at a much more modest rate, 9% year-over-year by quarter. (See Figure 6.3.)

Increasing Targeted Site Visitors through Contextual Paid Search Ads: HGTVPro.com

How can you target a vertical audience through search and drive them to your website? This was the challenge faced by HGTVPro.com, a Scripps Network Interactive site providing news and information to professional builders, contractors, and remodelers.

Scripps' Linda Fisk, who related this case (Fisk 2006), spoke of the need, early on, to deeply profile their targeted site visitors so that

FIGURE 6.3   An effective search engine marketing campaign placed National Instruments' listings at the top of paid listings for "virtual instrumentation."

they could craft the most relevant messages. Simple descriptive labels wouldn't cut it, so they launched a research effort to understand visitor psychology and motivations: what questions they are looking to answer, what problems they are trying to solve, what they care about most, what resources they most trust, and similar diagnostic questions. Scripps used focus groups, website intercept interviews, and trade show information gathering.

HGTVPro.com assigned contextually targeted search ads a leading role in placing the ads in front of prospects when they were actively searching or browsing. Scripps created the context, assembling a select network of sites tailored for their professional audience. Grounded in their customer insights, Scripps purchased relevant keywords that triggered the display of the right ad.

Campaign goals reported were click-through rate (CTR) and cost-per-click pricing. Linda Fisk informs us that contextual ad CTR exceeded 1.4%, which is "above the industry average and higher than some other campaigns run by Scripps." Because the campaign used "tightly bucketed keywords to intercept our well-defined audience," cost-per-click averaged a very affordable 25 cents.

Building Awareness by Leveraging Search Tied to Television Programming

The Apprentice: Martha Stewart episodes were hosted by various brands, two of which were Tide and Wish-Bone, the salad dressing. In this travel, packaged goods, and car-friendly reality show, contestant teams created solutions to fulfill advertising or marketing objectives. In Tide's case, the teams created a live/performing billboard supporting the introduction of Tide to Go, a new stain-removal stick. For Wish-Bone, the team developed a new salad dressing (Wikipedia 2006).

Capitalizing on the product interest generated by the program's episodes, each brand's websites and landing pages engaged viewers with uses/recipes and background and, in Tide's case, testimonials, problem solvers, store locators, sweepstakes, and FAQs—all of which work to build brand awareness, while the sweepstakes contest promotes trial and builds a prospect database.

Tracking keyword searches related to each brand tells how the shows generate consumer interest in the products. Google's analysis of searches performed in the weeks before and after airing reveal the impacts of television. "Tide to Go" searches rose 19 times over average search volume on the date the episode aired. One week later, following another installment of the program, search volume shot up 23 times. Wish-Bone showed a similar pattern: skyscraper-like spikes on its episode date and the day following. In both cases, search volume stayed above the preshow average. Google showed Tide to Go's bonus lasting for three weeks, and Wish-Bone sustained a 57% increase for two weeks (Google 2006a).

Drive Traffic to Website for Brand Learning: Honda Element

Honda's quirky "Element and Friends" campaign for its Element model aimed to position the brand as a different kind of vehicle that's utilitarian and fun. Honda and its agency created a website stocked with a driving game; cheeky, cartoony animals (possum, platypus, talking crab, burro, and rabbit); and short videos featuring the animals talking with their friend, an Element. Through dialogue, the Element subtly explained one of its features, like roominess, all-wheel drive, or interior configurability. Visitors could download the videos or, in a viral effort, send the website to a friend.

What drove people to the website? A combination of media: spot television, print ads, and tune-in outdoor boards offline; rich media ads and search online. Honda purchased a combination of car-related keywords, like "Honda Element"; keywords related to the campaign, such as "possum"; and those a little more distant—"funny videos" is an example. Why would Honda pick such a range of keywords? One factor: cost. On Google, "Honda Element" cost $1.15 per click, while "possum" and other low-demand keywords cost a dime to 15 cents per click. (See Figure 6.4.)

With offline and rich media ads providing an umbrella, Honda broadened its keyword list, and "extend[ed] the spirit of the campaign to search" (Heyman 2006). A second factor: consumer fit. Research showed that "funny commercials" and other keyphrases "have demographic profiles compatible with likely Element buyers" (Fine 2006). We usually think of keywords dutifully describing products, benefits, or calls to action, but Honda's effort shows us their creative side and their relationship to customer language.

FIGURE 6.4   Honda's Element advertising used a variety of animal characters, including a possum. Purchasing offbeat but campaign-relevant keywords tapped into consumers' search language and generated highly placed organic listings, all at a lower cost than traditional generic or brand-name keywords.

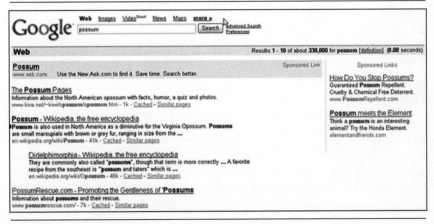

Winning Plays

- Search behavior has become the second most popular use of the internet after email. Online advertisers are learning that search activity is an excellent way to find prospects and customers. But they are also learning that search behavior helps develop a more relevant match of advertising content with search content. This relevant matching often leads to more engagement, further information searching, and purchase intent.

- The growth in search behavior has introduced a new selection and pricing model for buying advertising space—auction pricing and performance monitoring. It is critical, however, to pay close attention to data collected on clicks and click-throughs to ensure true value for money spent. Advertisers developing a comprehensive precampaign through postcampaign measurement strategy are in the best position to understand their advertising's effectiveness and brand performance.

- Search engine marketing has proven itself for traffic building, lead generation, and branding. The winning combination for search strategy appears to be a combination of search engine optimization and paid listings, which balance relevance and reach. Offline print and broadcast stimulate consumer searches. Their roles should be evaluated and planned as part of the search engine marketing program.

- Managing keywords and keyphrases, identifying and tracking the best performers are critical to successful search marketing. Successful online advertisers conduct research with consumers to learn the most common words they use for their searches in (or near) your category. Using consumer language has often resulted in a 60% or higher ROI.

- Advertisers should consider using highly specialized search engines beyond the big three—Google, Yahoo!, and MSN—because research shows that those searchers who are on more intense missions do spend more time at the specialized sites.

- Highly engaging ads, especially those having excellent titles, are critical when using search text ads, because we have learned that most search activity is time challenged. Searchers, being goal directed, "find and go" much like fast-food consumers who use the drive-through for "eat and go." Because searchers scan search results pages and ads, advertisers should continually test the language in the ads to make sure that they are always relevant. Moreover, it is important to make sure that the text ad or listing takes consumers to appropriate landing pages that meet their expectations and start to engage them in a compelling brand experience.

CHAPTER 7

Online Shopping and Buying

Search, shopping, and purchase all go together. No matter the purchase—car, airline tickets, camera, or camisole—shoppers research products throughout their buying journey. Online search plays a central role today, helping consumers find, consider, and select brands for purchase.

Anyone who has used a broadband connection at home or at work appreciates the speed and richness of the online experience, and the services now available, such as streaming music, video, and shopping. Broadband adoption, now mainstream (Pew 2006), provides consumers with greater ease and convenience for researching purchases online and shopping across all channels.

We take the view that calling shopping or researching products and services "search" is really too narrow; it easily misleads us to focus on online search (a big player) and ignore offline sources that consumers routinely consult—Yellow Pages, catalogs, stores, newspaper or magazine ads, or trusted opinions. We overcome this bias by broadening the term "search" to "shopping research," so we can be as inclusive as possible. We do the same with buying, emphasizing that customers shop online, but usually complete their transactions offline through stores, toll-free calls to catalog call centers, or mailing an order form. Customers routinely use multiple information sources and retail channels for shopping, then combine them in their own ways. And they follow their own paths, which may be quick and direct, as they are for low-consideration purchases like consumer packaged goods; for other products the route to the cash register often takes time and travels along roads with numerous twists and turns.

Retail Sales and E-Commerce

Overall Retail vs. Online Retail Sales Growth

Stores and all retail outlets rang up sales of roughly $3.5 trillion in 2005 (U.S. Census Bureau 2006b). From 2004 to 2006, retail sales grew about 7% year over year.

E-retail revenues command a small fraction of total sales but tell an exciting growth story. These, excluding travel, reached $114 billion in 2005, a 25% climb over 2004. Future prospects show continuing growth. (As we go to press, comScore reports a 25% increase in online sales during the 2006 holiday season over 2005.) After cracking $138 billion in 2006, Forrester Research (2006c) forecasts dollars rising to $171 billion by 2009; these are healthy double-digit rates in the neighborhood of 18% year over year. Increasing revenues but slowing growth signals the switch to the beginning of a maturing and more competitive channel—a point that takes on added importance when we outline the size of the online shopping population.

Consumers Fuel E-Retail Growth and Shop in New Categories

From the early days of online retail, shopper purchases for computers and software, books, toys, and video games drove sales. These early successes, eMarketer (2006i) forecasts, will continue. In fact, eMarketer expects computer hardware and software to capture more than half of the sales online. That's a major milestone, reflecting consumer acceptance of manufacturers' direct sales such as Dell, web-only superstores such as Amazon.com, and the online channels run by category retailers, represented by CompUSA.com and BestBuy.com. When you stop and realize that consumers spend an average of $500 for computer equipment (Google 2006e) and assume that there's little risk purchasing by typing credit card numbers into a web form, it's a remarkable development.

Online sales do not live by gadgets and gizmos alone. Shifts in three categories—jewelry and luxury goods, apparel, and health and beauty—signal change ahead. What's especially interesting and different about these categories? They require more purchase consideration and more research.

Online Travel Sales

Travel spending online for leisure and unmanaged business spending reached $65 billion in 2005 (Grau 2006, reporting eMarketer data). A combination of factors—including the growth of turnkey agencies like Orbitz, Travelocity, and Expedia; aggressive marketing by airline, rental car, and lodging supplier brands; broadband; and consumer acceptance—contributes to this growth. Travel analysts expect leisure and unmanaged business travel sales to rise markedly in the next couple of years (PhoCusWright 2005) and nearly double to $122 billion in 2009 (Grau 2006b). Historically, Grau points out, online travel, an early success story, outpaced retail e-commerce. Expectations are that online retail growth rates will be even faster from now on.

The Multichannel Marketplace

Today's retailers fully grasp online retail's potential, of course, and are aggressively moving to incorporate it into their complement of channels. Federated Department Stores' Macy's unit, for example, recently reversed its e-retail approach, changing from brochure-ware to sophisticated online operations. Why? Federated CEO Terry Lundgren explained to *Internet Retailer*: "Federated is more concerned with using the sites to drive multichannel sales rather than just boosting web sales" (quoted in Punch 2006).

Lundren's multichannel focus is well-placed. Trade magazine *Internet Retailer* classifies retail websites into four categories and tracks their revenues. Retail chain websites, like Neiman Marcus, Williams Sonoma, and JCPenney, claim the largest share, nearly 40% of sales. Catalog/call center operations like L.L. Bean and QVC (the TV and cable shopping network) took 15% of sales; and direct manufacturers like Dell and Sony garnered nearly 20%. Internet pure-play online retailers such as Amazon.com, BlueNile.com, Overstock.com, and NewEgg.com account for 25% (eMarketer 2006d).

Pure-play e-commerce business models have evolved into specialized channels with crystal-clear customer value propositions supported by disciplined business strategies centered around the "Treacy trio"—having the best product, best overall cost, or best operations (Treacy and Wiersema 1997). They have not become T. rexes devouring offline retailers as originally expected by internet economy proponents.

Today's Online Shopper Profile

Today's shoppers browsing online stores, researching and comparing products, cross the demographic spectrum, from age 14 on up (eMarketer 2006i). Nearly 118 million people, about four out of five internet users, shopped online in 2005. Due to the large numbers of people already online, growth will not be as rapid as in earlier years, but the numbers are impressive. For 2009, eMarketer (2006i) forecasts 133 million shoppers.

Shoppers like the anywhere, anytime convenience of online research and shopping. Most agree that online prices compete with offline costs, that sites are easy to use, that they have time to shop, and that they can get online. For these reasons, about 85% of internet shoppers 14 or older made at least one online purchase in 2005. Why doesn't everyone buy something online, then? Shipping's cost and delivery times can be showstoppers, but often the biggest barrier is that people want to see the product or be able to touch it. Does privacy matter? Concerns exist, but opinion varies on its extent (Copeland and Rogers 2005; eMarketer 2006i; Turow 2006). Online retailers, however, have generally taken steps to reassure shoppers of transaction security (Kim 2006).

Shopping Strategies

Shoppers research before they buy, firing up browsers for web work and combining them with offline advertising, catalogs, listening to word of mouth, or visiting stores or dealers (Forrester 2006; Freedman 2006; Yahoo! 2006c). Shoppers draw heavily on online research; nearly 90% conduct "some sort" of online research before buying from a web retailer or offline store (Reverse Direct Marketing 2005). This shopping activity is a major opportunity for online advertising.

Online, shoppers avail themselves of myriad research tools. Studies that looked into the sources used and their popularity generally agree that official manufacturer or merchant sites and search engines rank at the top. Those are followed by online malls with multiple retailers (like eBay or Amazon); specialty search engines dedicated to industries, categories, or topics; and then comparison shopping sites when purchases "involve more research" (DoubleClick 2005b; Goldman Sachs et al. 2005; Reverse Direct Marketing 2006; Yahoo! 2006c). It's a cross-referenced world.

Google, with research partner comScore Networks (2006a), studied the 2005 holiday shopping period, the time of highest online search and purchasing activity. During this busy season, 82 million consumers used web search, conducting 552 million searches, and tallied about $9.1 billion in sales across 11 different product categories, such as apparel, consumer electronics, flowers, jewelry, movies, and toys.

Even shoppers going to the local store check out the web before leaving home. They're finding or evaluating products, prices, or merchants. Shoppers engaged in seven research sessions on average prior to making a local shopping trip during the holiday period (ShopLocal 2005). (We would like to note that marketers are beginning to capitalize on this trend. EMarketer [2006c] forecasts local search revenues doubling from $1.3 billion in 2006 to $2.8 billion in 2008.)

When we look at individual purchases, DoubleClick's (2005b) study shows consumers search a number of times beforehand. How many times? Searches range from two and one-half searches for sports or fitness products to about five searches for apparel and computer hardware and six searches for travel. People spend more time researching purchases that require high levels of consideration (Yahoo! 2006c).

Importance of User-Friendly Shopping Sites

Recognizing the importance shoppers give to manufacturer or retailer sites, we're reminded of the need for top-notch site search. It's often overlooked, but 80% of all internet-based purchases involve searching within websites (WebSideStory 2006). Why so little attention? Two reasons.

First, when we talk about search, it's usually synonymous with internet search engines like the GYM trio (Google-Yahoo!-MSN), Ask.com, and others people use to find products and navigate to sites. About three out of four consumers use these search engines to find online shopping websites—much more than any other tactic (Kim 2006). With search engines aggregating consumers and creating audiences around their specific interests, marketers zeroed in on search engine marketing for front-end demand creation, but thought less about the site experience, which is where the real shopping and possible purchase takes place.

Second, marketing and advertising groups usually advise on brand marketing requirements, but selecting and implementing site search typically falls to information technology (IT) specialists. Often the discussion centers on how to leverage existing technical functionality rather than making the site search as responsive to consumer needs as possible.

Shoppers reach websites through internet search by typing web addresses directly into browsers, or through portals, specialty engines, or website links. Whichever ways traffic comes to your door, visitors need to be welcomed and shepherded through the site. Landing pages, website designs, and site search perform those jobs. Site search with its related navigational aids, such as menus, top-seller lists, or specialized departments, guide visitors to the products and product details, invite them to browse, and encourage them to learn about related products or add-ons that may be of interest. Through site search they access services that support branding and drive sales, like store locators, prepurchase support tools like FAQs, rich media demos, virtual models that show the way clothes look on customers or how customizations change appearance, customer reviews, and many other innovative features.

From the marketer's view, site searchers, WebSideStory's Steve Kusmer says, "are, in effect, prequalifying themselves as users interested in finding something very specific on a site" (quoted in Newcomb 2006b). It should not be overlooked.

Site Search Benefits

Susan Aldrich, Patricia Seybold Group

Customer activity that begins on an internet search engine doesn't end at the entry point to your site. You should sustain attention to visitors until they have either completed their objectives or abandoned them. Site search and the information it offers can help you determine how to surpass customer expectations and also reduce the number of frustrated visitors. The site search box itself is a tremendous gift to you from your customers: They are telling you exactly what they want, in their own words.

(Quoted in Susan Aldrich, "The Other Search: Making the Most of Site Search to Optimize the Total Customer Experience," The Patricia Seybold Group, 2006, p. 1.)

Listen to Shoppers: Chiasso

Full site redesigns too often leave the site search function untouched. This happened at Chiasso, the home decor retailer. Frustrated shoppers quit the revamped site because it was so hard to find the products they wanted. About 300 customers sent complaining emails asking the store to fix this problem. They wanted to buy, but were stymied. Chiasso responded. The retailer switched to an outsourced site search solution, and now reports an end to complaints and vigorous sales growth of 20% to 30% a year (Internet Retailer 2006b). (See Figure 7.1.)

How Easy Is Navigation? Northern Tool

Northern Tool provides another compelling story. Like Chiasso, motivated customers had unsatisfying experiences; site search returned long lists of partly relevant results and offered clumsy navigation. By six months after redesign, ease of use improved, the site search

FIGURE 7.1 Chiasso's revamped site search returns search results for "lamp" by categories, provides ways to easily filter or sort results, links to product details, and suggests related searches. The "popular searches" feature promotes browsing.

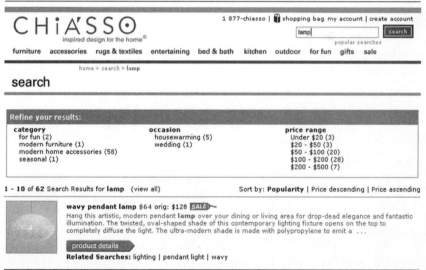

Source: www.chiasso.com.

conversion rate doubled, and sales credited to site search rose to 54% of online sales (Internet Retailer 2005b).

Great site search, of course, grounds itself in consumer insight. Understanding customers' motivations—why they're visiting, what they're after, what they need before they can buy—enables marketers to design compelling search approaches and navigational aids that furnish satisfying site search and brand experience.

Analyzing site search logs reveals the most important keywords, shopping patterns, related searches, abandonment points, and such. From that analysis marketers create consumer personas, a kind of segmentation, that characterize different types of shoppers and their behavior. With their shoppers in view, marketers are better able to make sure that keyword searches trigger the right pages, tailor product recommendations, offer promotions, encourage go-together buys, and stimulate impulse purchases. These techniques fully engage customers, increasing their desire to buy and raising their cart value or offline register receipt total.

Multichannel marketers should leverage their offline channels for cross-sell and up-sell opportunities. Over one-third of buyers picked their items up in stores, and about one-quarter returned products there. These are revenue opportunities for incremental sales. About half of people returning or picking up purchases reported buying additional items. Retailers, though, appear slow on the uptake, especially regarding in-store pickup: 82% don't offer it. The situation is better with returns, where 72% do (eMarketer 2006i). There's money on the table. Over half of web-to-store buyers spent up to $40 on other products, 20% spent between $40 and $80, and 23% spent more than $80 (Gartner 2007).

Routes to the Cash Register Are Multichannel

Shopping is more like a journey than it is a series of discrete, orderly steps. Shoppers use multiple information sources and channels as they learn, consider, and decide to buy. Because of all the education, emotions, checking, and cross-checking, consumers take different routes to the checkout; sometimes it's direct, sometimes it's not. The concept of "path" captures this idea very well.

Yahoo! (2006b), with OMD, studied shopping paths in a richly detailed study that combined ethnographic techniques (depth interviews, shopping trips, journals, etc.) with online surveys conducted among a high-quality panel. Their research looked at people who intended to purchase or made a purchase in five major product categories: auto, finance, technology and electronics, retail goods, and consumer packaged goods. Four paths emerged:

1. *Quick paths.* Characterized by a short time frame, fast decision making, little or no research prior to purchase, and immediate gratification, this type of purchase path is most common for routine purchases like consumer packaged goods, impulse purchases, and when people are distracted or under time pressure. Grab and go.

2. *Winding paths.* Shoppers move between different shopping channels and information sources on the road to discovering the right item. Winding paths typify retail purchases. Confidence using technology assists purchasing as shoppers search, visit sites. and compare. Sales conclude within a relatively short time frame (a few hours to a week). "Winding paths result from consumers trying to make the best purchase decision among many options, price comparison shopping, coupon use, and/or advice from friends or family." Educated, smart buys.

3. *Long paths.* This path emerges when consumers know what they want to buy, are determined to acquire it, and can wait weeks or months to do so after the start of search. Shopping typically takes place through only one channel, research is ongoing, and eventual purchase is very likely. "Long paths often result from waiting for the price on a specific product to drop, waiting for something (such as a new style) to become available, and/or waiting for delivery of an item."

4. *Long and winding paths.* Long and winding paths are often used for high-ticket and/or technology-related items. This path involves product research, learning, and comparison shopping, as well as professional and user reviews. Yahoo! points out that "eventual purchase is not definite, and could go either way. This path often results from having no fixed purchase deadline, unexpected complications in the shopping process, and/or uncertainty regarding the exact desired outcome."

The paths are somewhat predictive of purchase. Shoppers traveling the quick path or long path, about six of ten, are more likely to complete a purchase, whereas only three of ten winding path or long and winding path shoppers are likely to buy. The differences are due largely to goal—purchase is more certain when shoppers have clear ideas about what they want to purchase and why, and take a direct route to them.

No matter the path, at least four of ten shoppers in any category start shopping without a brand in mind. With the average number of brands considered to be around three for any purchase, marketers have opportunities to influence brand preference and purchase.

The path idea may provide marketers with additional ways to segment and target consumers and when combined with an understanding of consumers' use of search for product purchase, can suggest ways of reaching consumers with advertising that drive preference. However, consumers' shopping brings them into contact with new or unfamiliar brands, or nets them new information on familiar brands, throughout the purchase path. Shoppers start less often with a fixed set of considered brands; they begin with a starter set, then subtract or add brands as they search, research, and evaluate. Two risks we see are brand switching and shopper diversion.

Brand Switching and Shopper Diversion

The ease people now have to research products, prices, and merchants influences choice, and often causes people to switch. Switching may be lamented by brand marketers, but no one denies consumers this right. One early study (Deitlinger Research Group 2002) examined online information's impact on brand purchase. Its result: 40 million people changed their minds after studying online information, and 60% of them, 24 million, switched brands at purchase. Switching, of course, occurs frequently in services categories, too, with travel a well-documented industry (ComScore Networks 2006c).

AOL (2005), with partner Henley Centre, recently studied brand switching in the United Kingdom across a variety of retail and services categories including appliances, electronic, financial, travel, and home and garden. Their findings confirmed the value of search and online information as a way for consumers to learn about new products, develop more favorable attitudes toward brands, and eventually be motivated to buy new products offline or online.

But they also report two compelling, or troubling, findings, depending on your perspective. First, new information may turn people off to brands they planned on purchasing: 42% decided not to buy a specific brand they considered. Second, consumers are receptive to new information and new brands: 43% of online consumers switched brands after having one firmly in mind to buy.

Who switched most? The research-intensive and self-described internet experts. They're more likely than average to read product reviews, visit comparison shopping sites, subscribe to email newsletters, and give email feedback—and more likely to consult advertising. Brand switchers use internet ads to "help them find things they want."

A Classic Case of Shopper Diversion: "Google Pontiac"

Take the example of General Motors' "Google Pontiac" campaign. This innovative and controversial TV campaign blazed a new trail. Rather than create a traditional brand ad, Pontiac showed a screenshot of the brand name "Pontiac" entered into a Google search box. (See Figure 7.2.) Presented with paid ads and organic search listing after searching, the prospect decided what to look at and where to go.

The campaign worked. Hitwise data showed that searches increased on "Pontiac" during the time period the ad ran, and also when compared to site traffic from a year earlier. Pontiac.com benefited from increased visits. But Pontiac's home page received only 69% of the traffic. Where did the rest go? To auto portals, Pontiac enthusiast magazines, comparison shopping sites, and competitors.

FIGURE 7.2 Pontiac's ad urged consumers to "Google Pontiac" in order to learn more about Pontiac's offerings from organic search results and paid ads. Prospects decided where to go, but only 69% of people landed on Pontiac's home page.

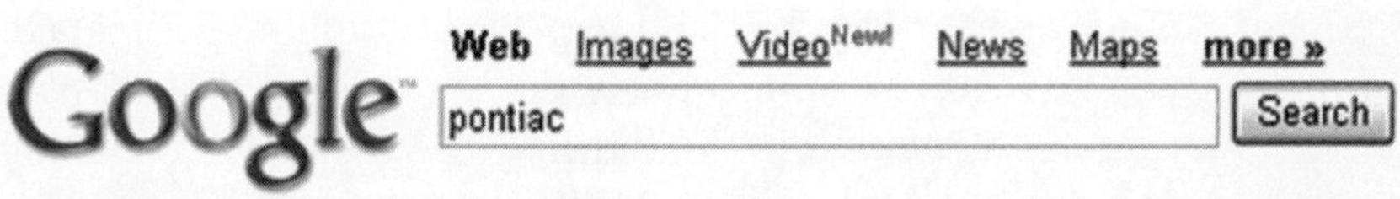

Google   Web Images Video^New! News Maps more »
pontiac   [Search]

Search marketing can be brutally competitive. Opportunistic marketers take advantage of competitors' marketing investments. These carjacked prospects were sent to Mazda's site, where they were encouraged to take test-drives. The result? Mazda's site received the second highest visit volume after Pontiac.com (Tancer 2006).

Smart Research Strategies for Retail Growth

We selected three cases that capture the importance of understanding customer shopping strategy, supporting customers through multi-channel marketing, and improving the brand shopping experience.

Support Dealers and Consumers with Web-to-Store Strategy: Waterford Wedgwood, WedgwoodUSA.com

Waterford Wedgwood, familiar and highly regarded makers of crystal and china, traditionally sold their wares exclusively through a retailer network. In 2002 the company started selling Waterford crystal online to buyers and, based on that experience, created and launched Wedg-woodUSA.com to showcase and sell its fine china, gifts, and replacement pieces online.

Their experience with Waterford enabled the company to develop a promising dual-channel strategy. (See Figure 7.3.)

Wedgwood retailers typically carry part of their line. Store size, shelf space limitations, specialization, and customer profiles all conspire to reduce the types and patterns for display. Incorporating the entire catalog, Wedgwood's e-commerce partner says, "[lets] people do a lot of research online before they order online or get to a store. Consumers report that they really trust product information that they get at manufacturers' sites because it's extensive and it covers their full product line."

Wedgwood capitalizes on the web-to-store trend and focuses on driving people to local retailers. The site provides a store locator feature in the footer on every page, not just the home page. This works hand in hand with the purchase research. Wedgwood's internet marketing director, Jennifer Korch, explains: "We see a huge percentage of people who go to the store locator after they've looked at 15-plus pages of product information [at WedgwoodUSA.com]. That tells me they've made a decision and want to go buy it somewhere. On the Wa-

FIGURE 7.3 Wedgwood's capable site search allows consumers to explore and research the full Wedgwood catalog online, and then offers consumers options to buy online or to find a local retailer.

terford site, we get considerably more people who use the store locator than purchase directly online" (Magill 2005c).

Wedgwood does not compete with retailers on price. The online site offers products for sale only at manufacturer's list price. As we learned earlier, consumers use search engines to find and compare prices. In most instances, Waterford Wedgwood points out, people have already decided where to buy; they're looking for more information. By keeping prices at list, the website effectively protects the retailer who may discount or negotiate with the buyer.

Second, the online site does not offer a bridal registry. Leaving a registry off the site means brides must register with a retailer. This effectively directs sales to retailers that complete offline.

WedgwoodUSA.com's site does provide shoppers with a capable site search and several navigation paths that enable people to browse according to their level of interest in, or knowledge of, pattern names, product categories, or collections.

Like many sites, WedgwoodUSA.com allows people to create accounts that simplify purchasing and shipping for online orders, create wish lists, and subscribe to email newsletters. These relationship-building features lay the foundation for meaningful communication, quick, convenient transactions, and future sales.

Revamp E-Retail Strategy Based on Consumer Insight: FirstStreetOnline.com

Web and catalog marketer FirstStreetOnline.com sells about 600 innovative products across a number of product categories—home solutions, electronics, lighting, healthy living, and such for healthy and comfortable living. Their core customer: baby boomers seeking cool lifestyle products.

The company, which spends about $50,000 per month on paid search, started bidding only on keywords for brands and items it sold. After a few campaigns, results showed "anemic traffic" and weak sales. FirstStreet revamped its strategy as follows (the details of this case were adapted from Brohan 2006a).

Using traffic analysis tools, the company learned that generic terms, like "keeping cool," "hearing aid phone," and "brighter reading lights," drove traffic, not the brand names and related phrases they historically purchased, such as Kool Down, a branded cooling product. As a result, FirstStreet shifted keyword purchases to more lifestyle-oriented words and phrases. (See Figure 7.4.) The company expanded from a narrow set of less than 500 keywords to nearly 11,000. Broadening keywords also helped raise page rankings, ad rankings, and click-throughs, presumably because of better matches

FIGURE 7.4 A lifestyle-oriented search for "hearing aid phone" returned FirstStreetOnline's ad in the top rank in the right-hand sponsored links section on Google (October 6, 2006).

among search terms, ads, and landing pages. Perhaps most important, adding so many new terms did not increase the monthly budget. The company reengineered the strategy while keeping the budget constant. "We aren't making wholesale changes in our paid search strategy," says Daniel Yonts, director of internet marketing. "We are working smarter and doing a better job of analyzing the keywords we should be acquiring."

While in the branded keyword era, landing pages showed only the product linked to the search term. FirstStreet got a lot of one-timers, people who viewed one page and possibly bought one product and then vanished.

FirstStreet analyzed visitor sessions, page traffic, and product placement. Realizing that people spent more time on category pages with multiple products, and more often bought products from them, FirstStreet followed its customers' lead. The company tied its broad search terms to categories, created category pages that exposed broader selections, and made them more appealing by using larger photos, improving descriptions, and including customer service tools, like live chat, on them.

FirstStreet's consumer-centric approach improved its site traffic (15% gain in average monthly unique visitors), conversion rates (up 2.5% in certain categories), and sales. First-time shoppers now spend more on average, rising from $130 to about $200 in some categories due to multiple purchases.

FirstStreet provided visitors with a "shopping cart quick order" feature, enabling them to type in item numbers and quantities from the print catalog and magazine ads.

The company is on track to increase revenues in 2006 about 10% over 2005. That's a major improvement; 2005 sales were about on a par with 2004 sales. Due to the changes, Yonts asserts, FirstStreet is "getting better results with our focus on category-driven search terms. It's paying off with more page views and sales from repeat buyers."

Improve the Brand Shopping Experience

Two ways to improve brand shopping experiences are to make it easier for consumers to find products of interest, and to provide consumers with tools or features that instill confidence in the purchase.

Here's what Home Depot did to improve a poor shopping-to-buying journey (Internet Retailer 2005a).

After a thorough review, the company decided to scrap its enterprise search system for the e-commerce site.

Home Depot implemented a new system that blended search and navigation functionality in order to provide a more consistent shopper experience, and added the capability to manage promotional links across the site. The change paid dividends. According to a Jupiter Research report (cited in Internet Retailer 2005a), "HomeDepot.com credits search technology . . . with a significant role in what have been double-digit conversion rate increases (including direct sales, referrals to stores, email sign-ups) and a lift in average order size since last year." This site search revamp improved customer satisfaction and enhanced customer experience at the website.

Furnishing assistance to shoppers based on their website behavior can work to reduce shopper uncertainty and lead consumers to take actions that lead to online or offline sales. "My Virtual Model," used by Lands' End and other leading apparel websites, lets customers try clothes on an avatar they conform to their body size and shape. Porsche's outstanding car configurator lets prospects design and experience a drool-worthy car that motivates dealer visits. And Bang & Olufsen's demo scheduler boosts qualified traffic to their local stores.

Search behavior is a new area that brands use to to help consumers when they seem stuck or indecisive. Clothing retailer Bluefly now initiates chat with customers when, for example, a shopper searched for more than three items in five minutes. Or, if a customer stalls on a checkout page, Bluefly initiates a chat session that helps the transaction complete. "Retailers that approach a customer with a chat," relates Robert LoCascio, CEO of chat vendor LivePerson, "are much more likely to generate a sale than those that rely on customers to find a chat button and click on it" (quoted in Tedeschi 2006). Of particular interest here is that business rules govern search/chat interactions, and can be developed for other types of assists that reinforce brand messages, shape preference, increase conversions, and close sales not only through search, but across all media.

Winning Plays

- Buying online is big and growing (133 million online buyers in 2006). Shopping online is even bigger and growing faster (85% of online users shopped online in 2006). Integrating advertising, online shopping, and offline and online buying into a multichannel experience strategy is critical for success. Multichannel shoppers often pick up extra items and spend more overall than single-channel shoppers, generating incremental revenue at little cost. Most offline retailers now have online buying, and even internet pure plays have adopted a multichannel approach. Determine how your brand can exploit a multichannel strategy.

- It is critical to make your online shopping site as engaging as possible, as only 4 out of 10 consumers come to a shopping site with a committed brand in mind. Innovation and creative offers have proven to find new buyers during an online shopping trip. Whether directed immediately to an online buying site or encouraged to visit a retail store via ads, these newfound buyers purchase at a high level of probability.

- Marketers are learning that online shopping and/or buying sites need to reflect a genuine commitment to the consumer. They need to reflect the brand or company personality and leverage in-depth knowledge of purchasing drivers. E-commerce afterthoughts don't cut it in today's competitive multichannel retail environment. The least effective shopping and/or buying sites are those designed just by the IT department that do not have a broader advertising plan to drive traffic to the shopping/buying site and do not utilize site behavior as strategic input for continuous improvement.

- The key for success is for marketing and IT to work together to create a user-friendly, brand-building, and action-driven experience with minimal hassle for the customer or potential buyer. Just as a bricks-and-mortar retailer invests time, creativity, and money in maximizing the shopping and buying experience for its customer, online marketers must do likewise in order to grow the business.

CHAPTER 8

Advertising Personally

EMAIL AND WORD OF MOUTH

Marketer interest from the beginning of online advertising in emailers is pretty clear: Email is a near-universal communications channel used by just about every American. Close to 90% of all internet users aged three and older—162 million kids, teens, and adults—used email at least once a month in 2006. By 2010 that number is expected to rise to 92% (eMarketer 2006a).

For most of us it's hard to imagine personal life and work life without email. DoubleClick's (2005d) study of email habits showed the role of email in contemporary life. Nine out of 10 email users check their computers, BlackBerrys, or other portable devices several times a day. Nearly half report "constant usage," made possible by broadband and wireless connections at home, at work, or away from these locations in city parks, coffee shops, health clubs, and other hot spots.

For smart marketers, email has evolved from tactical "spray and pray" blasts to strategic communications for managing customer relationships and promoting loyalty. This "new" email is sometimes called "email 2.0." In this chapter we look into the issues that affect email deliverability—without that advertising simply will not work—targeting considerations and strategies email marketers use to accomplish brand objectives.

Email is one source people use when sharing information and some use email to talk about brands. Because brand talk is relevant and credible when it comes from a trusted friend, family member, or authority, word-of-mouth marketing is emerging as a new discipline and strategic option. We conclude the chapter with a review of word-of-mouth marketing strategies and their role in brand building.

Win the In-Box Battle

Nearly universal email access means in-boxes filling up. Consumers receive over 360 email messages per week on average.

Consumers know what spam is: unwanted or irrelevant messages, email from unknown senders, and excessive email from senders to whom they gave permission. Consumers, with the aid of software companies and email services, have developed two sophisticated strategies for tackling spam so that relevant mail from family, friends, and marketers gets through.

The first strategy uses built-in features of email or spam-blocking programs that handle junk mail or let users click a "this is spam" button (After these, most people just zap unwanted mail with the delete key.) (Miller 2006). Spam clicks sent to ISPs may flag legitimate senders as spammers and block their email from being delivered. Because the "this is spam" button is so easy to use, many in-box owners are using it instead of unsubscribing. This impacts deliverability and may degrade consumers' perception of the affected brands.

Consumers know that spam filters are not foolproof and can catch wanted email. Over half of DoubleClick's respondents check their junk or bulk mail folders regularly to spot any misclassified mail, and an equal number have found legitimate mail in them.

The second strategy for many internet users is multiple email addresses. Over half the respondents in DoubleClick's study reported having at least three email addresses, typically a work address, home address, and free webmail address. Almost all consumers, 95%, designate one as their primary account, and 72% use one specifically for making purchases. Using accounts for specific purposes provides consumers with another way to control their email. Consumers using this strategy may pose problems for marketers, such as duplication of names on lists, mismatched targeting of the message to the recipient, or mailing to individual consumers too frequently. Any of these issues can negatively affect the brand-consumer relationship.

Email marketers need to persuade consumers to let their messages into the in-box intact, to open and read them, and to take actions on them that benefit themselves and the brand.

Nine Best Practices for Email Deliverability

Whitney Hutchinson, Avenue A | Razorfish

1. *Become a preferred sender.* Include verbiage at the top of your email communication encouraging users to set up your "from" address in their address books.
2. *Stay away from spam triggers.* Run your creative communication through a content evaluator tool to ensure that you are minimizing any spam triggers in your email copy. Most reputable email service providers (ESPs) should have such a tool.
3. *Utilize in-box monitoring.* There are many reputable companies out there that can help you seed your list and report back on the number delivered to each type of in-box (junk, spam, etc.). Check with your ESP to see if it provides these services. If it doesn't, utilize one of the leaders in the space.
4. *Get a dedicated IP address.* If you are sharing your IP address (through your ESP) with other clients, blocking issues that might be related to any of the other senders' campaigns can affect your ability to deliver your customer messages. An IP address dedicated only to your programs will help ensure your messages aren't blocked based on other marketers' email practices or programs.
5. *Make sure you're white-listed.* Stay on top of your ISP relationships to ensure white-listing status. This is a big job. Outsourcing your email deployment can help, as most ESPs have staff dedicated to this effort.
6. *Follow email authentication guidelines.* Specifically, Sender Policy Framework (SPF) and Sender-ID guidelines should be followed. This is a technical requirement that you may need to implement with the help of an IT resource.
7. *Manage abuse complaints.* Creating a feedback loop with the ISPs is vital in order to stay on top of your abuse complaints. As mentioned above, your ESP will likely have dedicated staff working on ISP relationships. Make sure they have created this feedback loop and that your list is immediately cleansed of those who report your messages as spam.

(Continued)

Nine Best Practices for Email Deliverability (*Continued*)

8. *Cleanse your list.* Make sure that your list is clean of hard bounces (invalid addresses) regularly. Each ISP has a different algorithm for bounce management, such as the number of times it will attempt delivery before bouncing it back. You should understand these algorithms and actively manage them. Again, outsourcing to a reputable ESP is helpful.

9. *Abide by the law.* Make sure that each commercial email communication you send out is in compliance with all applicable legislation.

(Hutchinson 2005)

Email Influences Consumer Purchasing

Each relevant email sent by marketers can offer consumers links to brand information and websites that may lead to sales. In addition to product offers, emailed statements and bills or updates from travel rewards programs, for example, are largely untapped opportunities for most marketers to communicate with consumers and stimulate sales (Epsilon Interactive 2006).

Email is a powerful purchase influencer. During the 2005 shopping season, email service provider ReturnPath found that 95% of the shoppers they surveyed used email to navigate to a retail website, read sites for gift ideas, and took advantage of the offers they contained (Miller 2006). Email works double duty as a branding and direct response channel.

Emailed coupons are effective purchase incentives and drive sales. Three-quarters of online purchasers redeemed an online coupon, and almost 60% redeemed an online coupon at an offline retail outlet. Special offers can help email get read and acted upon.

After purchase, customers expect to see order confirmations and shipping notices in their in-boxes. And customers in a Double-Click study expressed interest in follow-up offers for related products, membership rewards programs, and sweepstakes (Anfuso 2004).

Advertiser Spending on Email

Email is the most widely adopted electronic communications channel. Yet, compared with the major segments of measured online ad
spend (search and display advertising, which combined for 75% of
the $12.6 billion spent in 2005), commercial emailers' spending was
small—less than 10% of the total.

Much of email spending is not captured in widely reported
sources. Thus, we expect that the spending on email is much higher
because many companies handle their email functions in-house, usually spread across a number of departments, each of which is going
about its business and not necessarily coordinating email sends or
strategy (Beck 2006).

Seems low, doesn't it? Especially when you consider that more
than half of B2C (business-to-customer) marketers use email to communicate with customers, and B2B marketers use email to reach 80%
of their prospects. However, unlike search or display advertising,
email advertisers don't have to spend much on production, media, or
vendor costs that push budgets up.

JupiterResearch (2006) expects advertisers to allocate half
of their spend on email marketing in 2010 to customer retention
programs.

Advertiser spending for customer retention reflects the value
marketers place on email for managing customer relationships
through time. This is noticeably different from the way marketers
use online search and display advertising, for example, which are
used more for finding new customers, generating qualified leads, or
for building brand awareness.

Email for Relationship Building

"The fundamental purpose of email marketing," analyst David
Hallerman writes, "is to enhance a company's relationship with its
customers and regain lost customers" (eMarketer 2006a). Marketers
build and maintain the relationship through a variety of communications: newsletters, special offers and promotions, and customer
services.

Let's focus on the word *relationship* for a minute. Ethical email
marketing is permission-based, meaning that brand customers explic-
itly allow marketers to engage with them. "Yes, I'll accept your email,

Mr. Marketer," or "Thanks, but no," or "I'm no longer interested—please stop emailing me" (or words to that effect!). Customers are choosy about what they want to hear from individual marketers and how often. Good email marketing is a two-way street: a feedback loop where customer and brand continually refine their understanding of one another, but the consumer is at the controls.

Email marketing is all about relevance from the consumer's viewpoint. Campaigns that connect with subscribers at the levels they want them to get better results than those that interrupt the email activity without invitation.

Email pushes information out and pulls subscribers in and through to your brand's website, microsite, community and social networking destinations, or other location you choose. It's easy to get caught up in sending when your brand wants, but remember that brands engage in relationships with their email subscribers. Through all that your brand does, constantly think about customers' experience when they click through, because "products today," Paul Beck, Email Experience Council co-founder and executive director of interactive at OgilvyOne Worldwide, told us, "are not just things or packages, but the sum of those and their communications. Take a checking account. Your balance and transactions appear on web pages or in emails. Those are the brand, too" (Beck 2006). Managing email is managing the consumer-brand relationship for their mutual benefit.

When we look across all the different email campaigns out there, they conform to a relationship-building pattern: begin with engaging newsletters, follow with company or product information, then turn to the back-end aspects of transactions and customer service (ReturnPath 2006; Skylist 2006). Concentrate on branding and revenue first, then move to improving the efficiency of postsales support and loyalty.

We need to strike a cautionary note on newsletters. Most email marketers publish newsletters, and nearly 50% claim they will publish more newsletters (Nussey and Hallerman 2005). Newsletters get you a seat at the email marketing table. But remember that as you put your first one out or add another one to your list, which publishers do to meet special interests, the in-box volume for your subscriber increases. Couple that with competitors taking note and coming out with their versions, and your subscriber has much more to manage.

One challenge brands face is figuring out ways to keep their newsletters subscribed.

List churn is a fact of email marketing life. Faced with an average list churn rate of about 25% to 30% annually, marketers constantly need to replace lost names with new quality names. To get them, ExactTarget's Chris Baggott advises, "marketers using email need to focus on long-term list acquisition strategies, instead of quick fixes like co-registration and list purchase" (Baggott 2006).

Tips for Email Campaigns

- Build your list internally, even if it takes time, so the quality of your recipient list remains at a high level.
- Keep an accurate audit of how your company received permission to contact the subscribers to the lists—some people forget they signed up to receive information.
- Make membership to your list valuable.
- Provide recipients with a clear way to contact you for more information, including a staffed telephone number or email address.
- Choose software that is capable of performing as your lists grow, scans outgoing messages for viruses, and can measure the effectiveness of your campaign.

(L-Soft, "Successful Email Marketing Practices," 2002)

Build Quality Opt-in Lists: John Deere

Deere builds its opt-in list is by offering customers and prospects an exclusive sneak preview of the new season's farm equipment lineup. Deere runs a separate communications program, named "First-to-Know," that allows farmers to sign up for a single email (with confirmation) that will be delivered on a specific date and time. (See Figure 8.1.) An email link sends them to a branded microsite just minutes after the last of the dealers emerges from the

FIGURE 8.1   Deere's "First-to-Know" program captures email addresses from highly qualified prospects that are used to build lists and educate their best customers through relationship emails and a much-anticipated preview of new products.

annual meeting but 13 hours before the press embargo is lifted. Thousands click their mouses within seconds of receiving the email. With one suspense-building program, Deere acquires highly qualified farmers for its lists and educates its most interested customers. Deere builds other lists by promoting cross-registration on the confirmation pages it sends (case details from Marketing Sherpa 2006c).

MarketingSherpa (2006c) examined trends in open rates and click-throughs, discovering that response rates declined in a step-wise fashion: They were highest in the first 30 days, then dropped from 31 to 60 days, then dropped again, and afterwards remained reasonably stable. For this reason, email marketers now focus on the crucial first 60 days. Jeanniey Mullen, Email Experience Council co-founder and senior director of email at OgilvyOne Worldwide, tells us: "More and more research is pointing to the fact that the first three emails a recipient receives will determine the lifetime value of their email address. This means that the first email (in many cases, the thank-you message for registration) is critical to setting expectations for the type and frequency of communications" (Mullen 2006b). Send them.

Improve Segmentation Criteria for Email Lists: Brooks Brothers

Brooks Brothers wanted to increase its sales of women's clothing. Analyzing its opt-in list, the company determined that while it had permission to send email, many subscribers did not indicate gender on their profiles. To find out, Brooks Brothers, through its vendor, sent a real-time query to all subscribers who had clicked on any women's item in the prior three months. The query "produced a segment that was nearly twice as large as the number of subscribers who had self-identified themselves as female. Conversion rates from the campaign were 250% higher for the targeted women's line campaign than Brooks Brothers' general mailing" (CheetahMail 2006).

Increase Message Relevance through Personalization and Engaging Creative

Along with segmentation and targeting, email marketers make messages more relevant for recipients through personalization—inserting (your name here), listing (your favorite products), reminding (you of your important event), confirming (your purchase and shipping status), or specifying (an introductory interest rate). These and many other substitutions are common to direct postal mail and appear more frequently in marketers' emails. For example, Scotts, the lawn care company, well-known to those of us living in the suburbs, segments by geography, type of lawn, and whether a person grows vegetables or flowers. And this profiling is done for very grounded reasons. EmailLabs' Loren McDonald (2005a, 12), explains why: "Studies have shown that the greater number of personalization elements to an email, the higher the response rates. . . . Ultimately, however, true personalization means delivering emails that are tailored to the specific profile and preferences of each recipient. The types of personalization may vary in approach based on whether you are sending a newsletter, an announcement, or e-commerce email, but improved results are generally the outcome."

Dynamic content takes personalization an important step forward, assembling messages on the fly according to business rules, customer data, and customer behavior. Say a customer visits your site to look at dress shirts. As this individual explores, your database "knows" that the customer purchased a high-end blazer in the past two weeks and a cashmere sweater three months earlier. But the visit doesn't end in a sale. Using rules you defined, you send the customer a follow-up email concerned with the visit and the specific shirt and, to provide incentive, offer a discount on a tie when purchased with the shirt.

Establish a Loyalty Progression: Hotels.com and Petco.com

Experian, perhaps best known for its credit bureau services, is also one of the major email service providers. The company makes the convincing point that marketers should aim to move one-time buyers into potential loyalists, and potential loyalists into core loyalists. Why this progression? Core loyalists are the 10% to 15% of customers who generate at least 50% of profit.

Experian describes a best practice: "When a customer comes on the file, the well-devised new customer progression strategy takes every opportunity to make her feel like a valued, important customer. It is designed to find out who she is, what she likes, and why she bought, then to tie those insights into a series of promotions that improve the relevance and value of each subsequent communication with her" (Experian 2003).

Web travel service Hotels.com uses "email marketing/transactional hybrid messages to send an email before and after a customer's stay at a hotel. Messages include useful details (confirmation of booking #, preferences, hotel information) as well as marketing information (how to get more offers, items they can add to their trip, etc.). Many of these are banner ads, which link to up-sells and offers. Following the customer's stay, an email includes a link to a survey to determine their satisfaction" (Baggott 2006, 4).

Forrester Research reports (cited in CheetahMail 2005c, 2) that "event-based emails are 17% more likely to be opened than newsletter or promotional emails, and customers are 20% more likely to click through on them. They are read multiple times and are the last to be deleted." Conversions also run "well over the conversion average of other direct marketing programs."

One online retailer with a solid win-back strategy in place is online pet store Petco.com. Three days after a customer abandons an online shopping cart, the company sends an email featuring the product and three additional high-margin items. Tracking results, Petco reports that the click-throughs increased 85% and, more important, conversions 17% (Kuchinskas 2005).

CoreMetrics relates an example for PetFoodDirect.com, which used tests to vary email content, day, and time to find the most productive combination. "Testing showed that delivering promotional emails to correspond with days where sales were highest further stimulated visitor activity. By changing both the time and the day of its email campaigns, PetFoodDirect.com has doubled email click-throughs to its site and significantly increased email campaign performance" (CoreMetrics 2006, 7).

Add Value to Newsletters through Relevant Partnerships: Wild Oats Natural Market

As email newsletters morph into micromagazines, third-party ads for related products or promotions are making their way in. Upscale food retailer Wild Oats Natural Market, for example, sells about 15 ad spaces per quarter in "Wild Mail." In order to maximize the brand's value and maintain its high standards, the company carefully selects participants and exercises tight control. Only relevant products get the nod, and their creative executions must work hand in glove with Wild Oats' standards and formats. The tactic is meeting with success. Consumers view the coupons favorably, and often print them out and redeem them at stores. (See Figure 8.2.) Vendors

FIGURE 8.2 Upscale food retailer Wild Oats allows select brands to advertise in its email newsletter. Partners carefully track performance. Consumers view the coupons favorably, frequently printing them out and redeeming them.

track redemptions and sales, which are "very strong" (ExactTarget 2006b), providing performance insight into the partnerships. Another benefit: The ad space sold can fund, or defray certain costs of, email campaigns.

Rethink Email Strategy to Build Loyalty: MotorcycleSuperstore.com

Oregon-based MotorcycleSuperstore.com is everything motorcycle: apparel, parts, and accessories for every type of rider. The in-stock selection alone totals over 50,000 items.

This web-only retailer's goal is to increase sales through its website or call center. An online multichannel strategy embracing search engine marketing, affiliates, and email newsletters drives enthusiasts to the website. We did a search (September 10, 2006) for "motorcycle tires" on Google.com and found the MotorcycleSuperstore.com pay-per-click ad in the first rank and its organic listing at number four. A click-through on the organic ad took us to a relevant landing page. And we found some affiliates pretty easily. These components are working well today, as is the company's email campaign. But a few years ago in 2004, the email program wasn't, so they sought to fix it.

To get the email program on track, Motorcycle Superstore's team and vendor concentrated first on improving deliverability and understanding the factors that would stimulate subscribers to open their emails. Afterward, they shifted toward higher-order factors for driving web- and phone-based sales.

Step one focused on cleaning the list of undeliverable names. Names were removed after three undeliverable attempts, as recorded by the vendor. Eliminating the "dirty" names reduced the list size by only about 12%, but even this relatively small improvement would eventually prove to have salutary effects on delivery. How? By retaining white-list status with ISPs through fewer bounces, having fewer messages marked as spam, and otherwise becoming a trusted sender. The cleansing effort paid off; deliverability increased from 86% to over 99%.

With available information they knew that open rates held steady at about 30% for their monthly email. Testing showed that upping the frequency led to more revenue, but depressed open and click-through rates and raised unsubscribes. As we discussed, consumers usually greet extra email with a punch of the delete key or a hit to the "this is spam" button.

Motorcycle Superstore now sends emails to different segments on different schedules. Some receive weekly emails, others less often. Erick Barney, the chief marketer, states their aim pretty succinctly: "Ultimately the challenge is to define acceptable performance levels with regard to our overall email marketing strategy" (ExactTarget 2006a, 2).

Reasoning that motorcyclists ride on weekends and therefore might be interested in replacing parts and buying new clothes or accessories on a Monday or Tuesday in order to get their packages in time for the next weekend's ride, Motorcycle Superstore tested email sends twice, and measured delivery rates, open rates, unsubscribes, the number of orders, and order value. Differences in the days' results were negligible, so they decided to go with Monday. Sometime later trade press buzz suggested that Thursday was a magic day for opens. That led the company to test Monday against Thursday. The results favored Monday; response to Thursday's emails sharply decreased over the weekend. Why? The marketing director explained: "We attribute this to the 'weekend warrior' nature of motorcycle industry consumers, especially during peak riding seasons." MotorcycleSuperstore.com stayed with Monday email sends. The company's experience shows why it's critical for brands to conduct their own testing and not rely solely on norms.

In order to classify more of the Motorcycle Superstore list, the marketing team sent emails featuring products specific to each riding style. (See Figure 8.3.) This worked well, according to Motorcycle Superstore's vendor, ExactTarget, which observed, "Using purchase activities and email click activity, Barney's team successfully categorized nearly 70% of their master list." (If this strategy sounds familiar, recall that our Brooks Brothers example used a similar approach to classify people it wasn't sure about.)

With the list more accurately classified, the company created an eight-group segmentation based on "riding style exclusives," "combination riding styles," and the entire list. For promotional emails, eight different sends go out with variations in offers that speak directly to the interests of each segment, making each one relevant. "Email variations," ExactTarget says (2006a, 6), "can be subtle—or drastic—depending on the nature or seasonality of the promotion."

Tuning all the factors in a measured, building-block fashion

FIGURE 8.3   MotorcycleSuperstore.com first send emails with products specific to riding styles. From purchasing, the company learns each consumer's preferences and assigns individuals to segments based on purchase behavior. Customized emails are sent following classification.

resulted in a doubling of open rates and a tripling of click-through rates for the new segmented, targeted emails.

Word of Mouth

Emails can be a personal, opt-in marketing tool, especially suited for building relationships with customers. Another fast growing personal activity over the internet can be conceptualized as word of mouth. Word of mouth is very impactful, but is not under the control of the marketer like email or online advertising.

Word of mouth researcher Keller Fay Group pegs the number of person-to-person brand mentions at 56 per week. Fortunately for marketers, good comments outweigh the bad ones (2006a). Yet with about 25% of the comments critical or negative, word of mouth cuts both ways, and marketers must be prepared for both positive and negative.

Buzz, word of mouth, grassroots marketing, even word of mouse refer to people talking about brands, movies, financial products, the Numa Numa dance, meals, cars, celebrities, or just about any topic, really, taking place online in addition to consumers talking directly with each other via email, land and mobile phones, texting, or instant messaging.

Because people share their personal thoughts and opinions, advertisers have less control over the points made and passed on. Word of mouth involves risk to brands.

As a practice, interest in stimulating and tracking word of mouth is high but adoption by marketers is still at an early stage.

Word of mouth as a discipline is becoming institutionalized through the efforts of two associations, the Word of Mouth Marketing Association (WOMMA) and the Viral and Buzz Marketing Association. They work to develop the professionalism of the field through educational activities, research, and conferences.

The Word of Mouth Marketing Association and its members distinguish between two classes of word-of-mouth campaigns—organic and amplified.

Organic Word of Mouth

Organic word-of-mouth advocates come forward based on their experiences with a brand or company, and have a "natural desire to share their support or enthusiasm." Campaign activities are more back-end, focusing on customer satisfaction, improving product quality and usability, responding to customer concerns and criticism, opening a dialogue and listening to people, and earning customer loyalty (BoldMouth 2006). Online, organic word of mouth spreads (and is measured) through email, message boards, chats, and text among people who are generations removed from the original sender. Social networking site HotOrNot.com, for example, owes a large part of its phenomenal success to the monumental buzz spread organically by devoted fans, major media coverage, online sites, and blogs (Hong 2006; Tweedy 2006).

Amplified Word of Mouth

Amplified word-of-mouth campaigns are designed to raise brand awareness by getting people talking through techniques similar to marketing-support public relations. Some of the techniques used include creating communities, identifying and reaching out to influential individuals and communities, motivating advocates to actively promote products, giving advocates information they can share, using advertising or publicity that creates buzz, or making tools available that help people share their opinions (BoldMouth 2006). These campaigns typically come to mind when we think about word of mouth, and we concentrate on them in this chapter.

What prompts people to gab about and advocate brands? Bzz-Agent, a company that generates and tracks word of mouth through a network of 200,000 agents—"everyday consumers who have volunteered to sample products for the company's clients and share their opinions with people in their personal networks," helps us understand why.

A majority of the BzzAgents, nearly 60%, fit into a group Keller Fay (2006b) calls "conversation catalysts." (This is about four times their proportion in the general population.) These influentials shape the opinions of colleagues, friends, and family and, as such, provide real-world insight into factors that work and don't work in word-of-mouth marketing. The study gives us two very key insights:

1. Word-of-mouth success is about communicating solutions—providing answers that consumers want to pass along to others.
2. The leading reasons for spreading the word are in-depth product knowledge and the enjoyment that comes from sharing that knowledge and their experiences with colleagues, friends, family, and brands.

Word of mouth is practical and commonsensical, a way for one person to help others navigate the world of brands and purchase those that best meet their needs.

Word of mouth is part of our grand oral tradition; what are being passed on are not just strings of words, but personal stories synthesized from individual experiences, thoughts, and reflections that are imbued with meaning. Sharing brand stories personally is like sharing oneself as well. Consider providing your talkers or bloggers with stories that help them fully connect with the brand at deep levels, so that they can internalize and then embed them into their conversations or messages.

Keep in mind that storytellers are invested in the quality of the knowledge and perspective they pass along. Consultant and author Joseph Jaffe points out (2005) that senders have a reputation for independence to uphold: "People are very tuned in to the fact that whatever you forward to your email list says something about you. . . . And hardly anyone would ever send a salesman over to a friend's house." Treat them as ambassadors, not shills.

Use Word of Mouth to Build Brand Interest and Trial for a Brand Extension: The Tide Coldwater Challenge

Procter & Gamble's Tide brand's growth is based in part on the new Coldwater brand extensions to generate incremental sales. New sales for Tide Coldwater have done well, propelling Tide to its best market shares in years (Neff 2006). P&G discovered that many consumers, sensitized to skyrocketing energy costs, looked for ways to cut energy use. The company also found that these energy-conscious consumers were reluctant to wash in cold water because they felt laundry detergent lacked sufficient cleaning power to get the job done. Tide Coldwater's value proposition allows customers to save on energy costs and deep clean their clothes in cold water. The company developed and ran an extraordinarily innovative multichannel campaign, with word of mouth at its center.

P&G partnered with the Alliance to Save Energy (www.ase.org), an advocacy group headquartered in Washington, D.C., dedicated to promoting energy efficiency worldwide, a healthier economy, and a cleaner environment. The Alliance sent emails outlining the benefits of cold-water washing and mentioned Tide Coldwater, giving the brand a very powerful endorsement. That email drove people to Coldwater's microsite where they could register for samples, opt into an email list, and learn more the product. (See Figure 8.4.) Tide Coldwater supplemented that effort with a test mailing to a randomly selected group.

The brand donated $100,000 to the National Fuel Funds Network, an organization that works with state and local agencies to help defray the costs of energy bills for low-income families in different regions throughout the country. Tide Coldwater allocated the money proportionally, based on the percentages of people taking the Challenge (i.e., registering) from each region. By taking the Challenge,

FIGURE 8.4   The Tide Coldwater Challenge minisite presented branding messages and engaged consumers to learn more about the brand's benefits by encouraging them to calculate actual savings and request product samples. The campaign's word-of-mouth component encouraged consumers to spread the word.

Note: This extract is from a recent page. Although the original page was not available at the time of writing, its key elements are captured here.

consumers influenced the disbursement of funds; this provided another reason to pass the email along.

Tide Coldwater's site furnished visitors with a fun, easy-to-use, and eye-catching energy savings calculator, modeled after a washing machine. After estimating savings for themselves, consumers could press a "send to a friend" button that launched the word-of-mouth action. Many marketers provide that function and thank the sending consumers afterwards. It's routine.

But P&G broke new ground, adding a social networking touch. Friends received personalized emails, with site links and opportunities to take the Coldwater Challenge themselves and request product samples.

Tide set a goal of distributing one million samples. Word spread quickly; P&G met almost half its target in the first month, then reached its full target just two months later (Leavitt 2005b; Promo Magazine 2005).

Tide Coldwater created an enormous opt-in list of people agreeing to receive regular communications from Tide Coldwater. Subscribers receive exclusive coupons, special offers, sweepstakes, and product samples; new articles for saving time and effort on fabric care; and quick tips and helpful solutions for removing stains. Hitwise data confirms that email continues to generate substantial upstream traffic to Tide.com.

P&G supplemented the launch-period word-of-mouth campaign with a variety of communications campaigns. Public relations programs factored in heavily, such as media tours with the Alliance to Save Energy president, additional mentions in the Alliance's E-efficiency newsletters, and Hispanic outreach. In-store and point-of-sale educational and promotional materials were distributed. And two 15-second TV spots aired that spoke to the benefits. About six months later, Tide Coldwater initiated a direct response campaign on national cable created to educate consumers and stimulate retail demand (Leavitt 2005b; Red 2005).

The Tide Coldwater Challenge succeeded in creating a goodly number of site visits from that buzz, search intelligence firm Hitwise found. "Visits to Tide.com increased by an astounding 90% in just one week and the average session time spent on the website increased from less than four minutes to over nine minutes that same week. We know that the campaign was viral because 56% of visits to Tide.com originated at internet email services like Hotmail and Yahoo! Mail, up from 1.3% before the launch" (Prescott 2005).

Generate Interest in Brand Offerings through an Influencer Campaign: Sprint Ambassador Program

Sprint's Power Vision family of services provides mobile users with just about every available voice, web, and multimedia feature. Subscribers can stream or purchase music, watch live news or NFL TV, shoot and send pictures, and have a constant "web tone." Aiming to publicize Power Vision and its newest phones to the mobile media savvy, the company undertook a six-month word-of-mouth influencer campaign, the Sprint Ambassador Program.

Sprint recruited influencers through personal invitations emailed to A-list bloggers across a variety of industries, ranging from advertising, media, and marketing to technology. Bloggers accepting the invitation received a Samsung A920 phone, and Sprint picked up all the charges for six months. With unlimited use and budget, Sprint figured bloggers would get the full experience. A very important point was that the email asked for feedback only to Sprint about the phone

FIGURE 8.5   Bloggers posted pieces on the Sprint Ambassador Program.

Source: Jeff Jarvis BuzzMachine blog, January 6, 2006.

or services; there was no "play for publication" scheme at all. Bloggers decided for themselves whether they wanted to comment about the phone. (See Figure 8.5.)

David Dickey, Sprint's online and interactive advertising manager, reveals that bloggers did write about the phone. The campaign generated searches on Google to the tune of 389,000 hits (Wood 2006b).

Measuring Word of Mouth

Realizing that word-of-mouth campaigns generate positive and negative comments or actions, how should marketers evaluate their brands' results? Experienced word-of-mouth marketer Sprint advises, "define specific success metrics before beginning a word-of-mouth campaign" (Wood 2006b). That's especially good advice because there are so many ways to research, analyze, and gauge results. Personalize your brand campaign metrics to its specific marketing objectives.

Winning Plays

- Email is the most frequent activity by people using the internet and is highly valued by marketers to reach customers and increasingly to attract customers. On the surface, email would seem identical to direct mail (or at least a close cousin). There are, however, a number of factors unique to email that can limit its effectiveness:
  - It needs to be opt-in or permission-based, as consumers increasingly use spam blockers and quick delete buttons.
  - Use of email in newsletters or offers not only must be relevant but should also optimize convenience and simplicity.
  - In order for email to be highly effective, it must connect with action-shopping site, website, or information search.
- The personalization and dialogue potential of the internet is just beginning to be fully recognized by marketers. Email newsletters are the most popular tool used by marketers, but they must be integrated with other elements in the go-to-marketing strategy to be effective.
- The primary strategy for email (newsletters, offers, and others) should be to retain customers and build loyalty. Think of email as relationship building with the potential for continuous dialogue among invited guests rather than an interrupt-and-repeat model of the classic push mode of mass broadcast advertising.
- Done well, email marketing, integrated with shopping, buying, and dialogue, leads to additional word of mouth for the brand (which, in essence, is free). Research shows that word of mouth from friends or trusted experts is the most credible and potentially motivating advertising for a brand. Unfortunately, word of mouth is not controllable, and negative word of mouth can often disseminate quicker than positive word of mouth. It is critical therefore to integrate all email marketing with positive product

usage experience and service experiences. In essence, total brand delivers.

- Decentralized and noncoordinated email strategies are inefficient and potentially (and probably) harmful to brand image. Without a clear connection to marketing strategy, brand personality, and contact management in place, brands risk sending mixed messages and, worse, irrelevant messages. That risks alienating customers, and weakens the brand's in-box penetrating power and ultimately its performance.

CHAPTER 9

Futures

A Look Ahead at Emerging Plays

The mission of *The Online Advertising Playbook* has been to aggregate, evaluate, and integrate what has been learned about advertising online during its initial decade. This final chapter attempts to look ahead into the next decade of online advertising. More of the same? Or significant changes?

Much of the effort to use the powerful new technology called the internet for advertising in the early days was a transfer of practices proven useful in electronic mass media like radio and television. While this transfer provided some value, the big breakthroughs came through e-commerce learning, email adoptions, targeting thinking from direct marketing, and creative leaps congruent with the interactive nature of the internet and most recently the growth and adoption of information and shopping search by consumers.

In order to peer a little more clearly into the future, we asked some experts to share their thoughts via interviews and written contributions. The most interesting part of this futurology exercise was the emergence of three new models of advertising different from the mass-media-rooted interrupt-and-repeat model and the search-based targeting model currently in vogue.

The first model is the permission-based (opt-in) model, centered on engagement, not exposure. The second new model is the one of consumer empowerment where both the time spent with messages and even the generation of messages or word of mouth emanate *from* the consumer. The final model is a model of advertising as service to consumers.

It is our view that all three of the new models will override the push model of advertising that is based on interrupting large media audiences with a message as many times as the advertising budget will permit. These new models of advertising, while stimulated by experimentation online and emerging media forms, will become valuable models for advertising in general, not just online advertising. It is an exciting time for marketing and advertising practitioners and for consumers as well. We hope the following views will stimulate your own thoughts about future possibilities between now and 2017.

Comments on the Future

Changing Rules and the Rules of Change

Jeff Cole, Professor, University of Southern California

After only a few years it is already easy to see that the internet (and now wireless technologies) has changed the rules of everything. Everything that we have learned and become accustomed to has been affected, and in most cases, transformed. Nowhere is this more true than in the world of advertising and the ways in which we reach consumers with commercial messages.

While the origins of the internet can be traced back to 1969 as a federal project of the Defense Advanced Research Projects Agency (DARPA), the World Wide Web as we use it today began in the early 1990s. Advertising, or any kind of commercial activity or message, was actually illegal on the internet until the end of 1995. By the time Congress got around to lifting the ban on commercial activity on "its" internet, buying, selling, and advertising were already commonplace. By allowing, if not embracing, private interests, Congress, whether it realized it or not (and it probably did not), was forever changing the advertising business and a whole lot of other businesses as well.

An advertising executive retiring in 1995 with 40 years' experience could have looked back on a stable, exciting, and rewarding career. As dynamic as the business must have felt, in retrospect it (like the television and print businesses) really did not change that dramatically during the course of those years, especially in comparison to what was about to happen. In 1955 a big agency juggled advertising budgets among television, newspapers, magazines, radio, and a few other venues such as outdoor advertising. Throughout that period television became and remained the dominant advertising medium. Although television audiences began to fragment with the introduction of satellite channels and VCRs in 1975 and advertisers had more targeted channels to choose from, the business fundamentally remained the same. That can also be said of newspapers, which in 1955 relied on display and classified advertising and still did 40 years later. Someone trained to work in advertising in 1955 certainly had to learn new players and techniques and remain nimble, but the business stayed relatively constant during all those years.

Everything began to change in 1995. Entering the advertising business after the rise of the internet means participating in a dynamic industry that changes every six to nine months, and all past training and lessons must be relearned—and not relearned once, but constantly as new players, media, technologies, and wisdom change at a pace that has never been seen before. A year ago, MySpace, YouTube, and Facebook would have barely warranted a thought, but now they are vital forces changing everything about advertising and distribution and how consumers use media. But it is not enough to learn these new rules and players and sit back. New players are about to emerge on the internet, and new rules will have to be written as conventional wisdom is scrapped. And this goes on and on and on. It is highly unlikely that advertising will ever again enter a period of long-term (or even short-term) stability. Those beginning careers there must crave a life of constant change and chaos, as everything must be reconsidered, and want a workday that is completely unlike the one before.

From 1995 until the dot-com meltdown of 2001 and 2002 it was easy for advertisers to dismiss the internet as a passing fad. Users quickly registered their distaste for pop-up ads and threatened to boycott products from companies that employed them. Although many start-up companies in that period created business plans seemingly written on the back of napkins with financial strategies that began and ended with bringing pairs of eyeballs to websites, users also demonstrated little interest in banner ads. By the time start-ups ran out of funding and disappeared en masse during the meltdown, it was easy to dismiss the importance of the internet.

Two things changed after the meltdown that will have enormous significance for advertising in the decade ahead and beyond. First, with many heralding the demise of the internet, it actually grew in importance after 2002. Levels of access, usage, and especially broadband continued to grow steadily irrespective of the financial retrenchment. At the Center for the Digital Future at the USC Annenberg School we have been tracking users' attitudes and behaviors online and offline since 1999 (www.digitalcenter.org). Our work shows that in the 2000–2006 period the internet steadily became an essential part of everyday life. Strong growth of broadband, especially due to its always-on function, integrated the internet into all the tasks and rhythms of daily life. Our work clearly demonstrated that during the years of the meltdown and beyond, users bought more online, checked their email more often, became more comfortable in a wired world, and considered the web more important in their daily lives than television. Out of this growth emerged user-generated content, online communities, a movement to mobile, and other developments that sapped classified advertising from newspapers and attention from television viewers.

The second thing that emerged in this period was sophisticated search, especially Google, which became essential for anyone looking for anything on the internet. Search companies tied effortless and reliable search to paid adverting. That development changed all the rules and for the first time advertisers had to pay only when their audience demonstrated interest in their products. With that development, ad budgets were reconceived and began to be rearranged.

The naysayers about the future of the internet have all but disappeared. It is almost impossible to find anyone now who says it is going away or declining in importance.

Trying to predict change in a world that is constantly changing is a foolish effort. In a previous era it could take a decade or more for predictions to be demonstrated to be prescient or just plain wrong. Now, that proof emerges in a matter of months, and the predictors are quickly confronted with their folly.

That being said, there are a couple of trends that can guide us in the path ahead.

The Audience Continues to Grow Empowered   The days of watching television on someone else's schedule or passively engaging in media are coming to an end. Teens in particular make it clear that they do not simply want to receive information, but want to generate it and share it with peers. Whether the 30-second advertisement is dead or not, audiences demand a far higher level of engagement with their ads, and advertisers insist that engagement be proved. Teens want to move their content freely from platform to platform, irrespective of anyone's desire to restrict them. They will use the immense amount of information on the web to empower themselves politically, in negotiations with salespeople for automobiles and many other products (including funeral directors), and in relationships with doctors, teachers, and elected officials. Advertisers need to prepare themselves to deal with the most empowered generation ever seen.

People Like Choice, but Not Too Much Choice   In 1975 when most people could receive seven to nine television channels, 90% of all viewing was in three places, ABC, CBS, and NBC. A generation later when many households could receive hundreds of channels, 90% of all viewing was on only 8 to 12 channels. On the web, 90% of all time is spent on about 16 websites (although the other 10% is spread among tens of millions of possibilities). People want choice, but not too much choice. Too many options overwhelm and immobilize consumers. Studies have shown that rather than finding a restaurant menu filled with pages and pages of choices appealing, most people stop reading after two pages and feel frustrated. Most restaurants have found that diners actually like about 8 to 12 options, enough to offer real choice but not so many as to overwhelm.

The Role of Peer-to-Peer Continues to Grow   As much as teens look to major media for content, they are now looking to each other as well. One of the strange axioms that have emerged is that in many cases young users trust unknown peers more than recognized experts. Fortunately, this changes as they move into their 20s and need reliable information from people who have knowledge and expertise. Users of peer-to-peer networks have made it clear time after time that they do not want to see government or corporate influence in "their" sites. This does not mean that advertisers must stay away from these sites, but rather that they must move gingerly and be up-front rather than hiding their presence or goals. Nothing works better than true viral messages on the web, and nothing fails more definitively than what appears to be peer viral and actually is a manipulated or hidden message from a big company. Peer-to-peer changes the role of everything and those who venture there must learn, relearn, and relearn again the rules of playing in that world.

Brand Is More Important Than Ever   Although many predicted that the web's direct access to consumers would diminish the value of brand and marketing, the exact opposite has occurred. As people face thousands of choices on the web from sources they recognize and even more from companies or places they have never seen before, they do not know what to trust. This is true of sources of news as well as products. In the past one could rely on the quality and integrity of mainstream media (with occasional exceptions) and know that the sources of misleading or fraudulent information could be found. This is not the case on the internet. As users are not sure who or what they can trust, they are quickly gravitating away from peers (except teens) and unknown names toward names and brands they recognize, frequently from the offline world. While there are serious questions about the future of brands like the *New York Times* in the offline world, in the online world their names mean everything. This is equally true of commercial brands as well. Some new brands will emerge only online, but whether online or offline, the value of brand has never been more important.

The Challenges of Change: Relevance, Empowerment, and Authenticity

Vincent Barabba, Chairman, Market Insight Corporation

It is no longer a question of whether internet advertising will alter how advertisers engage current and potential customers; the critical question is the speed and extent to which the change occurs. An answer to the latter question will be partially determined by how advertisers come to understand and address two important and interrelated actions.

The first action is to challenge the traditional models of allocating resources based on cost per thousand and exposure rates and start spending the time and energy to take full advantage of the internet's ability to engage the right people with the right message rather than attempting to get in front of the most people with the same message.

The second action is to discourage attempts to monetize internet advertising applications that are more focused on providing advertising space at the expense of the focused content or service for which the particular application is promoted. In essence let's make sure we don't fall prey to the same pattern of behavior of allowing sellers of traditional advertising space to accomplish what might be described as having the tail wag the dog.

As an example, why it is that television news (be it morning or evening) has an allotted amount of time, no matter whether there is sufficient news to warrant the time allocated, and, with the very few exceptions of major events, is always shown at the same time of day? One of the reasons is that the network or program has been able to sell the ad space that fits between the allocated news content at a time when it is expected that certain people, usually described by age and economic demographics, will be watching. This, of course, leads to the question of whether it is the purpose of network news to present the news that is timely and relevant or to present enough news (be it relevant or not) to fit around the advertising space that has been sold—often months and years in advance. Are news department budgets based on getting the news, or getting enough news to fill the space between the ads?

Of course, as many argue, advertising allows traditional and new media the ability to provide free news and entertainment. But viewing news and entertainment supported by advertising is far from being completely free. Consider how much we pay for goods and services because the cost of advertising (whether it is effective or not) is built into the price of the products we buy or the amount of time we waste observing (or fast-forwarding through) advertisements that are not relevant to everyone watching. This is not to say that advertising has no value as a method of informing people of what is available to meet their needs and desires. This is a question of finding the most efficient and effective ways to accomplish the task.

When Television Was the Next New Thing   In the 1960s the majority of communication that took place between the manufacturer and the customer was impersonal and through mass communication. Around that time, television replaced newspapers as the primary source of information and radio as the primary source of entertainment. The transition to television for advertisers, given the more enduring homogeneous behavior of large sections of society, made a lot of sense. For example, given the number of women watching soap operas on television, an advertiser could reach approximately 80% of all women aged 18 to 49 in a week through three minutes of daytime television. The 1960 cost to reach these women, in today's dollars, was approximately $325,000.

Today, the cost of trying to reach 80% of all women aged 18 to 49, using network TV broadcasts only, would be approximately $15 million—46 times more expensive than in 1960. That startling comparison also puts into perspective the promise of more targeted advertising placements. By the use of cable programming to supplement the more expensive network reach—with 2,000 spots in a carefully selected combination of daytime, early news, late night, and network morning shows—the advertiser could reduce the cost of reaching those women dramatically to some $5 million. Even with this more efficient placement, however, the cost would still be over 15 times greater than in 1960. Because of changing and more fragmented consumer behavior, broadcast television has now reached the point where it often reaches fewer *relevant* customers while actually costing more.

The Continual Evolution of the Internet as the Next New Thing

In the late 1990s information technology and the internet promised to change everything. But, given the reality of product and service fulfillment requirements, it did not change everything. It did, however, change a lot!

Understanding the impact of the internet is not found in the technology that enabled it. It is best understood by appreciating the behavior of successive new generations of people who approach and engage the internet (and life) in different and continuously evolving ways. Major portions of these generations did not grow up believing that you had to be at a certain place at a certain time to see, hear, or read something of interest to them. What seems new to many of us who grew up before these technologies were available has been available to them for quite literally all their lives. For the older members of these generations eBay and Amazon have always been there; for the younger ones, MySpace and YouTube have always been there.

These generations have also learned that there is advantage to collaborating and have turned traditional transaction economics on its head. They live in social structures that are both virtual and real. They give away music, songs, and extra storage space because they like doing so. To them advertising is not a bad thing; to them it is how you advertise relative to their interests and needs (i.e., search) that is important.

Today, any individual customer, and particularly one who has grown up using multiple channels of communication, has the potential of knowing as much as or more than any one individual seller about categories of products and their various selling prices. For example, over two-thirds of purchasers of new vehicles obtain detailed information about all vehicles in which they are interested in a fraction of the time it used to take to watch the television shows that showed the advertisements during commercial breaks.

As these consumers have come to understand the economics and the behavior of information providers, be it offline or online, they have also become more concerned and have raised questions about the value and the integrity of the information. Much market research tends to support the belief that consumers are not satisfied with information received through advertising. The same, with some variation, can also be said of the internet. Customers are now looking for information sources that not only are helpful in guiding decision choice but also can be trusted to provide unbiased information. Evidence is also beginning to come to light that enterprises can benefit from providing helpful and trusted advice.

How does all this relate to the future of internet advertising? Today we have technology that has the potential to provide individuals the ability to choose what they want to hear, see, or read—when they want. This is an opportunity that could lead to greater and more meaningful engagement between the customer and the provider of products and services. This opportunity could be diminished, if not lost, if advertisers, based on the lingering memories of past successes, encourage the development of programs and applications designed to attract large numbers of eyeballs to a particular site over a selected time period and selling that mass audience to advertisers—in essence, as has occurred in broadcast media, allowing the tail to wag the dog.

What does the future hold for internet advertising? Promise! The promise, however, will be achieved only if advertisers take the advice attributed to Albert Einstein: "Without changing our patterns of thought, we will not be able to solve the problems we created with our current patterns of thought."

Advertisers seeking to benefit from the internet need to move beyond allocating resources based on cost per thousand and exposure rates and start investing the time and energy to make the transition to take full advantage of the desires and competencies of internet users to reach the right people with the right message rather than the most people with the same message.

The Personally Relevant Future

Bobby J. Calder, Charles H. Kellstadt Distinguished Professor of Marketing
and Professor of Psychology, Kellogg School of Management,
Northwestern University

Any attempt to predict the future will be wrong. It is useful to think about the future, however, because this may lead us toward a future to be desired. So what might be the future of online advertising, say 5 to 10 years out?

The one thing I would hope for most is that online advertising will continue to reflect the evolution of the web itself. Currently online advertising is valued most for responsiveness, epitomized by pay-per-click, and the ability to assess return on the advertising investment. This has been a direct reflection of the interactive nature of the web as a medium. But in the future the web will be much more than an interactive medium. The general shape of this development has come to be referred to most often as the "Web 2.0." (This itself, again, is more useful as a vision than a prediction.) The central tenet of this vision is that the web will be more of a platform than an application (think Google versus Windows). Web pages will have more the feel of running an online program than simply viewing information. These dynamic websites will be backed by direct-access databases and RSS-type links so that users can easily search for relevant information and be informed of relevant updates and changes in information. Sites will also combine applications and data from other sites (think incorporating MapQuest into a site). And perhaps stretching into the Web 3.0, dynamic websites will routinely incorporate participation such that users actively add to content, network (including blogging and podcasting) around content, and generally add collective intelligence, either actively or passively through usage, to the content—all of this within the scope of the "long-tail" view that says that the entire distribution of users can be addressed, not just typical users.

What will it mean for online advertising to keep pace with the Web 2.0? Consider a financial services ad for a retirement product, a category certain to increase in the future.

The message of a television ad currently running in this category is, "The best book on retirement is the one you will write." An online ad in the future might serve up this same message in a dynamic Web

2.0 way. Either playfully or seriously the ad could invite users to name their book or otherwise indicate what they would include in it. Users could compare themselves to others. They could access a database of retirement information—for example, places to retire, state taxes, housing costs (from another site). They could see how many other people are thinking of moving in general or to a specific place, and they could request updates about this, or even network with similar others. The Web 2.0 possibilities are endless. The point is that the ad, like the web itself, becomes dynamic—explorable, searchable, and participative—but not in an overwhelming way; users see only what they want to see.

All of this Web 2.0 functionality should make current trends in online advertising even more meaningful for users. The contextual and behavioral targeting of ads becomes not only possible but meaningful to the user's experience. They enable the user to create the online experience that they want from the ad. IPTV addressable video becomes something that the user is *pulled* to rather than a device for pushing more intrusive ad content on the user. Users are led to the richer experience of film because they want to see something in this mode.

The web is already a rich experience for many users. Research by Ed Malthouse and me has demonstrated that it already engages users in a way that enhances advertising effectiveness. We call one of the 22 distinct experiences our research has identified "Entertains and Absorbs Me." It can be described as follows: *I look forward to visiting this site. I have fun while I'm there and don't want to leave. It has a distinct personality and often surprises me. It's a contrast to the mainstream media.* A big part of this experience is a feeling of compulsive attraction, of not wanting to break away from the site. It turns out that this specific experience is a major driver of site usage (at least for the content sites we have studied). Moreover, the extent to which a user experiences Entertains and Absorbs Me is highly correlated to the effectiveness of advertising.

Now it is perfectly possible that online advertising could follow the model of old media in which the medium is simply another vehicle for potential static, albeit clickable, ad exposure. What I hope does not happen is that we merely serve up a retirement ad, addressed to over-55 book lovers, about writing your own book in retirement, an ad that includes a link to the company's web site. A preferable vision is that online advertising uses the emerging dynamic properties of the web to become part of an even richer web experience encompassing both content and advertising.

Future: Fast-Forward

Joanne Bradford, Corporate Vice President, Global Sales and Marketing; Chief Media Revenue Officer, Microsoft Corporation

There are many keys to success in digital marketing, but the most fundamental is understanding the consumer. At Microsoft we've built a very successful software business from understanding the cross-roads of consumers and technology. Now we are bringing these in-sights to marketers who need to understand how advertising can stand inside that same intersection. Consumers have moved out from our old models and are interacting in a way that media and marketers have never seen before. They're communicating and getting informa-tion faster than ever before. Their media behavior has evolved with technology and they've moved on. Now we as marketers have to catch up with them. It's a playground of opportunity.

Consider the profound changes that are going on in the world today solely around the area of personal communication. People are connecting, sharing, and expressing themselves in ways that were not even dreamed of just a few years ago. Instant messaging, email, video cams, blogging, in-game chat—it has become a very blurry world compared to not long ago when phone, fax, and letter were pretty much all we had for personal communication. Amidst all of this change, however, what we are learning is that the mode of communi-cation matters less and less to more and more people. As marketers we need to focus less on what application or device our customers are using. We need to focus on how we can facilitate connections among people and the information they care about most. Understanding how we can satisfy these core human needs should come first. Figuring out how the technology enables this should follow.

In this context, marketers need to think not just about how you reach your consumers, but how you engage them. Digital marketing opportunities are far more active than traditional passive media—and consumers are expecting more and more to control their content and communications experiences. We have to think very creatively about how we develop advertising that engages and embraces these con-sumers' emotion and attention.

On top of this shift in thinking, we have to grapple with measuring the effectiveness of our campaigns. In this world of accountability we have to ensure that our research and measurement techniques are keeping pace with the innovations in the media landscape. We know that for many marketers the risks of experimentation in interactive advertising will remain an obstacle until we have reliable measurement mechanisms in place to judge successes and failures. We must drive innovation within our research tools.

All of this change requires dramatic shifts in thinking among both individual marketers and their organizations. Recognizing the changing consumer media landscape is one thing; the next key to success is leveraging technology to build stronger relationships with customers. Think about Nike's inspiration to put iPods in their shoes. Nike identified that many runners are also passionate about music, especially when they exercise. Nike used technology to satisfy two important needs among their consumers, who are eating this stuff up.

Starwood Hotels is another great example of a company using technology to enhance the customer experience. The company has a great rewards program and a website loaded with convenient time-saving features for its most loyal customers. Starwood studied people's passions for the brand, and built an experience that weaves together connections, rewards, and loyalty.

Bottom line: Don't start your ad planning with a media spend allocation, but rather go back to the consumer to understand what drives people's passion for your products and services and how you can use technology to deepen those relationships. And we believe that this principle will hold even for direct marketers who focus primarily on response metrics and sales. The future of direct response is measurable, meaningful brand interaction.

At Microsoft, we get lots of questions from marketers who ask us to predict the future for technology and advertising. We don't have any magic crystal balls, especially when technology twists and turns in so many unexpected ways. I remember when my brother bought one of the first-generation $1,500 fax machines and we all thought this was the ultimate in instantaneous communications. Did anyone back then predict the revolution that was yet to come?

Still, we can anticipate some basic changes on the road ahead. We know the traditional television delivery model is evolving rapidly as technology has brought consumer control and mobility into the picture. This is a trend that has significant implications for advertisers and how they reach increasingly fragmented and mobile audiences.

Search is another area where we are sure to see big changes as it becomes more personal, intuitive, and relevant. Search right now is not much more than asking a machine for an answer. The experience will continue to evolve significantly over the next few years—we have only scratched the surface.

The very nature of the content that we consume will evolve. The field of journalism, for example, has already begun adapting to a world that includes user-generated content and blogging. Individual content producers, some of whom might be credentialed journalists (and others who might not be), will develop relationships with readers that could supercede established publications.

Finally, there is the question of what all this technology change means for the advertising business itself. Will the future mean the end of advertising sales teams and the traditional buying process? I don't think that the advertising business will cede to an automated buying and selling environment, because people care too much about their brand. You can't turn your brand over to a machine; you can't turn your brand and your advertising placements over to an online tool. People's brands are too important to them, they're too important to the consumer, and there's too much real human creativity and thought (as demonstrated in the pages surrounding this one) that are necessary to make a successful campaign.

Real-Time Targeting

Greg Rogers, Vice President, Sales Strategy, TACODA, Inc.

Chapter 2 on targeting speaks of how media planning has evolved from broad demographics (e.g., women aged 25 to 54) to a more comprehensive set of characteristics (e.g., males aged 18 to 34 who purchase four or more DVDs a month, exercise, and attend sporting events). This refinement in targeting was driven by the development of audience-specific media. The rise of cable programming like the Discovery Channel and online programs like ESPN.com has increased the opportunity to deliver targeted messaging, which requires a better understanding of consumer behaviors. The importance of focus groups and lifestyle-based surveys has grown in direct relation to the vertical media outlets being created in both the online and offline worlds.

However, an inherent problem with survey-based planning arose from the constant demand for more nimble competition. In mid-2006, the head of online marketing for a major movie studio summed up the quandary he faced: "We release a DVD or new movie about every two weeks. We have some general insights as to who the audience is, but there is little time to get any more granular than the basics." While the studio's time to market represented an extreme, the manager's sentiment reflects a greater industry need for rapid and concise targeting methods. In the past, marketers gave up either timeliness or precision when researching their consumer behaviors, the conventional wisdom being that the two objectives run counter to one another. However, the online space has begun to address this trade-off as behaviors are captured at the moment they occur and are stored in massive databases awaiting analysis and action.

In the not too distant future, the movie studio will utilize those databases to instantly understand its audiences. Behavioral targeting solutions will be employed to analyze visitors to the websites created for upcoming theatrical releases. Every time a user comes to the movie's site, the database will build a profile of the behaviors that person has exhibited in the past. Website visitors who exhibit the same behaviors will be identified in intricate detail and clustered together, with the clusters taking on a life of their own, much like the people that they describe.

The movie studio will suddenly move from a generic understanding of its audiences to a concise map of consumer behaviors by which to target its advertising. Using behavioral targeting ad networks, the studio will find millions of people online who look just like their consumer clusters and serve them an advertisement. The studio will have a repository of targeting data for use in planning sequels and DVD releases. It will also have research to support its offline marketing activities. Perhaps most important, it will have a way of uncovering the complex DNA of its consumer groups within days, even hours—something that would normally take months using traditional survey research methods.

Employing behavioral targeting solutions as a means to understand consumer interests requires two leaps of faith. The first is whether the people who visit the company's website represent an adequate sample of current customers. The second leap is whether people's online surfing behavior is an accurate reflection of their psychology.

These two assumptions that online advertisers currently have to accept will no doubt be tested in the days to come. If they are proven to a good extent to be true, the ramifications on how we delineate our customers and target them will be profound. Time to market for new products as well as advertising campaigns will shift to warp speed as we instantly create the micro-audiences that Chris Anderson has termed "the long tail of the marketplace," a tail that will begin wagging the dog as behavioral targeting moves beyond the online space with the convergence of media technologies. If consumer behavior is indeed an indication of interest, and we can collect and cluster those consumer behaviors in intricate detail, we will shift from the monochromatic targeting that prevails today to the technicolor vibrancy that looks just like real people, a long-sought-after marketing ideal.

Learn as You Do

Rishad Tobaccowala, CEO, Denuo

There are three sets of things any advertiser should know. The first is that there are some trends occurring externally and these trends seem to be quite clear. The traits seem to be well known in the world of media and technology. They are trends of an on-demand environment, a participatory environment, and a reaggregated environment.

What this means is, first, electronic media are moving from a broadcast push, programmed schedule to an "I want it when I want it" on-demand schedule. Second, participation is at the core of everything from blogs to broadcasting to MySpace to Facebook to just about everything else. Third, a lot of marketing was traditionally about segmentation taking large audiences and making them into smaller audiences for targeting. In an on-demand world, you have audiences of one whom you need to reaggregate into large enough audiences to target with both scale and relevance—almost "backward segmentation." The entire search phenomenon is all about how you reaggregate groups of a few large enough groups to market to profitability.

So, three key trends—on-demand, participation, and reaggregation—clearly play off each other, but those three trends seem to be driving a lot of the trends of where electronic marketing is going. These three forces have huge implications for planners. In a changing environment, you need to learn while you are doing. This is a very iterative model, and it's not a model where you scenario plan and think and spend years and years writing decks. You *do* because things are moving too fast for you to think too long or research the situation too much; by the time you've thought your way through something, the world has changed. This brings huge organizational challenges, and *the real challenges are not necessarily technological, but organizational.*

It's essential to remember that while the web is 2.0, people continue to be 1.0. While technology can morph quickly, behaviors and people and organizations and power still remain like soap operas. You have to embrace this change, and the only way to do that is really to make change be part of your homework. You should set aside two hours a week regardless of what level you are at (maybe it has to be on a weekend at home) to actually participate in a lot of these new roles, because only when you do it yourself will you understand what it implies both for you, your brand, your company, and your future.

Taking a broader industry view, today the companies that understand the digital world best tend to be in the software and technology businesses. By the nature of those companies, they tend to have a particularly heavy population of younger workers. These companies have a tendency to feel like they're only five years old. Apple Computer has been around for 20 years or so, but there's a new Apple out there that feels like it's five years old since Steve Jobs came back. Companies that think young feel young, because by their very nature they tend to be a little bit more experimental, and they are succeeding in the digital world. It is also critical to have a highly diverse workforce, because by their very nature they're used to chaos, which is people having different opinions and different perspectives. Thus, they're trying different things and that comes to a certain extent from diversity of experience and perspectives.

Choice, Control, and Trust

Dan Stoller and Jane Clarke, Time Warner Global Marketing

Many great visionaries and institutions have tried, unsuccessfully, to paint a picture of the future:

> "There is not the slightest indication that nuclear energy will ever be obtainable."
>
> —Albert Einstein, 1932

"The problem with television is that people have to glue their eyes to a screen. People won't have time for it."

—*New York Times*, 1939

"I think there is a world market for maybe five computers."

—Thomas Watson, IBM, 1943

"Two years from now, spam will be solved."

—Bill Gates, 2004

When it comes, specifically, to the future of marketing, Jim Stengel, chief marketing officer at Procter & Gamble, may have said it best: "I can't sit here—no CMO can—and say which way marketing is going to unfold in the next 10 years."

Ten years is a long time away and the accountability factor is quite low, so why not take a chance at predicting the future of that slice of marketing called advertising?

At Time Warner Global Marketing, we have a unique perspective on the future of media and advertising because of our wide array of media platforms and advertising strategies, extending globally.

Choice, Control, and Trust   We believe the future of advertising lives at the intersection of media *choice*, consumer *control*, and consumer *trust*. As content choice increases and on-demand consumer experiences (control) become pervasive, consumers will look for trusted media brands to point the way. We believe trust or, more specifically, openness in marketing is a key factor to the future of advertising in a noisy, fragmented world.

- *Choice.* Media is pervasive in today's society. Limitless content can be consumed over a growing number of access points—in all rooms of the home, on the road, and at work (e.g., laptop and desktop PCs, mobile devices, TVs, iPods, gaming devices).
- *Control.* On-demand technologies like digital video recorders, video on demand, iPods, and online search engines put consumers in control of their programming. These technologies will become pervasive across all media platforms over time.
- *Trust.* As more and more choice and control become available, the importance of trusted media brands to help consumers dis-

cover, experience, and transact will grow. Over the next 10 years, trusted media brands that recognize the need to help consumers navigate through endless options will become the user interface to simplifying and managing choice. Media companies will fight to gain the brand permission to play this role, forming more relevant relationships with consumers, thus becoming even more important to advertisers.

Trusted media brands will have an open window into audience behavior. As consumers become comfortable with the benefits of on-demand or consumer control and managed choice, they will be more willing to share personal data.

More choice and more control will lead to more data about consumer preferences and more opportunity for targeting relevant content, services, and advertising. Only trusted brands will be allowed to access highly valued information about consumers.

This intersection between choice, control, and trust, if managed correctly, will create a game-changing environment for the advertising and media industry—an environment where targeting consumers will not be about message intrusion but about message invitation. Message invitation leads to a high probability of relevance. At the end of the day, successful advertising is about relevance. The media that best leverage technology to enhance ad targeting (relevance) and measure marketer ROI as well as drive consumer ROA—"return on attention"—will benefit most from the choice/control/trust paradigm. We believe internet media and those media influenced by the internet will be the big winners in this new paradigm.

Internet influence is the advertising industry's version of convergence. We see the early stages of internet-like advertising concepts moving to traditional media platforms (i.e., Visible World will be for television just as DoubleClick was for the internet), and we also see the continuous flow of traditional media moving to the internet (i.e., as the internet has become a viable distribution platform for magazine and newspaper experiences, it will become a viable platform for video and audio experiences). Both of these trends, a kind of two-way convergence, will only accelerate over the next 5 to 10 years.

The inherent targeting, tracking, and optimizing capabilities found online will become more sophisticated and at the same time easier to use. Internet-specific platforms like search will continue their dominance, becoming more pervasive and more specialized and creating even better environments for advertisers. Some of these capabilities will be extended to mobile and interactive television environments. We believe consumers will interact with content across small screens (mobile), medium-sized screens (computers), and large screens (plasma HDTV screens), creating opportunities for new types of advertising models. Each screen size will require its own environment-specific search capabilities and rich media formats for gathering and displaying detailed information about new products relevant to each consumer's specific needs.

We believe online advertising will continue to grow at a rapid pace over the next 10 years as the internet influence accelerates. Internet ad revenue will grow by (1) generating incremental ad revenues to internet-specific platforms (e.g., search); (2) share-shifting revenue from traditional media environments to traditional media experienced on the internet (e.g., television vs. video); and finally (3) continuing to drive direct marketing dollars online.

The internet influence on traditional media and advertising is about technology as well as an approach or philosophy or way of doing things that is inherent to the internet—being dynamic, accountable, interactive, open, and communal. The knowledge and insights gained from building the internet into a $12 billion advertising platform over the past 10 years will have a fundamental impact on the way we market to consumers over the next 10 or 20 years through all media. At the most general level, the accountability and trackable nature of the online medium has brought a renewed focus to marketing effectiveness and consumer behavior across all media. The qualities that define the online programming experience (control, choice, convenience) have impacted and will continue to impact other media programming environments in a big way. Consider how online qualities like limitless access to niche content; consumer-generated content; search; and deep, rich, local content will impact what consumers expect of other media.

Collaboration across media types and between industry disciplines will allow us to truly leverage, in a breakthrough way, the potential impact the internet can have in serving consumers and advertisers alike. In understanding and managing for the choice/control/trust paradigm, the internet can help to align consumer and advertiser goals and create more relevance in advertising.

Think Differently

Noel Capon, R. C. Kopf Professor of Marketing, and Jeremy Kagan, Adjunct Professor, Graduate School of Business, Columbia University

As the starting point for our speculation on the future of advertising on the internet, one thing is surely true: It will be very different from what we see right now. What will characterize the future is creativity; and that creativity will emerge from many different places. Some of these places will be existing players who adapt as the medium evolves, but it will also come from the most unlikely places. After all, who had heard of Google eight years ago?

While productivity in detail is a fool's errand, there are areas where we believe there will be important advances.

Information on Audiences   Internet advertisers have different and more valuable information than is available from traditional media. With traditional media the advertiser typically has access to demographics on a broad audience group. Using the internet, advertisers have data on individuals. Whereas internet advertisers may know little about individual audience members' demographics, they often have detail on interests, purchases, and locations. This data will allow far more precise targeting, but will raise the required skill levels of media planners as advertisers seek their targets in many microniches. As a special case, integrating the internet accessed from mobile devices (PDAs, cell phones, etc.), advertisers will direct messages to individuals based on physical location.

Intelligent Personalization   More information about an audience, in some cases individual preferences, will allow firms to conduct advertising campaigns with surgical precision. Advertisers will be able to maintain and reinforce the desired message across multiple media, and use behavioral information to dynamically adapt the message in real time. Amazon already uses recommendation systems to send site visitors personalized messages about products judged relevant based on past purchases. An extension is to combine data on past purchase behavior with search behavior to divine future intentions. Hence a person who researches information on Tonga could receive a campaign message that included travel guide recommendations or links to an online travel partner.

Cross-Channel Creative Campaign Delivering an integrated creative campaign is not a new problem for advertisers. Traditionally, advertisers have integrated among media alternatives in radio, television, newspapers, and magazines. The internet has complicated this challenge by sharply increasing media types to include websites accessed by personal computers (desktop and laptop), portable handhelds, cell phones, and others. To be effective, advertisers will require a broad range of back-end technology managing digital marketing assets, to modify and encode them in real time and ensure appropriate delivery and tracking.

The Webification of Old Media Online innovation will leverage old media and continually blur the lines between old and new media. For example, by integrating with Global Positioning System (GPS) technology, taxicabs in New York City can already display the closest automated teller machine (ATM) for a bank advertiser, or the nearest Subway franchise. Advertisers will be able to customize messages to specific, and sometimes unlikely, locations: For example, how better to target a beverage ad customer than with an online-enabled poster in a bar's washroom?

More subtle options exist as well; the advertisements for clothing seen by a particular user can feature a model with the race, build, and gender of the viewer, dynamically and repeatedly updated. Similarly, cable infrastructure provides both internet access and television service to households that can be targeted with far more precision if technology enables economical deployment of creative campaigns. Ultimately, as shown in Figure 9.1, advertisers will converge behavior, identity, and location to deliver highly personalized messages as part of a unified campaign.

Cost and Revenue Models Investment in personalized, unified, multimedia messaging should increase advertising efficiency. Revenue models will have to shift from variables like cost per thousand (CPM), awareness, and similar variables toward variables that get closer to purchase behavior. Some revenue models will focus on actual purchase behavior; others will focus on behavior like click-throughs that get closer to purchase. Advertisers have already been pushing agencies for pay-for-performance models; the internet will accelerate that trend. Concurrently, media owners that deliver per-

FIGURE 9.1 Targeting improvements will come from combining demographics, location, and behavior.

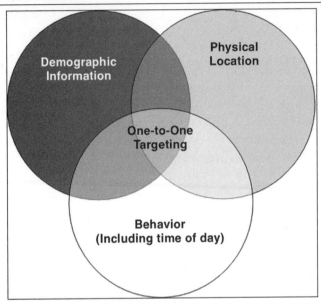

Source: Noel Capon and Jeremy Kagan, 2006.

formance should gain by reducing the advertiser's buying risk through better segmentation and results-driven models. Average revenue yields per audience member should increase dramatically.

Reaching target consumers across multiple media and aggregating them in real time to meet advertisers' needs will take advantage of personal information about the audience that is available in other media only in aggregate. However, these trends will give rise to some new problems:

Click Fraud As payment systems come to depend more heavily on actions by customers, the opportunities for cheating increase, and any pay-for-performance scheme other than actual purchase behavior increases the possibilities of fraud. A critical issue for advertisers will be the level of trust they put in the specific media vehicle—the website, network, brand, or advertising system— that they choose to use. Advertisers may pay a premium for more trustworthy media vehicles. We can already see the signs of that trend in the price-per-click deltas between top-tier search engines and other search engines whose search traffic may be less engaged and responsive.

Automatic Censorship   When many small audiences are aggregated automatically in internet advertising, automatic censorship may occur due to automated algorithms that protect advertisers from objectionable content when searching for ad. Placement through internet networks may unwittingly censor news sites. For example, the *New York Times* includes significant content on war, violence, and other disturbing topics. Online "censorbots" from Google and others may block such objectionable content pages from advertising use and severely impair the online revenue model.

Ad Blocking and the Privacy Backlash   As advertisers increase their abilities to target people personally, individuals will demand an anonymous option to shield themselves from certain types of behavioral profiling. They may not be happy about being tracked across different media types. For example, a person using the internet for research on a personal medical condition may actively object to receiving messages for that condition. Making no distinction between an individual's leisure interests and the workplace raises similar issues. Examples include dating and social activities, medical issues, political preferences, and career research. With these sorts of issues on the horizon, can marketing persona management and anonymous buttons on individuals' web browsers be far behind?

The future of online advertising will rest on a balance of trust and information sharing: for consumers, the privacy they sacrifice and the control they relinquish to receive marketing messages of value; for advertisers, the expense and complexity from a logistical, creative, technological, and even regulatory basis of managing advertising campaigns versus the greater efficiency in audience targeting; and for media owners, maintaining the bonds of trust with individuals and advertisers by developing acceptable standards and ensuring that actual behavior is consistent with those standards.

Experiment, Learn, and Adapt

Brian McAndrews, President and CEO, aQuantive

It is my view that the future of advertising will need to accommodate increasing consumer empowerment; it will have permission-based aspects and also "advertiser as service" aspects. Consumer empowerment is clearly on the rise. The digitization of media means that consumers are increasingly in control of when and how they receive their media and, in turn, their marketing messages. Further, the evolution of marketing will involve elements of permission-based marketing. For example, this will continue to be a key component of successful email marketing and will likely be an important component of successful mobile advertising as it evolves. And, finally, elements of "advertising as service" will also be prevalent: enhanced targeting and personalization, plus the ability for consumers to get richer, deeper content in areas of interest, will allow consumers to more readily obtain the information they want when they want it—and nothing else.

What should the marketer be doing now to be better prepared for this future? The marketer's response should involve a multipronged strategy that can be broadly categorized:

- Target and personalize every marketing interaction.
- Make your website the central expression of your brand.
- Integrate your digital messaging vertically.
- Test and experiment in emerging media.

Let me discuss each of these.

Target and Personalize Every Marketing Interaction The expansion of the internet and the eventual transformation of all media into digital media means that consumers have increasing control over content. In an on-demand world, the consumer gets to decide when she wants to consume content and, to a large degree, whether or not she wants to consume advertising. While the internet has been the first true on-demand medium, other media are rapidly following. With the growth of the internet, the growth of digital radio, the increased proliferation of digital video recorders (DVRs), and the growth of video-on-demand (VOD) offerings, consumers are increasingly gaining the ability to consume media on their own timetables. With technology enabling the avoidance of advertising, marketers need to ensure their messages are better targeted to their audience and are relevant.

Studies have shown that, even when people can skip through ads in a DVR environment, not all ads are skipped. In fact, in many cases, consumers drill deeper into advertising content—reviewing longer-form commercials, for example—when that content is particularly relevant to them. Relevant content resonates.

In the online advertising world today, we have the capabilities to target and personalize advertising based on many variables, including segmentation based on past customer interactions, context, time of day, broadband connection versus dial-up, and many others. We also have the ability to "frequency cap," providing a benefit to consumers who, even if they are interested in a product or service, do not want to see the same advertisement over and over again. Over time, and in emerging digital media, these capabilities will only get better. And the consumer will benefit. At aQuantive, we are working toward a day when no advertising dollar is wasted, when every marketing message is perfectly targeted and delivered to a person who is receptive to that message: the right message at the right time to the right person. While this may represent a digital nirvana that we may never fully achieve, the progress we have already made is remarkable.

Make Your Website the Central Expression of Your Brand   I believe that the website is rapidly replacing the 30-second TV commercial as the central expression of the brand. The television commercial remains an effective way to generate awareness for a brand and can sometimes establish some differentiation for the product or service featured. However, thanks to the increased penetration of broadband and the proliferation of new technologies such as rich media, web video, and Ajax, the website is able to offer a marketer and consumer the ability to engage in a far deeper, immersive, more meaningful, and ongoing dialogue.

Marketers who understand this are considering the website as part of their marketing spending and are recognizing that this should, and will be, an ongoing investment. The web is a unique medium in that it can be three channels in one: an advertising channel, a sales channel, and a customer relationship marketing (CRM) channel.

However, to take full advantage of its capabilities, marketers need to realize that the website is no longer "brochure ware," something you build and then let sit for a few years before you revise it. It is a living, breathing communications vehicle that needs to be constantly tended and nurtured, analyzed and optimized.

Integrate Your Digital Marketing Vertically   The ability to gather data on customer interactions and on the performance of elements of the marketing mix is significantly enhanced in the digital world. From basic measurements of how effective advertising has been in generating online sales to how much time a customer has spent on your website, where the consumer has gone, where they dropped out of the purchase cycle and why, to more sophisticated measurements such as the impact of advertising on offline sales, online marketing has trumped its offline counterparts.

What is often overlooked in this equation is the critical importance of *integrating vertically within the digital channel*. This integration across all digital channels (including display advertising, search, the website, email marketing, etc.) allows a marketer to have a single view of the consumer, enhancing the marketer's ability to effectively and efficiently engage that consumer in a meaningful dialogue. As all media become digital, of course, this expertise and experience can be utilized to take on the challenge of vertically integrating all media. Eventually, this will include video on demand, IPTV, mobile, and other emerging digital media channels. In the meantime, tremendous benefits can be achieved by integrating within those components of the digital channel that exist today—which leads right to the final part of the marketer's strategy:

However, to be the most effective marketer possible, it is ideal to have a single view of the customer—that is, to be able to message to a customer across all touch points in a coordinated, coherent, and measurable way. There is a lot of talk about horizontal marketing integration across TV, print, and online media. And it is important to ensure that this is done as well as possible, with a consistent brand message and coordination among the different components of the various elements of the marketing mix.

Test and Experiment in Emerging Media   Today's emerging media will be tomorrow's commonplace marketing vehicles. And consumers all over the world will decide how quickly those markets evolve. It is noteworthy that the growth of mobile devices in some emerging countries far outpaces the growth of the personal computer. Technology companies around the world are making large investments in everything from video-on-demand capabilities to wireless infrastructure to the digitization of out-of-home advertising. Because it is impossible to predict the exact timing and location of these new developments, it is critically important that marketers be testing emerging media now. This does not necessarily require significant financial investments by the marketer. In fact, many of the emerging media do not yet have enough penetration to make a significant investment for a major advertiser even possible. Also, there are risks that can accompany new media opportunities, which necessitate caution. For example, today's experimentation for marketers may be social networking, blogging, or podcasting, all of which present some risks to advertisers; tomorrow it will be something else. What is required is some investment of time and resources on the part of marketers and their agencies to sift through the myriad of choices and target the ones that offer the most learning for the minimum investment and manageable risk.

Advertising as a Service

David Kenny, Chairman and CEO, Digitas Inc.

There's an allegory about parallels in the evolution of Digitas Inc. and the world of consumer media consumption and advertising. A decade ago, we were direct marketing driven. We were a single agency with a penchant for data and analytics. About five or six years ago, that began to evolve as we became more convinced that our skills, our clients, and, in fact, our industry should be focused on digital media as the future of direct marketing. And we took on scale as more players bought into this belief and as our early partnerships with the likes of Yahoo!, Microsoft, and Google began to scale. Partnering allowed us to do bigger things through digital direct marketing. More and more, we were driven by the idea that the internet would become a place to build brands. This underscored some fundamental changes that we saw coming in the world of marketing: Brands would approach and engage their consumers in a very different way, and the agencies that served those brands would look and act differently than they had in the past. At the same time, we'd begun to focus on recruiting extraordinary talent, updating our media game, committing to new beliefs about content and creativity, and complementing and deepening our beliefs—the Modem Media and Medical Broadcasting Company acquisitions—to build the foundation of what we believed to be the agency-of-the-future approach.

Core to our belief system—and the digital revolution—is a new way to view advertising: It's about brands as a service. Service in different contextual and content forms. Brands as contextual and content service to consumers. At Digitas Inc.'s agencies, we prompt new employees to think about it this way: In certain countries, when you say, "I'm going to market," it means, "Can I bring you back something?" Essentially, I'm offering you service. Looking at marketing and advertising this way, we believe that all content for consumers starts with a series of service-focused questions. For example, what service does somebody who is considering buying a car need? What service does a PC buyer need? What information do they need and do they want? Today, providing these services also prompts another question: How much of it is branded versus unbranded? Ultimately, we try to define the highest level of service we can provide to the customer and we make the message or the experience relevant to that need. Defining service drives the content approach. Serving messages, information, and experience to the customer today takes the form of both branded and unbranded (or less branded) content.

The natural next step is to consider the functionality of this service. That's to say, how do we need it to work? The functionality could be the kind of information that gets served up to somebody searching for a car, or it could be how a payment system works once you've found what you're looking for. It can certainly be about how search keywords get you all the way through to the right information you need—as in getting you important information about a recent health diagnosis.

After we consider functionality of service, we brainstorm. Who else can help us provide this service? Sometimes it's the media platforms. Sometimes it's other content providers. Sometimes it's other consumers who share their stories, and sometimes it's the clients themselves. Our ultimate strategy is to provide for our clients' customers' service needs.

This service perspective helps pull together all elements of marketing strategy (media, creative, analytics), which is very different from the monologue approach of buying space for your brand and trying to fill it. You might not fill it with the right thing or the desired service—you're just filling space. It's also hard to develop media strategy without the creative strategy in mind. Under the same service strategy, it's very important that analytics be at scale. It's critical to know how individual campaigns are working and how they are being optimized. We define our work largely around the way consumers behave. They don't always behave in a linear fashion (they're often more random than that), and we're driven to make sure that messaging, and experience, work alongside consumers as their behaviors change.

This requires a strategy that is more about service than selling. This idea is easier for some clients to get than others. Naturally service-oriented companies such as airlines and financial services got it quickly, adopted it first, and today lead the new approach to marketing. Increasingly, considered-purchase product companies such as auto and computer hardware makers are driving service as key to what differentiates them.

A natural question is whether our approaches are changing because of the internet or because the internet is a powerful metaphor of the way consumers and their behavior are changing. Clearly, it's the latter. For sure, the internet isn't a panacea. It's just the medium through which more and more data is going back and forth at high speed. There are things we do through live events and sales force automation and with call centers providing customer service. Good marketing is still built upon some fundamentals: consumer inspiration, insight, and a lot of good listening skills.

Consumer behaviors have evolved in two important ways. First, for most consumers in the Western world time equals money, and consumers are increasingly focused on using their money and time wisely. As a result of that, anything that saves time is viewed as beneficial. For example, TiVo helps you skip commercials, so you can get information you want when you want it; search helps you get to the right product when you want it. The need to save time is what fundamentally drives search, because you can get to what you want really fast. The notion of being able to control the time element of media is what has changed the consumption patterns and changed the terms under which brands must communicate.

Second, consumer trust in iconic brands is not what it used to be, and this has influenced consumer behavior. Consumers are wary because trust has been eroded by political figures, by government, by companies that have gone bad, and by other abuses that have compromised individuals' belief in the words of anything bigger than themselves.

Increasingly consumers trust word of mouth, especially from friends, which has always been the best form of advertising. Today, there are all these different ways that people can seek word-of-mouth opinions beyond face-to-face conversation. If you've got a great product and you've got engaged consumers, how do you get them to tell that story to others, to get people fired up? Young people are using technology to create ongoing communities, a powerful word-of-mouth platform. Teens' physical community at school becomes part of their extended electronic community at home, and it's within those communities that they're often making decisions. People remain socially driven.

And, as we prepare for the future, the service approach to advertising has brought us much closer to our clients—figuratively and literally. We're often living their culture, and their customers' experience, as a result of being on-site. This builds a higher level of trust for us to work with them and to be part of the communities they're going to serve. More than something akin to an outsourcing partner, we're becoming like an adjunct relationship. We're helping them reengineer consumer relationships by reengineering our own with them.

In summary, we're going to continue to see changes in the way our industry does business. You see this even more when you look at advertising as a service. For all of us, it's going to be about knowing what you do well, knowing where to partner, where to be broker, and repeating the process over and over again in real time for the benefit of one person—the customer. Old industry structures are destined to change, and traditional silos undoubtedly will crumble. It's an exciting time to redefine marketing and advertising as true services.

Online Audience and Advertising Effectiveness Measurement

Online advertising is now over a decade old, and has finally secured its rightful place in the media mix. Companies from Fortune 1000s to small start-ups now realize how critical maintaining a presence online is toward building their brand, creating engagement, and improving sales. However, despite the fact that the internet has moved from media planning afterthought to line item, much of the promise of online advertising remains unfulfilled.

The original promise of online advertising was its greater accountability compared to other media platforms. The internet allowed more accurate measurement, the ability to gauge effectiveness, and the opportunity to optimize performance in real time. While it is true that digital media are more trackable and accountable than most other forms of advertising, the noise-to-data ratio remains high. There is such an overwhelming amount of information that can be collected, it becomes increasingly difficult to discern actionable metrics and insights under the avalanche of data.

The universe of online measurement can be bewildering. There are competing methodologies, competing products, and competing claims that create a great deal of confusion in the marketplace. To address some of this confusion, we need a better understanding of the measurement landscape. This Appendix discusses some of the most prominent measurement services available (from the broad array of possibilities), their product offerings, methodologies, and areas of expertise.

205

Offline Audience Measurement

The universe of advertising and audience measurement for offline media such as TV, radio, and print is far less bewildering, but it has not always been that way. Whenever a new medium emerges, competing measurement systems are typically launched, with each hoping to become the standard currency for ratings. In more established media those battles played out long ago, and advertisers and media companies have agreed to a single standard to measure audience size, cumulative reach, and ratings. In radio, for instance, Arbitron is the accepted audience ratings standard, used by both advertisers and broadcasters as the basis for setting prices in their media buys. In television, the road to ACNielsen's dominance is littered with would-be competitors who have tried and failed to offer an alternative: RD Percy & Co., AGB Group, Arbitron, and the $40 million Systems for Measuring and Reporting Television (SMART) TV initiative from Statistical Research, Inc. (Mandese 1999). Traditionally, both Arbitron and Nielsen use a random sample of the population to gather viewing habits using a written diary. Both have also made recent strides using so-called people meters, devices that measure what is being watched or listened to, and by whom.

Whereas Nielsen and Arbitron use random samples to project audience size and composition to measure media, the newspaper and magazine industry uses auditing services such as BPA Worldwide and the Audit Bureau of Circulation (ABC). These organizations provide third-party, independent verification of circulation and audience composition. While each industry may have an accepted, singular form of ratings currency used to help set pricing, these are not without controversy as well.

Audience measurement and advertising effectiveness are never an exact science, and are always disputed at some point. Both media buyers and sellers complain bitterly about methodologies, functionality, cost, and accuracy. Advertisers would like to know more precisely what is working to grow the brand. There is a broad array of measurement services available, and the following pages examine their methodologies, offerings, and core competencies.

We begin by looking at the audience measurement landscape in the online space, using metered tracking, surveys, and internet service provider (ISP) data for national and local markets. These audience measurement companies are most useful in the prebuy phase for me-

FIGURE A.I Metrics span the range of online ad campaigns, from prebuy planning to delivery, branding, and site performance. Campaign management needs to select the most important metrics from each group for their brand and advertising goals.

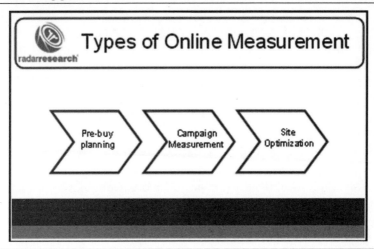

dia planning and competitive analysis. We then profile companies in the ad serving space, which provide real-time campaign data analysis for advertisers, followed by companies that provide site-side optimization analytics. (See Figure A.1.)

Lastly, this chapter explores emerging niche measurement companies in the brand assessment, buzz quantification, and cross-media measurement industries, which do not fit neatly into the standard categories. Depending on your online advertising goals, budget, and degree of sophistication, you may need to utilize several of these services to get a holistic view of your online marketing.

Online Audience Measurement

There are two prominent methods of measuring online audience activity: metered tracking using panels, and telephone surveys. Both methodologies have their merits and weaknesses, and the major audience measurement companies such as Nielsen//NetRatings and comScore Networks use a combination of both, depending on the service. Metered tracking data services utilize technology that records which websites an internet user visits via software that panel members voluntarily install on their computers. While metered panels can get a more accurate view of online media consumption than telephone surveys might because they track actual behavior rather than self-reported visitation, metered data typically comes under fire for underrepresenting the at-work audience—an audience that is crucial for many publishers. Few companies permit metering software to be installed on their company network, especially medium-sized to large companies. As a result, much of the at-work data is collected from smaller businesses and then projected to the full at-work audience.

Audience surveys such as the ones conducted by The Media Audit and Scarborough Research, to measure local usage, employ aided recall (e.g., respondents are asked which websites they visited and are given a list to choose from) or unaided recall (no list is provided and respondents must answer from memory). While both methodologies probably skew slightly toward larger, more well-known brands and properties since respondents self-report their visitorship, this is one of the few ways to understand cross-media usage.

ComScore Networks

ComScore Networks has a suite of measurement offerings, including both syndicated measurement services and customized information and consulting services. Its flagship service is comScore Media Metrix, a syndicated measurement service tracking over two million continuously measured internet users worldwide. The core panel consists of 50,000 home users and 50,000 work users recruited through a mix of random digit dialing (RDD) and online incentives, as well as 20,000 university users recruited entirely online. RDD is a probability sampling technique where each household in the United States has an equal chance of been selected in the sample. The online recruitment takes place primarily via affiliate marketing in order to cast a wide net for potential panelists and offers several types of incentives, including sweepstakes and technological inducements such as virtual storage. ComScore claims it has tried to develop an incentives program that has broad appeal without incurring the costs of cash incentives. The tracking software is opt-in for panelists and requires a log-in for each session. This allows comScore to track not only web usage but also digital applications and software usage such as instant messaging and AOL's proprietary services.

The syndicated measurement service offers a mix of audience

measurement reports and planning tools designed specifically with agencies and advertisers in mind. The megapanel of two million users reports on the surfing and buying activity of consumers, offering information that can be used to perform market and competitive research, as well as media planning and analysis. ComScore Media Metrix provides its clients with demographics analysis of who is visiting specific sites as well as online buying power metrics that can be used to segment audiences based on actual purchases captured in its tracking software.

As publishers, advertisers, and agencies have become more sophisticated, demand for more powerful measurement tools has increased. Content owners and media buyers now need to go beyond simple demographic information as they refine their online planning and analysis. ComScore Media Metrix has responded to this demand by expanding its syndicated services considerably to include detailed psychographic and behavioral measurement on 101 local U.S. markets, better measurement of key ethnic segments such as the growing online Hispanic population, and more qualitative consumer information.

Additionally, comScore Media Metrix measures activity on the advertising networks, reporting on actual rather than potential reach. It also allows clients to use its Ad-Focus tool, providing planning lists only on sites that accept advertising, eliminating much of the so-called noise in metered measurement.

ComScore's AiM product suite uses an extensive consumer survey to gain qualitative insight into lifestyle and behavior trends. AiM matches and appends behavioral data from its metered measurement service to the survey responses. Media buyers and advertisers can use the service to develop a profile of their consumer target through cross-tabulation with other AiM targets, evaluate media duplication and cross-visiting behavior, and analyze their overall media plan's reach/frequency. ComScore has also developed somewhat more sophisticated reach/frequency tools for media planning over the past few years. There are reach/frequency tools in both the core product as well as AiM, allowing clients to define the length of their overall campaign and duration on each site. Clients can also input either gross impressions or target impressions for the campaign.

ComScore's most recent product introduction attempts to measure the universe of search behavior with qSearch. The product cuts a fairly broad swath across the spectrum of search, capturing activity at

TABLE A.1   ComScore Product Offerings (2006)

	ComScore Reports and Release Schedule	
Report	Report Description	Data Release Schedule
Core reports	Audience ratings (U.S., local, Hispanic, international), source-loss, digital calculator, daypart, trends	Monthly Total U.S.: 10th–15th of following month Local U.S.: 20th–25th
AiM (qualitative survey)	Various reports based on 4,600+ audience targets	Semiannual (winter, summer)
MediaBuilder	Custom audience aggregation/competitive insight	Monthly (15th–20th)
Reach/frequency	RF analysis for online campaigns	Updated with monthly total U.S.
Search/search planning reports	Search tracking and planning reports	Monthly (25th–30th)

more than 25 search properties and collecting data at the site level, user level, and day level. Marketers are able to conduct a prebuy analysis for their search marketing, as well as use comScore's profiling tool in order to understand more about searchers within a particular keyword set. ComScore's future product offerings will include streaming media measurement. To help you better understand the diversity of product offerings from comScore, Table A.1 illustrates the syndicated tools the company offers.

Nielsen//NetRatings

Nielsen//NetRatings (NNR) offers a suite of services that compete directly with comScore Networks. Nielsen//NetRatings offers products for media planning as well as market research and competitive analysis. Nielsen//NetRatings essentially offers two services for online advertisers: @plan for media planning and NetView for online audience measurement. Nielsen//NetRatings employs panel-based research to measure the online audience, using similar tracking technologies to those of comScore. (See Table A.2.)

Nielsen//NetRatings takes an extremely disciplined approach to measuring web audiences, first enumerating the universe of online

TABLE A.2 Nielsen//Net Ratings Product Offerings

	Nielsen//NetRatings Reports and Release Schedule	
Report	Report Description	Data Release Schedule
NetView	Audience ratings	On the 9th of every month
MegaView Local, Search, Retail, Travel	Syndicated vertical product based on megapanel	Monthly
@plan	Media planning tool based on consumer lifestyle data	Quarterly
AdRelevance	RF analysis for online campaigns	Monthly

users (both web and digital applications) using RDD and a telephone survey.

NNR's core syndicated product, NetView, provides measurement of both home and work users, reporting on unique visitors, page views, and time spent on websites; families of brands; and channels, with 28,000 individuals engaged in metered tracking. NetView also reports on audience demographics, site trend reports, unduplicated audiences, and loyalty metrics such as frequency. NetView goes beyond measuring web usage to also include applications such as instant messaging, media player, ISP applications, information toolbars, and shopping or auction assistants. NetView also allows clients to filter their results to include just sites that are ad-supported.

NetView's meter measures usage at the individual level. Consumers recruited to the panel are required to install software on their computers that tracks their usage. Consumers on the panel are required to log in each time they go online, and all members of the household have their own log-ins so NNR is able to track individual usage. While requiring panelists to log in is undoubtedly more invasive, the trade-off is a more balanced, accurate measurement. Currently, NetView reports on individual usage while NNR's MegaView, its megapanel used as the data source for several syndicated products today, reports on household usage. As NNR integrates NetView and MegaView into one reporting source, the company's aim is to move to individual-level reporting for every product.

All telephone numbers in RDD used by NetRatings have an equal probability of selection; thus panelists are randomly chosen and there is minimal bias in the panel. It is the recruitment methodology long accepted as the most reliable for research panels by marketers and analysts. However, the cost of recruiting entirely through RDD is becoming prohibitive as the panel grows, and, although the data gleaned from this panel is suitable for top-line analysis, it wasn't meeting the needs of clients who demanded deeper data sets. Thus NNR began to build a platform for a megapanel (dubbed MegaView) via online recruitment to build the sample base, using the core RDD panel from NetView to calibrate the rest of the sample.

NNR recruits panelists online through partnerships with other panel-based research companies such as Greenfields and Harris Interactive and offers incentives such as cash sweepstakes. To ensure the panel is not skewed toward broadband users, NNR recruits dial-up users through ISPs such as NetZero.

While NNR plans to integrate the two panels into a single, integrated product in 2007, currently the two are distinct from each other. Today, the MegaView panel acts as the platform for several vertical, syndicated products, including Local, Retail, Travel, and Search products.

The MegaView service currently has 300,000 panelists who are actively tracked, comprised of 120,000 households. Currently the service only reports on a household, rather than on an individual, basis. Panelists are required to opt into the panel rather than automatically join when they download other software.

In addition to NetView and MegaView, Nielsen//NetRatings' suite of products includes @plan, a media planning tool similar to comScore's AiM service. The tool is used to gain insight into individual lifestyle and brand choices, on par with Simmons or Mediamark Research Inc. MRI in the offline media planning realm. The information in @plan is based on survey data and is thus self-reported but has proven useful for media planning purposes to select target audiences. The surveys are conducted 364 days a year (New Year's Day is the exception) and is released on a quarterly basis. Only adults 18 and over are included in the survey. The product is geared toward media planners, allowing planners to determine their target audience and estimate the market size. Ultimately, the company considers @plan a complementary service to its metered panel measurement.

The last product in Nielsen//NetRatings' suite of advertising measurement is AdRelevance, an advertising tool that allows marketers to see online advertising activity across formats, channels, industries, and platforms for their own and competitors' campaigns.

NNR's AdRelevance technology captures ad data across 2,000

sites, permitting advertisers to see advertising impression data, esti-mated spending based on rate card value, and creative content for their own ads, as well as competitors'. AdRelevance reports on 15 dis-crete but commonly used ad dimensions in addition to rich media formats and paid search placements. Given the disproportionate amount of house ads on many sites, AdRelevance also allows clients to remove house ads from their calculations, to give a clearer view of actual ad activity.

More recently, AdRelevance has added features that provide more competitive insight into paid search marketing, including an overview of all search activity across all categories and the top key-words on a weekly basis.

Hitwise

Hitwise bills itself as an "online competitive intelligence service," but rather than using a metered tracking method, Hitwise employs a network-centric methodology, partnering with ISPs to capture online usage, including search and conversion behavior. Hitwise sees itself not as a competitor to Nielsen//NetRatings (NNR) or comScore Media Metrix but as a supplementary tool that is able to provide more de-tailed insights than panel methodology can provide.

Hitwise readily admits its approach precludes the company from having the type of direct relationship NNR and comScore have with panelists, thus giving up some of the lifestyle and attitudinal data those companies are able to capture. However, the company tracks the usage and clickstream data of 25 million people globally in real time. Thus, while the metered tracking companies release their data on a monthly basis, Hitwise can provide more seasonality in its data, reporting on weekly or even daily usage. Additionally, comScore and NNR data are oriented toward the largest sites online; once the data analysis becomes too granular, the number of panelists becomes too small to be considered statistically significant. Hitwise believes its sweet spot lies in the small to midsize sites not included in comScore and NNR, providing greater breadth than those companies can offer.

Scarborough Research

While comScore, Nielsen//NetRatings, and Hitwise all track online us-age (albeit via differing methodologies), there are two companies that use survey methodologies to provide data on local audiences specifically. These companies are probably far more useful for media owners than for advertisers, but they are worth mentioning for their insight into local audience behavior.

Scarborough Research has already carved a large niche in the local newspaper measurement industry, tracking audience media consumption, shopping patterns, and lifestyle habits on local, regional, and national levels. The company was founded in 1974 as a newspaper measurement service owned by VNU, Inc. In the 1990s, the company expanded to include websites for local media such as newspaper sites and local TV station sites.

Scarborough Research's core service measures the top 75 local DMAs and also maintains a national database. The company reports on 1,700 categories and brands, including retail shopping behavior, lifestyle, demographics, and media usage. Scarborough Research uses a two-phase data collection methodology, beginning with a telephone interview that is followed by a mail-in survey. Rather than tracking actual behavior, the company relies on aided recall to determine media consumption behavior through a survey conducted twice a year.

The consumer survey booklet is a self-administered questionnaire that measures consumer lifestyle and media behavior in more detail, including detailed questions on retail and shopping habits as well as broadband access and internet use.

Scarborough uses aided recall to prompt consumers. Rather than ask an open-ended question that may skew unreasonably toward the more popular sites and punish lesser-known brands, the company asks consumers about particular websites for their local market. In the mail-in survey, Scarborough also looks at the online search marketplace as well. The company asks respondents about both their online and offline media viewing habits, drilling into which TV station websites and newspaper websites consumers view. The company also only looks at the individual website usage rather than corporate ownership. As a result, it cannot report on usage for a family of local websites owned by the same corporation.

Unlike the panel-based services, Scarborough Research does not maintain a panel for its surveys. The company recruits a random sample from the top 75 DMAs. Rather than maintain a panel over time, the company does continuous measurement that is constantly refreshed. The sample frame consists of adults 18 and over living in households with a landline telephone. The respondents are randomly sampled to ensure balance. Data is delivered on disk to clients twice a year with a 12-month rolling average database. Scarborough surveys over 200,000 respondents aged 18 or over on an individual basis (as opposed to household tracking).

The Media Audit

The Media Audit is a syndicated research company that covers local audiences and markets, primarily for the newspaper and local television station industries, and now covers online media as well. The Media Audit relies on surveys to measure media consumption and lifestyle preferences. The company was founded in 1971 in Texas. Its primary product is a syndicated local-market audience survey currently conducted in 86 markets throughout 37 states and sold as annual subscriptions to individual members of the communications industry.

The survey covers over 450 target items for each rated media's audience. These data points include features such as demographics, lifestyle preferences, products purchased, credit cards used, and other selected consumer characteristics. The Media Audit uses random digit dialing to recruit a random sample of adults in local markets. The company surveys only adults over the age of 18 and does not cover the media consumption or lifestyle habits of children or teenagers.

The Media Audit uses a single-phase telephone data collection process (i.e., all of the data is collected in a single telephone interview rather than in a multiphased process of phone and mail-in surveys, as Scarborough Research does). The Media Audit data is gathered within four-to-six-week time frames and delivered within 30 days following the close of the interviewing process. For the top 45 markets the survey is conducted biannually and data is released twice a year; for the smaller markets, data is collected annually.

The Media Audit collects website ratings data for local newspapers, television stations, radio stations, city guides, and alternative weeklies in each of 80+ markets. The company also collects self-reported visitation data for national sites that consumers turn to for local information such as MSN, AOL, and Yahoo! or national classifieds sites such as Monster and HotJobs. The Media Audit asks in an aided-recall survey what sites the respondent has visited in the past 30 days, the past week, and in the past 24 hours. This information is most relevant to local advertisers and advertising agencies.

Online Campaign Measurement

Despite the internet entering its second decade as an advertising vehicle, there is still some debate over how to count an impression. To advance the medium toward standardization, the Internet Advertising Bureau (IAB) launched a Measurement Task Force in November 2004, with the support of many of the leading corporations in advertising and research. The goals of the task force were to develop a global standard for counting online advertising impressions and to provide industry transparency to the systems that measure ads. While the impression argument is not completely settled, the standard established by the IAB has put to rest much of the debate.

The IAB maintains that the task force represents a number of significant firsts in advertising. It is the first time "that any advertising medium has developed a measurement standard that measures the ad itself, as delivered to a consumer, versus other media that measure the programming or content" (IAB 2006c). It is also significant that this marks a global effort toward standardization, as it included stakeholders from the United States, Europe, Asia, and Latin America.

The guidelines have the support of many major online publishers as well as close to 40 major proprietary third-party ad-serving technologies. In addition to proposing a detailed definition for counting an ad impression, the task force also recommends third-party independent auditing and certification guidelines in the United States for ad-serving applications. In 2006 the task force developed a set of Broadband Video Commercial Measurement Guidelines, in anticipation of greater broadband advertising adoption by more marketers. The guidelines will determine at what point a broadband video commercial is counted, and define it as a commercial that may appear before, during, and after a variety of content including streaming video, animation, gaming, and music video content in a player environment. This definition includes broadband video commercials that appear in live, archived, and downloadable streaming content (IAB 2006c).

Companies that have completed the certification process include Atlas Solutions, DoubleClick, CNET Networks, Walt Disney Internet Group, and Yahoo!, among others.

This section examines two companies that are crucial to understanding an advertising campaign's online effectiveness: DoubleClick and Atlas Solutions.

Atlas Solutions

At the most basic level, Atlas Solutions is a third-party ad server for advertisers, agencies, and publishers. Its origins can be traced to the late 1990s as a proprietary ad-serving solution for the interactive agency Avenue A. Around 2000, the strategic decision was made to separate Atlas from Avenue A (although both are today owned by the same corporate parent, aQuantive) and sell Atlas' services as a stand-alone company. Born out of an ad agency, the product was geared toward media buyers more than publishers and remains so to this day. Launched as a competitive product to Dart for Advertisers (DFA) in 2002, Atlas estimates the two companies combined today own 80% to 90% of the North American ad-serving marketplace.

The underlying technology for both ad servers is fairly straightforward. When a page loads on a website and an ad request is made to the publisher's server, there is a redirect to a third-party server, such as Atlas. The third-party ad server counts an impression right after the publisher does, sometimes causing discrepancies in reported impressions between the publishers and ad server. However, both Atlas and DFA have very similar counting methodologies, and discrepancies between the two tend to be very low and predictable (relative to publishers' proprietary ad servers).

Not long after this technology was introduced, it became apparent that simply counting impressions and clicks was not enough. Both Atlas and DoubleClick use a similar technology to track actions such as sweepstakes entries, registrations, and sales conversions. The third-party ad servers use a beacon to track action by placing a 1 × 1 pixel invisible graphic interchange format (GIF) image on landing pages, with a cookie. Suddenly, the ad servers became much more valuable in terms of offering fairly sophisticated campaign analytics and optimization tools, capable of telling a much more complex story for online advertisers.

Atlas provides marketers with the tools to measure impressions, clicks, and, if they're using action tags, conversions as well. For a large campaign with multiple creative units on diverse placements, deployment and optimization pose a logistical challenge.

Atlas provides an automated solution for creative optimization at the campaign level, weighting a creative unit's performance based on a particular placement on a particular site. By adopting a champion versus challenger mentality (setting benchmarks for the top-performing ad placements), Atlas' system recommends which creative units to drop because of underperformance and which units should increase their impression load.

According to Young-Bean Song, vice president of analytics at Atlas Institute, there are two major trends in online campaign measurement taking place today. The first is cross-channel analysis between discrete forms of online advertising, such as paid and organic search and display advertising. As marketers increase their search marketing budget at the expense of display advertising, Atlas has undertaken research to understand the synergy between the two methods. Attempting to quantify the impact of display advertising on search marketing, Atlas found a 22% higher possibility of conversion when advertisers employ both search and display in conjunction with each other.

The second and related trend also attempts to tell a more complex advertising story by rethinking conversion attribution. With more media bought on a cost-per-action (CPA) basis, it becomes critical for a marketer to correctly attribute action to the proper source, or rather sources. The prevailing mentality typically attributes the conversion to the last click that occurred before an action took place; budgets and creative departments tend to be optimized accordingly. Atlas is currently attempting to develop metrics that shed light on what happens before the last click, or ad view.

This becomes a slightly more daunting task when you consider that many of the ad networks swap impressions with each other. If a marketer does a media buy with five separate networks, the networks' reach is conceivably broad enough to reach the same user multiple times. If one sale occurs, each network may take the credit for that customer, with the advertiser paying multiple times for the same conversion. Atlas estimates that there is an average duplication rate of 170%, with potential overpayment per campaign averaging $255,000. Atlas is working to build conversion attribution tools that will explore all the potential touch points and brand exposures well before the purchase decision point in order to more accurately measure performance.

DoubleClick

Although DoubleClick offers a suite of advertiser and publisher management tools, for the purposes of this discussion, we are focusing on tools that help marketers measure their campaign effectiveness. Dart for Advertisers (DFA), like Atlas, is a hosted, third-party advertising management and serving product. While marketers can access their campaign data from any web browser, the hardware and infrastructure for delivering ads are centrally managed by DoubleClick.

Some of DFA's central features include a creative library, allowing advertisers to manage their creative assets in a central repository and schedule start and end dates as well as test periods for campaigns. Marketers can also batch upload and assign assets to multiple ads, saving time trafficking and deactivating creative units. DFA allows marketers to roll up multiple ad placements into a single roadblock for better reporting and more accurate pricing. DoubleClick has also designed DFA to support myriad pricing models, including cost-per-click, cost-per-action, and flat rates. The system can also be customized or expanded by clients and integrated into existing in-house billing systems.

DFA also includes a reporting feature, ReportCentral, providing a centralized tool to track campaign metrics such as click-through rates, costs, conversions, and return on investment (ROI). The company claims its interface streamlines the time it takes to generate customized reports, and includes reporting features such as cross-site duplication, frequency to conversion, and time lag to conversion. Additionally, the reporting tool features network-level reporting, allowing users to perform trend analysis across advertisers and campaigns, and planned media queries, comparing actual costs to planned campaign costs.

Like Atlas, DoubleClick also places a strong emphasis on creative measurement and optimization. Clients can set their own criteria to optimize creative elements against click rate, postclick conversion, postimpression activities, or a combination of both. DoubleClick uses the same methodology as Atlas to capture actions that take place after impressions are delivered, using what they term "spotlight tags." The third-party ad-serving companies are marketers' best hope to accurately attribute conversions and attain a richer, more complex view of the total impact of their online advertising.

Site-Side Analytics

The audience measurement companies, like comScore and NetRatings, provide valuable insight for marketers on where to find their target audience, the size of the audience, and the audience's online behaviors. The campaign measurement companies, like DoubleClick and Atlas, give marketers a real-time view into how their online advertising is performing, based on clicks and responses. The third piece in a marketer's online measurement toolkit should be a site-side analytics platform, offering a comprehensive view of not just how his or her advertising performs post-click, but also search and affiliate marketing, organic search performance, and the myriad ways consumers find a site.

The types of analytics these companies offer tend to be extremely sophisticated, and overlap among advertising, marketing, merchandising, and editorial departments, as they provide intelligence across a broader swatch of initiatives than just advertising. There has been little consolidation activity in this sector and there are still many competing companies and technologies, such as Coremetrics, Google Analytics, WebTrends, and WebSideStory.

Marketers have a wide selection of analytics vendors to choose from; however, the differences between them tend to be slight. As Forrester Research noted in its June 2004 report "Selecting a Site Analytics Product": "The wide array of Web analytics choices presents a challenge for buyers. Web analytics products are often nearly impossible to tell apart on first—or even second—look" (Forrester Research 2004).

The analytics companies listed here, as well as others, produce reports that companies can use to redesign their websites to sell more effectively, alter market segmentations, and simplify processes to boost consumer response. The tools can tell a manager which search words generate the most visits or the highest rate of conversion or what to offer in a follow-up promotion.

For marketers using multiple service providers for their campaign management, the benefit of using a site-side analytics tool is the holistic view across all internet media these companies provide. As Matthew Lawson, director of product marketing at Coremetrics, explains, "On the internet, people's behaviors are complex. Consumers consider items over time. They may browse online, click through an email a week later and still not purchase, search for related terms and browse, click on an ad another week later and browse, and then purchase at another time." These more sophisticated analytics tools go beyond gauging traffic to a site to measure ROI across multiple campaigns in a single interface, helping to identify underperforming placements or creative elements.

If an organization is a commerce company, these tools can help identify and track consumer conversion points such as completing a purchase, creating a wish list, finding a bricks-and-mortar store, or signing up for a loyalty program. For some companies, the goal may not be to sell directly online, but rather to generate leads for sales in another channel. Again, these companies can measure conversion points such as newsletter registration, completing an application, finding a local store, playing a game, or participating in a forum. Another goal for a company's website may be self-service and customer support, allowing customers to find information that would otherwise take place through more expensive channels such as a toll-free number.

The analytics tools allow a marketer to not only create a baseline for these conversion points but also establish his or her own target metrics to better improve the performance of marketing dollars as well as merchandising and promotional campaigns on the site itself. The aim is to bridge the gap between external marketing campaigns and what takes place on the site. Site-side analytics complete the circle of measurement and optimization begun in the prebuy planning phase. Additionally, these tools are useful not just for understanding and evaluating an advertiser's acquisition tactics, but also for increasing the efficacy of retention programs such as targeted email.

Brand Campaign Measurement

Not long ago, the internet seemed to be the exclusive domain of direct marketing companies, and the impact on brand image or trial of the medium was considered dubious. However, as the number of brand-oriented marketers using the internet increased, it became clear that online advertising plays an important role in brand building, capable of increasing awareness, interest, and engagement. There are several companies that specialize in quantifying the branding impact of online advertising.

Dynamic Logic

One of the leading online brand measurement companies is Dynamic Logic, founded in 1999 and today owned by Millward Brown Intelli-Quest. Dynamic Logic helps marketers measure advertising effectiveness online through traditional brand metrics, beyond clicks, helping to identify the most effective creative executions. The company methodology measures effectiveness through control/exposed surveys. Essentially, an exposed group of users who have seen an ad is compared to a control group of users who have not. The exposed group is randomly intercepted and surveyed immediately after the ad has appeared on their browsers. Typically, they are notified by pop-up or floating windows, with an incentive to win a small cash reward in exchange for their participation. The control group is recruited on the same sites during the same time period. Dynamic Logic then uses the survey to gauge metrics such as brand awareness, ad recall, message association, and purchase intent.

There are several advantages to the control/exposed methodology. Marketers only need several hundred respondents to achieve statistically significant results. This methodology doesn't measure the effectiveness of the entire campaign, since most of the testing is done on a subset of the total creative executions in a campaign. Additionally, to test each creative unit in a campaign would be expensive for most advertisers and overwhelming for the publisher and audiences.

A less commonly used online methodology is pre/post testing, although it is frequently used offline. Using this method, a sample of users on a site is surveyed before and after a campaign is deployed. If the campaign was effective, the brand impact statistics should be higher in the postcampaign survey than in the precampaign assessment. One of the advantages of this methodology is that advertisers can evaluate how an entire campaign impacted an entire group of users, not just the how a few creative units impacted a subset of exposed users. However, the weakness of this methodology is that it requires a larger number of respondents than the control/exposed methodology does, and as a result often costs more. Given the immediacy, lower cost, and flexibility of the control/exposed methodology, its no surprise it has become the more widely adopted testing technique online.

Dynamic Logic's flagship brand measurement product is AdIndex, which typically uses the control/exposed methodology to collect attitudinal data from users. Dynamic Logic has designed the tool to be easy to implement, and allows advertisers, agencies, and publishers to customize and filter the data they collect. Additionally, Dynamic Logic has partnered with rich media providers to integrate its technology into products such as PointRoll, Bluestreak, and Eyeblaster. To ensure marketers make informed decisions, the company uses a minimum significance level of 90% to reduce the likelihood of a sampling error.

InsightExpress

InsightExpress is a full-service online market research organization. Leveraging a combination of innovative technology and market research expertise, InsightExpress enables its clients to harness the power of online market research to make the right business decisions. Founded in 1999, the company is headquartered in Stamford, Connecticut, and maintains offices in New York, Los Angeles, and San Francisco. InsightExpress is affiliated with General Atlantic LLC.

InsightExpress offers a range of research solutions, including AdInsights, an industry-leading online media measurement offering. In addition to the in-market testing via AdInsights, the company also offers precampaign testing with the Creative Pre-Test and postcampaign analysis. With its latest solution, ADI Plus, a joint offering with Marketing Evolution (reviewed later), InsightExpress also provides clients with Interactive Gross Rating Points (iGRPs) that, for the first time, allow them to include online ad measurement in traditional marketing mix models.

AdInsights is a customizable research solution that measures key attitudinal components of live campaigns, such as unaided/aided brand awareness, persuasion, brand favorability, and purchase intent. AdInsights employs a standard test/control design, inviting users to participate in a brief survey while on a given website where the online ad may appear. Survey participants are invited via banners, leaderboards, and skyscraper units. The differences between the responses from the two groups are measured, and any lift can be attributed directly to the online ad campaign. Because this all happens while the campaign is live, and respondents have the same potential for exposure to other online media, this methodology allows for the online advertising to be isolated as the single driver of results.

Prior to launching a campaign, InsightExpress' Creative Pre-Test acts as a diagnostic tool designed to determine the optimal message, size, technology, placement, and format. As a result, clients can identify possible improvement opportunities before a campaign goes live. Postcampaign, AdInsights Reconnect uses opt-in email addresses provided by survey participants to conduct additional research over time. Marketers can access these respondents to conduct a variety of follow-up research including continuous ad tracking and competitive analysis.

InsightExpress recommends sample sizes between 500 and 600 survey completions per cell (such as site, ad size, creative execution, etc.) or an aggregate of 3,000 completions per project. In certain cases, it's possible to use as few as 300 survey completions per test/control group. The company estimates it's possible to launch a project in five to seven working days, depending on the level of customization needed.

Emerging Measurement

With the proliferation of blogs, online video sites, social networking sites, online forums, and other forms of consumer-generated media, marketers have less control over how their brands are discussed and viewed by their target audience. Word of mouth has become increasingly important at the same time that marketers are losing absolute control. As a result, there is a new generation of niche online measurement companies designed to help a company understand its brand's imprint in these environments.

Nielsen BuzzMetrics

Nielsen BuzzMetrics started as three separate companies that consolidated in 2005, all with similar goals: developing technologies and tools "to help companies measure, understand, and leverage the increasing amount of consumer activity, influence, and content—the 'buzz'—that was migrating to the internet and new forms of media" (Nielsen BuzzMetrics 2006). BuzzMetrics was founded in 1999 to create technologies that would help companies leverage word-of-mouth activities. Intelliseek was established to help marketers delve into immense amounts of company feedback and consumer-generated content to form real-time measurement of buzz about the brand. The third company, Trendum, developed linguistic analysis technologies.

In 2005, the three companies came together through a partnership with VNU, Inc. to form Nielsen BuzzMetrics.

Today the company's objective is to create a new measurement standard for consumer-generated media. The intelligence gleaned from Nielsen BuzzMetrics' services is valuable not just for media planning and buying but also for new product launches, customer service, and crisis management.

Essentially, consumer-generated media have exploded in the past few years. While Usenet and other online forums have existed (in some cases) longer than the graphical web has, in the past few years blogs, social networks such as MySpace and Friendster, and video-sharing sites such as YouTube have exploded. According to the Pew Internet & American Life Project, over a third of American users have posted content online, including having a blog or web page or sharing self-created content such as a story, artwork, or a video (Horrigan 2006). Consumers today share their brand experience not only with friends and family, but with the rest of the world, and much of this content is passed along virally from consumer to consumer. These sites provide an immense archive of content that can be tracked and measured, providing both broad and deep market intelligence of consumer interests and brand-related content.

Nielsen BuzzMetrics views itself as a complement to traditional media planning and research, rather than a competitor. In many advertising and research circles today, there is mounting support for new standards that measure consumer engagement, which may include actions such as consumer conversations, passing along of information, and recommendations as a counterpart to traditional exposure metrics. The company's greatest expertise is in the automotive, consumer electronics, nutrition, pharmaceutical and health, and television categories.

The two products that form that cornerstone of Nielsen Buzz-Metrics are BrandPulse and BrandPulse Insight. BrandPulse is a solution that provides an online reporting interface to help track and measure the volume of consumer-generated media (CGM) about a particular brand, and the latter centers on issue-specific reports that highlight consumer trends, opinion shifts, and marketplace predictions. Nielsen BuzzMetrics' future goal is to move more closely to a syndicated model of data delivery, rather than building a new taxonomy for products, feature attributes, or consumer attitudes a client was interested in measuring each time. A syndicated model will allow the company to create benchmarks and norms for each industry segment, while allowing clients to create custom segments or their own tracking terms.

For the most part, Nielsen BuzzMetrics is selling its services to the brand or marketing teams within an organization. Within the market research department, BuzzMetrics tends to augment traditional brand equity tracking. For instance, within the television sector, a network launching new shows for the fall season might compare its half dozen shows to 40 others launching in the past year and in the same season, identifying their share of online conversation before, during, and after their marketing campaigns. The service can be used to track the effectiveness of a specific new advertising campaign to evaluate how much buzz the campaign has generated. More recently, corporate communication and public relations departments have partnered with Nielsen BuzzMetrics to monitor potential crisis situations, using the trend data on the amount and tenor of conversation about the event and the company to help spot early warnings of an impending crisis before it enters the orbit of mainstream media.

Marketing Evolution

One of the burgeoning areas of measurement that is important to measuring the value of online advertising is cross-media marketing measurement. A significant challenge marketers face is accurately gauging the effectiveness of their marketing dollars across television, print, radio, out-of-home, internet, wireless, and other advertising and marketing vehicles. Additionally, marketers must figure out how best to optimize their spending, creative aspects, and positioning across multiple media vehicles. Marketers need to understand how the internet fits into the overall marketing mix. There are now several companies centered on developing research protocols and tools for more accurate cross-media measurement and optimization.

Marketing Evolution is a company that specializes in cross-media measurement, providing its clients with dollar-for-dollar comparisons among their TV, radio, print, direct mail, email, websites, events, and internet spending levels. The company provides custom research and consulting services to help its clients test their marketing efforts and provide learning from those tests.

Marketing Evolution's core service is dubbed ROMO, for return on marketing objectives. ROMO is designed to provide in-market, continuous feedback on advertising performance and, not unlike Dynamic Logic or InsightExpress, quantify brand impact metrics such as awareness and purchase intent. Marketing Evolution differs from the online brand measurement companies in key ways. While Dynamic Logic and InsightExpress focus exclusively on measuring online advertising effectiveness, Marketing Evolution subsumes those initiatives by measuring online and offline together in a patent-pending methodology reviewed by the Advertising Research Foundation (2006). A full cross-media study typically ranges in cost from $200,000 to $400,000. For marketers with $10 million or more in advertising budget, the relative investment is well worth it if their marketing spending is optimized across media while maintaining the total budget.

ROMO offers specific results for each of the media in the marketing mix and suggests adjustments to the overall allocation in order to maximize return. Marketing Evolution claims the key benefit is better results within the same budget. The company's methodology seeks to understand individual media performance and the resulting ROI, as well as to gain insight into brand positioning within a competitive set.

ROMO begins by understanding a marketer's goals and objectives—what is the marketer ultimately trying to achieve? For instance, is a marketer's strategy to build brand awareness and differentiation or to reinforce the brand message and generate immediate sales? Marketing Evolution translates these goals into a measurement design that works hand-in-hand with the media plan (creating exposed and control groups) and measurements of marketer's goals (ranging from sales to branding). The measurement design almost always includes a survey, and the survey questions ask branding-related questions. To get a more complete understanding of effectiveness, Marketing Evolution has integrated sales metrics into the ROMO analysis, at the client's request. The end goal of the analysis is to paint a detailed picture of each channel (including online) in the marketing mix and understand its contribution in terms of relative cost efficiency.

Integration

Integration is a consultancy firm founded in 1994, dedicated to designing tools that measure the effectiveness of marketing communications. Its core product is Market ContactAudit (MCA). Essentially, it audits both the effectiveness and the cost efficiency of a brand's marketing plan across media. The goal of the audit is to provide marketers with a common currency for comparison so companies can manage the total brand experience across channels.

The first step in an MCA audit is what the company calls calibration: "mapping contact influence at category level before measuring brand-contact associations to determine brand performance in the category" (Integration 2006). The cost for this phase of the audit is $35,000. The initial phase is designed to establish benchmarks for the Brand Experience Point, the common currency that will be used to compare marketing across channels and brands. Integration believes this step is critical in order to make informed comparisons between different marketing channels, and between a brand and its competitors. It sets the groundwork for future Integration studies.

After the initial calibration, Integration recommends brands regularly measure their marketing's effectiveness and efficiency against their competitors'. Toward that end, Integration offers MCAtrackers, a series of periodic research waves to regularly update the brand-contact associations.

As an advertising platform the internet has allowed marketers to effectively gauge success and measure performance in real time. However, online measurement can be a daunting task, with myriad tools and services available to help marketers track their advertising expenditures and optimize their campaigns. The greatest challenge for marketers is to be able to form *actionable* marketing strategies based on the data they measure.

For most marketers, to get a truly holistic view of their online advertising performance they need three core measurement tools, each designed to strengthen a particular phase in their campaigns. First are the audience measurement services, which are critical for the prebuy phase and are used for media planning and competitive analysis. Second are the ad-serving companies, which provide real-time campaign data analysis, allowing marketers to see what is going on in their campaigns at that moment. Third are the site-side analytics companies that bridge the gap between what takes place in advertising and marketing campaigns and what takes place on a company's website.

Perhaps no less important, however, are the companies that measure branding, cross-media performance, or buzz building. Whether a company should subscribe to one of these services depends on the marketer's goals, budget, and ability to synthesize the insights into actionable tactics. Marketers must have the internal resources not only to measure their campaigns, but also to be able to nimbly optimize their creative, their media, and their spend. Measurement without optimization is useless.

Business Metrics for Online Advertising

Marketers gain additional insight into campaign effectiveness by analyzing business metrics. Business measures gauge the brand's ability to meet business objectives and perform on criteria essential to success; these fall into a number of categories:

- *Customer satisfaction.* Search marketers look to understand and improve the linkages between the text ad or listing and the brand experience.

- *Business process improvements.* Marketers reengineer problematic processes, like newsletter sign-up, checkout, or customer service, for example, in order to create or sustain compelling brand experiences and assess their impacts on criteria like customer satisfaction, revenue, or customer retention.

- *Financial indicators.* These measure the economic value of the search advertising campaign. They often include return on investment metrics. The most common ones are campaign related: cost-per-lead, cost-per-acquisition, cost-per-sale (or transaction), revenue generated, and profitability. (The Glossary defines many of these and related measures.) After these, metrics typically become more personalized to brand requirements. They can include subscriber renewals or cancellations for publishers, lead-to-close ratios for e-commerce or B2B sites, or changes in cost factors that result from moving a business process to the web or improving an existing one.

Winning Plays

Metrics need to be tailored for each brand and company with respect to its particular objectives. There is no magic number. Instead, smart marketers use a constellation of metrics that are guided by four considerations:

1. *Determine your online advertising goals.* Define what you're looking to accomplish with your online campaign—site traffic, lead generation, online sales, offline sales, and so forth. Ask if your goals are relevant to the business results you seek. If they're not, why measure? Don't confuse tactics with objectives.

2. *Make sure they're realistic.* Are the goals achievable within the time frames you've established? Are you able to assign the right resource levels to them with the right level of capability and focus? Do they require some future event to occur in order for them to be accomplished?

3. *Ensure that they're measurable.* We all know that business objectives need to be stated clearly and quantifiably. Objectives that specify capturing 300 qualified leads in 30 days or gross product sales of $9 million in the next quarter leave no room for interpretation. Progress against them is easily measured, and you can use a variety of tools for tracking, from local spreadsheets to rich analytical systems.

4. *Be certain you have the right metrics to measure your objectives.* There's no point in tracking a specific metric, say average sale per visitor, if you don't have the sales data, visitor data, and dates of sale at hand. Recognize that some metrics are easily available, some are easy to compute, some may need to be derived from multiple data sources, some may be proxies because direct measurement is not possible, and data quality may be quite variable. Be very clear about why you're measuring, what

you're measuring, the quality of your metrics, and the confidence you have in them. Don't waste time with metrics that don't matter. Merely accepting data, no matter how cool and persuasive its presentation, will not give you the guidance you need to manage your brand, search advertising campaign, or budget effectively.

Above the fold Any area of a web page that is viewable without the viewer having to use the vertical scroll bar. Ad space in this area is usually more expensive since it is more likely to be viewed by the visitor.

Ad banner An advertisement on a web page using text, often animation and sound, that links to an advertiser's website.

Ad flight The duration of time an advertising campaign is live.

Ad inventory The number of page views a site has available for advertising.

Ad request The request of an advertising element recorded by the ad server software as a direct result of a visitor's action (e.g., clicking on the ad), also known as the ad impression.

Ad server A computer, normally operated by a third party, that delivers and tracks advertisements independent of the website where the ad is being displayed. Use of an ad server helps establish trust between an advertiser and publisher, as statistics are maintained by an objective third party.

Adult words Words that are censored by search engines, including the Federal Communications Commission (FCC)'s seven naughty words. Search engines often maintain two databases, one containing uncensored terms to keep away from children searches, and another that is approved for the general public. Often called "stop words" by the search engines because the indexer stops when it finds one of these words.

Ad units A classification of ad types. Ad units on the internet include banners, buttons, microbuttons, pop-ups, skyscrapers, text links, interstitials, superstitials, and others. Most commonly defined by the Interactive Advertising Bureau (IAB) as voluntary guidelines.

Advanced match type A keyword matching option offered with Yahoo! Sponsored Search. The Advanced match type enables an advertiser's listing to appear in a broader range of relevant searches, even when the bid keyword is not an exact, word-for-word match with the search query.

Advertising network   A network representing many websites in selling advertising, allowing advertising buyers to reach broad audiences relatively easily through run-of-category and run-of-network buys.

Advertorial   An advertisement styled to resemble the editorial format and typeface of the content in which it runs. Often generates higher response rates.

Affiliate   The publisher/salesperson in an affiliate marketing relationship.

Affiliate marketing   A type of advertising system based on the cost-per-action (CPA) payment method whereby websites run advertisers' banners for free but get paid on any sales or registrations that result from visitors clicking on the banner.

Affiliate merchant   The advertiser in an affiliate marketing relationship.

Affinity group   A group of people with common interests, identified for the purposes of targeting specific ads.

Affinity marketing   Any marketing effort, including email promotions, banners, or offline media aimed at consumers on the basis of established buying patterns. For example, a bookstore might send an email advertisement to all customers who had previously bought mystery books with a headline of "New mystery books released this week."

AIDA   The acronym for attention, interest, desire, and action. A historical model of how advertising works, by first getting the consumers' attention, then their interest, and so on.

Algorithmic search results   Nonsponsored listings that appear in the main section of the search results page. Search engines use proprietary algorithms to crawl websites and create indexes. When users search for specific keywords, a search engine retrieves relevant listings from its index that match the queries. The ranking of these listings is based on relevancy. Also known as natural, or organic, search results.

Alt text   Short for alternative text, alt text is HTML code that allows an HTML coder to add text to a graphic that is visible to those who have images disabled or those who position their mouses over a banner advertisement. Often used by advertisers to reinforce a message or call the visitor to action, such as: "Click Here."

American Association of Advertising Agencies (AAAA) National trade association representing the advertising agency business in the United States.

Anchor text The text that is surrounded by a hyperlink (the part you click on, in a browser). Used by some search engines to rank search results.

Animated ad An ad with movement, often an interactive Java applet, Shockwave, or GIF89a file.

Animated GIF An animation created by combining multiple GIF images into one file. The result is multiple images, displayed one after another, that give the appearance of movement. Useful for attracting/distracting web surfers.

Association of National Advertisers (ANA) The national trade association dedicated to serving the interests of corporations that advertise their products and services in the United States.

Authority site A system that counts inbound and outbound links to identify central sites in a community.

Autoresponders Automatic replies sent by the email software of the recipient after receipt of an email.

Backlinks Also called inbound links, comprised of all the links pointing at a particular web page. Most major search engines allow the visitor to see who is linking to a page or site. That process is called "checking backlinks."

Banner A graphic image that appears on a web page that is usually hyperlinked to an advertiser's website. It may be in a variety of formats including GIF, JPEG, Flash, HTML, Java, JavaScript, and more. The standard banner ad is 468×60 pixels; the most common size for tile ads is 125×125 pixels.

Banner blindness The tendency of web visitors to ignore banner ads, even when banners contain information visitors are actively seeking.

Banner burnout The description of an event when a banner has been shown to the same visitor(s) to the point where the click-through rate has dropped dramatically. Rotating banners helps to reduce banner burnout.

Banner exchange An internet service that provides free banner impressions to those willing to place free banners on their sites. A typical exchange ratio is for every two banners shown for free, they get one of their banners shown for free on someone else's site. The company running the banner exchange takes the other impression and tries to sell it.

Banner/link exchange   A cooperative advertising program where participating businesses work together to promote each other's products/services and websites on an exchange rather than paid basis.

Banner rotator   A program that randomly swaps out banner ads on a website so that each time the site is visited or refreshed a different banner ad appears on the screen. Online advertisers frequently use banner ad rotation because it is usually less expensive than paying to place a static ad on a website.

BBBOnLine   The Council for Better Business Bureau, BBBOnline is the respected consumer protection agency.

Beacon   A line of code placed in an ad or on a web page that helps track the visitor's actions, such as registrations or purchases. A web beacon is often invisible because it's only 1×1 pixel in size and has no color. Also known as web bug, 1 by 1 GIF, invisible GIF, or tracker GIF.

Bits per second (bps or bits/sec)   A measurement of how much data, or number of bits, can be transferred through a network connection in one second. When the amount goes over 1,000,000 bps it will often be shortened to Mbps (millions of bits per second or megabits per second).

Blind link   A text or graphical hyperlink that does not clearly indicate the page or web address the hyperlink will lead to. A controversial practice.

Blog   A hybrid form of internet communication that combines a column, diary, and directory. The term is short for "web log," which is a frequently updated collection of short articles on various subjects with links to further resources.

Bluestreak   A rich media vendor's proprietary technology for creating ads, allowing more interactivity with the ad unit.

Bookmark   A saved link or URL (website address) to a web page within a World Wide Web browser that you can revisit at a later time. Most web browsers provide a bookmark feature.

Broad match   Your ad appears when the words in your keyword are contained in the query, regardless of their order and even if other words are also included. For example, a broad match for the keyword "tennis shoes" would include "shoes for tennis" and "tennis dresses and shoes." Usually less targeted than phrase or exact matches.

Button ad   An interactive online ad in the form of a small graphic (usually 88 × 31 pixels) generally placed in the margin of a web page.

Button exchange   Network where participating sites display button ads in exchange for credits, which are converted (using a predetermined exchange rate) into ads to be displayed on other sites.

Cache bursting   A process, also known as "defeating cache," that ensures banner ads are not cached and thus banner advertisement impressions are not undercounted.

Citation count   The count of references to a page on the internet. Some search engines work on the theory that pages with high citation counts are better.

Click-and-mortar   Stores that have presences both online and in physical retail space.

Click-down ad   Refers to displaying another file on the user's screen, normally below or above the initial ad, allowing the user to stay on the same web page while viewing requested advertising content.

Click fraud   A crime that occurs in pay-per-click advertising when a person, script, or computer program imitates a legitimate user of a web browser clicking on an ad, for the purpose of generating a charge per click without having actual interest in the target of the ad's link. Click fraud is the subject of increasing litigation.

Click index   A scoring system designed to help understand how well listings are performing. It evaluates the listing's click-through rate relative to competitors, taking into account current position.

Click protection   A system designed by Yahoo! Search Marketing to help ensure that unqualified clicks are not charged for. Uses a variety of techniques to filter the clicks before they show up as a charge within the account report.

Click rate   The percentage of impressions that resulted in a click-through, calculated by dividing the number of clicks by the number of impressions. For example, if a banner is clicked on 13 times while being displayed 1,000 times, the banner would have a click rate of 1.3% ($13 \div 1,000 = .013$). This is also commonly known as a banner's click-through rate.

Clicks   The number of click-throughs that have occurred as a result of a user clicking on a banner and being redirected to an advertiser's web page.

Click-stream   The path a visitor takes while navigating from site to site or from page to page within a website. Click-stream data is useful to publishers to see what path potential prospects are taking before leaving their site.

Click-through   The action of clicking on a banner and having the browser automatically redirect to the web page that the banner is hyperlinked to.

Click-through rate (CTR)   The response rate of an online advertisement, typically expressed as a percentage. Calculated by taking the number of click-throughs the ad received, dividing that number by the number of impressions, and multiplying by 100 to obtain a percentage. Example: 20 clicks/1,000 impressions = .02 × 100 = 2% CTR. Same as click rate.

Click-through URL   The action following a hyperlink within an advertisement to another page outside of the current site the user was on.

Click tracking   Counting clicks on links via a redirected counter program that counts the clicks.

Cloaking   The practice of displaying different pages on a website in different situations. Usually involves showing one optimized page to search engines but a different page to live visitors to the site.

Comment tag   HTML comment tag that marks some HTML as a comment rather than displaying it in a browser. It is notable in relation to search engines because search engines have been known to index comment-based text.

Compound   An ad that is comprised of many pieces or images, all of which link to the same click-through URL.

Content integration   Advertising woven into the editorial content or advertising placed in a special context on the page, typically appearing on portals and large destination sites. Also known as web advertorial or sponsored content.

Content match   A feature offered with Yahoo! Sponsored Search that displays existing listings near relevant articles, product reviews, and more, enabling increase in customer reach through online publishers, newsletters, and email.

Contextual advertising   Online advertising targeted to the particular individual visiting a website. A contextual ad system scans the content of the page for keywords and responds with ads based on what the visitor is viewing.

Contextual link inventory   Generated when listings are displayed on pages of websites (usually not search engines), where the written content on the page indicates to the ad server that the page is a good match to specific keywords and phrases. Often validated by measuring the number of times a viewer clicks on the displayed ad.

Contextual marketing   The broad term that refers to making marketing efforts relevant to the demonstrated interests of a particular consumer. Contextual advertising is one type of contextual marketing.

Conversion rate   The number of visitors who respond to an ad's call to action divided by the number of impressions, multiplied by 100 and expressed as a percentage. For example, your conversion rate is 1% if a hundred people are shown your ad, five people click through to your site, and one person makes a purchase.

Cookie   A process by which a small file is sent from a web server to the local users' computer to store information unique to that browser. Often used by advertisers to keep track of the number and frequency of advertisements that have been shown to a visitor or by sites to help them determine the number of unique visitors.

Cookie file   A memory function of an internet browser, storing cookies in a format allowing for easy retrieval.

Cost per acquisition (CPA)   The cost to get a customer, determined by dividing the total cost of your advertising by the number of customers you acquire. Sometimes referred to as cost per conversion, cost per inquiry, cost per lead, or cost per sale.

Cost per action (CPA)   One of the online payment models by which advertisers pay for every action completed (sale or registration) as a result of a visitor clicking on the advertisement. Prices typically range from $1 to $25 or a percentage of a sale, 5% to 25%. This is an ideal method of payment for advertisers who want to guarantee paying for only the number of customers generated as a result of an advertisement.

Cost per click (CPC)   Pricing based on the number of clicks an ad receives. The CPC is the cost of advertising divided by the number of clicks. A typical range is 5 cents to $1 per click. Also known as pay per click (PPC).

Cost per inquiry (CPI)   The cost of getting one person to inquire about your product or service. This is a standard used in direct response advertising. CPI is the same as cost per lead (CPL).

Cost per lead (CPL)   One of the types of CPA, the CPL method allows advertisers to pay for every lead or customer inquiry that resulted from a visitor who clicked on their advertisement. Prices typically range from $1 to $10. This is an ideal method of payment for advertisers who want to guarantee paying for only the number of potential customers with an interest generated as a result of an advertisement. Also known as cost per inquiry (CPI).

Cost per order (CPO)   Pricing based on the number of orders received as a result of your ad placement. Also known as cost per transaction.

Cost per rating point (CPP)   The cost, per 1% of a specified audience, of buying advertising space in a given media vehicle.

Cost per sale (CPS)   Pricing based on the number of sales transactions the ad generates. Since users may visit a site several times before making a purchase, cookies can be used to track user visits from the landing page to the actual online sale. Also known as cost per acquisition or pay per sale.

Cost per thousand (CPM)   The cost, per 1,000 people reached, of buying advertising space in a given media vehicle. Pricing is based on the number of impressions served over a period of time. A $50 CPM means payment of $50 for every 1,000 times the ad appears. ("M" is the Roman numeral for 1,000.) Also known as pay per impression.

Cost per transaction (CPT)   One of the types of CPA, a CPT method allows advertisers to pay whenever a visitor who clicked on their advertisement generates a transaction, usually a sale. Prices typically range from $1 to $25 or a percentage of a sale, 10% to 25%. This is an ideal method of payment for advertisers who want to guarantee paying for only the number of paying customers as a result of an advertisement.

Crawler   A component of the search engine that gathers listings by automatically "crawling" the web. Makes copies of the web pages found and stores these in the search engine's index.

CRM   The acronym for customer relations (or relationship) management. CRM entails all aspects of interaction a company has with its customer, whether it be sales or service related. Encompasses methodologies, software, and usually internet capabilities that help an enterprise manage customer relationships in an organized way.

Daughter window   An ad that runs in a separate window associated with a concurrently displayed banner. In normal practice, the content and banner are rendered first and the daughter window appears a moment later.

Dead link   An HTML link where the destination page no longer exists. Many search engines routinely check for dead links by spidering the page again. Dead links used to be a serious problem on some search engines, but with increased link checking dead links are becoming rare.

Deep linking   Linking to content buried deep within a website, often two or more directories deep within the site.

Defaults   Term used by ad networks to describe a type of banner that is served to a site when no paying banner is available. Usually a PSA type of advertisement unless the ad network permits publishers to specify their own default advertisement.

Defeating cache   *See* Cache bursting.

Delisting   Occurs when pages are removed from a search engine's index. This may happen if the pages have been banned or for other reasons, such as an accidental glitch on the search engine's part.

Description tag   An HTML tag used by web page authors to provide a description for search engine listings.

Dimension   Various measurements are used to define vertical and horizontal interactive marketing units (IMUs) or ad units used for ad campaigns. These sizes are per voluntary standards set forth by the Interactive Advertising Bureau (IAB).

IAB Dimension Name	IMU Pixel Size
Button 1	120×90
Button 2	120×60
Full banner	468×60
Half banner	234×60
Large rectangle	336×280
Leaderboard	728×90
Medium rectangle	300×250
Microbar	88×31
Nonstandard	Sizes that do not adhere to IMU guidelines
Rectangle	180×150
Skyscraper	120×600
Square button	125×125
Vertical banner	120×240
Vertical rectangle	240×400
Wide skyscraper	160×600

Directory A compilation of websites reviewed and organized by human editors into useful categories and topics, similar to the organization of the Yellow Pages. Examples of directories are the Google Directory, About.com, and the Open Directory Project.

Domain name The unique name that identifies a website on the internet. Domain names are derived from a hierarchical system, with a host name followed by a top-level domain category. The top-level domain categories reflect the purpose of the organization or entity—for example, "com" (for commercial enterprises), "org" (for nonprofit organizations), "net" (for network services providers), "mil" (for the military), and "gov" (for government).

Doorway domain A domain used specifically to rank well in search engines for particular keywords, serving as an entry point through which visitors pass to the main domain.

Doorway page A web page created expressly in hopes of ranking well for a term in a search engine's nonpaid listings and which itself does not deliver much information to those viewing it. Instead, visitors will often see only some enticement on the doorway page leading them to other pages (i.e., "Click Here to Enter"), or they may be automatically propelled quickly past the doorway page. With cloaking, they may never see the doorway page at all. Several search engines have guidelines against doorway pages, though they are more commonly allowed in through paid inclusion programs. Also referred to as bridge pages, gateway pages, and jump pages, among other names.

Double opt-in An email subscription practice that asks consumers to confirm their subscription to a list before the subscriber actually receives the information. The double confirmation is considered by many email marketers to be the best guarantee of user interest.

Dynamic content Web page content that changes or is changed automatically based on database content or user information.

Dynamic rotation Delivery of ads on a rotating, random basis. Dynamic rotations allow ads to be served on different pages of the site and exposes users to a variety of ads.

Earnings per visitor (EPV) Calculated by dividing the total earnings from visitors by the number of visitors.

E-catalog Similar to paper catalogs, e-catalogs provide customers with prices, descriptions, and pictures of products for sale, presented on the internet.

Effective CPM (eCPM)   A useful way to calculate the average CPM across all sites or within a category. This is calculated by dividing the total estimated spend by the total number of impressions in thousands. *Example:* Total spend of $10,000 divided by (1,000,000 impressions/1,000) equals an effective CPM of $10.

Effective frequency   The number of times an ad should be shown to one person to realize the highest impact of the ad without wasting impressions on that individual.

Effective reach   The number of people who will see an ad the most effective number of times.

E-form   An electronic form that is filled out by a user and sent over a network. They are typically used to place orders or provide feedback. E-forms can be placed on web pages or in Java applets and usually contain text boxes, buttons, and other components.

Electronic magazine (e-zine)   An electronic version of a traditional paper-based magazine. Instead of distributing the magazine via the postal mail, an e-zine is emailed to your subscribers via the internet.

Electronic mailing list   A list of email addresses identified by a single name or Listserv, such as clients-list@sbdc.com.au. When an email message is sent to the mailing list name, it is automatically forwarded to all the addresses in the list.

Exclusive   Refers to an ad that appears every time the page is loaded. Exclusive ads do not rotate.

Exit exchange   An arrangement between two or more sites in which each site shows advertisements for other sites in exchange for the others doing the same. When you sign up for an exit exchange, you get a small piece of code, usually a script that can be placed on your web page. When your web page is accessed, the script is executed, allowing the visitor to see your site, not just an advertisement or banner that you have created to entice them in.

Exit page   The last page a visitor saw before leaving a website. Content of page may be the reason for interest lost in your website.

Exit traffic   Type of web visitor traffic in which visitors leaving a site click on a pop-up or pop-under advertisement—otherwise known as an exit console.

Expandable banner   A banner ad that can expand to as large as 468 × 240 pixels after a user clicks on it or after a user moves the cursor over the banner.

Extramercial   Banner ads placed in the extra space in the right column of internet web pages.

Facilitated chat   Within a facilitated chat, a host or facilitator controls the messages that appear on the chat screen. Commonly used when there is a guest speaker. Facilitated chats provide an orderly environment for the guest speaker and ensure that he or she is not overwhelmed with dozens of questions all being asked at once.

Filter   A method of isolating a selection of items from a longer list. A way of hiding certain file types by their file names or extensions.

Filter words   Common words that search engines remove from web pages before adding them to their databases. This saves search engines enormous amounts of database space. Filter words are: the, is, an, of, for, do.

Flame   A public post or email message that expresses a strong opinion or criticism.

Flash   A software plug-in that enables browsers to play multimedia animations. Some rich media advertisements require users to have this plug-in downloaded.

Floating ads   An ad that appears within the main browser window on top of the page's normal content, appearing to float over the top of the page.

Floating/overlay   An out-of-banner ad delivery type appearing outside the predesignated ad placement areas via a transparent dHTML layer over the page. They are often non-user-initiated and float and/or animate over the page's content.

Forced click   Type of click-through that is forced upon a visitor without his or her consent.

Frequency cap   A restriction on the number of times an advertisement is displayed to a particular website visitor.

Geotargeting   The distribution of ads to a particular geographical area by, for example, using a place name in your keyword, such as "Minnesota multimedia" or "Sacramento farm equipment." Some search engines allow targeting of specific countries and languages without using keyword relevance.

Graphical search inventory   Banners and other types of advertising units, including pop-ups, browser toolbars, and rich media that can be synchronized to search keywords.

Graphic interchange format (GIF)   One of two most common graphic file formats for graphic images on the internet (the other being JPEG). Most banner advertisements are created in the GIF format and it is more popular than the JPEG format. GIF89a or animated GIFs are sequences of standard GIF images combined to create animated banners.

Gross exposures   The total number of times an ad is shown, including duplicate viewings by the same person.

Heading tag   An HTML tag of six sizes. Search engines can rank a keyword higher if it appears in a larger heading.

Hit   Occurs when a surfer downloads a file for viewing in his or her web browser. Every time a site's web server passes information (text, graphics, calls to CGI scripts, MIDI recordings, QuickTime movies) to an end user, it records a hit in the log file with that file's path name. For example, if you download a web page containing text and three images, you will have registered five hits—one hit for the HTML page, one hit for the text file, and one hit for each graphic file. The web server hosting these files keeps track of the number of accesses made by each viewer and stores this information in a log file. Hits are not the best measure of how many people are viewing your site; however, they do tell you exactly what your viewers are downloading.

House ads   Self-promotional banner advertisements that a website publisher runs in an ad space when no paying advertisement is available to fill the space. Typically these are advertisements promoting one of their websites' services, products, or features.

Hover ads   Hover ads uses dHTML layers to display a message on your web page. Hover ads are used by more site owners instead of the pop-up window since pop-up blocking software cannot block the new hover ads. A new window is not being opened and the pop-up blockers can't figure out that an advertisement is being displayed; messages get more attention as a result.

Hybrid search engines   The new-generation hybrid search engines combine a directory with a search engine to give their visitors the most relevant and complete results. Today the top 10 search sites are hybrids.

Hyperlink   HTML code that when clicked on redirects a user's browser to another web page either within the same window or in a new window. Most banners are hyperlinked to the advertiser's web page.

Hyperstitial   An application running alongside a browser that allows advertisers to display full-screen ads while visitors wait for a web page to load.

Hypertext   Any text that contains links to other documents. Words or phrases in the document that are hypertext links can be selected by a reader and cause another document to be retrieved and displayed.

Hypertext markup language (HTML)   A computer programming language that helps control the format of a document's content and design on the World Wide Web. An HTML editor is a software program that enables one to easily create HTML pages.

Icon   A small graphic image that represents a file or application and when clicked upon launches it.

Identification   The process whereby customers identify themselves with the companies that provide them with products or services.

Impressions   The number of times a banner ad was requested and presumably seen by users. It is often hard to obtain an accurate impression count, as they can be undercounted due to issues relating to the cache or overcounted due to noncompleted requests.

Inbound link   Link pointing to a website when a user arrives at a website from another site.

Incentivized click   A type of click-through in which the person clicking on the advertisement does so in order to receive some reward. Often results in low visitor quality.

Incentivized traffic   Visitors who have received some form of compensation for visiting a site.

Incoming link   A link on another website that when clicked opens up to your website.

Index   The collection of information that a search engine can look up a query against. With crawler-based search engines, the index typically copies all the web pages found from crawling the web. With human-monitored directories, the index contains the summaries of all websites that have been categorized.

Indexer When a search engine spiders (downloads) a web page, it must process the page to store it. A spider is responsible for the downloading, while the indexer is responsible for processing the page. A search engine indexer will typically process a page by removing all HTML tags, checking all hypertext links, often compressing the page by pulling out filter words, looking for stop words, and finally storing the page in an online searchable database.

Inline An ad delivery type whereby the ad is delivered within predetermined placement areas on the publisher's website. Inline ads generally are contained within the IAB ad dimension specifications.

Insertion order (I/O) A contract that specifies the details of a search advertising campaign, including placements options, keywords, ad creative content, landing page, pricing, geotargeting, and language options.

Instant messaging A method of online communication in which two parties have a conversation in real time by alternately typing text into an instant message window that displays the text right away so that both parties may see it.

Interactive ad formats Text-based ads on search sites that complement a broad selection of ad formats, encouraging internet users to take immediate action. The Interactive Advertising Bureau (IAB), a nonprofit trade association devoted to the use and effectiveness of online advertising, offers standards and guidelines for many ad formats or interactive marketing units (IMUs).

Interactive Advertising Bureau (IAB) Founded in 1996, the IAB is the leading online global advertising industry trade association, with over 300 active member companies in the United States alone. IAB activities include evaluating and recommending standards and practices, fielding research to document the effectiveness of the online medium, and educating the advertising industry about the use of online and digital advertising.

Interactive marketing units (IMUs) Voluntary ad format guidelines introduced to enable marketers to utilize greater interactivity as well as expand the creativity in their online messaging. Sponsored by the Interactive Advertising Bureau (IAB).

Internet Relay Chat (IRC)   A chat network that operates over the internet. Originally evolved from the UNIX talk program, IRC is similar to the chat systems found on commercial online services.

Internet service provider (ISP)   A business that delivers access to the internet, usually for a monthly fee.

Interstitial ad   An intrusive type of advertisement that loads between web pages without having been requested by the visitor. It is similar to a superstitial except it does not load in the background. The ad page appears for a short period of time before the user-requested page is displayed. Also known as a transition ad, splash page, or flash page.

Inventory   The number of ad spaces available for sale on a website during a certain period. Determined by taking into consideration the number of advertisements on a page, the number of pages with advertisements, and the number of page views during a specific period.

Invisible web   The group of dynamic or large database sites that search engines will not index.

IP address   An IP (internet protocol) address is a string of four numbers separated by periods (such as 111.22.3.444) used to represent a computer on the internet. When a PC accesses the internet through an ISP, it sometimes receives a temporary IP address.

IP delivery   Refers to the process of delivering customized content based on the user's IP address. This allows websites to protect their proprietary code designed to rank high on search engines.

Island position   An advertisement that is surrounded by editorial material with no adjoining advertisements to compete for the audience's attention.

Joint Photographic Experts Group (JPEG)   A graphics format that displays photographs and graphic images.

Jump page ad   A microsite reached by clicking a button or banner. The jump page itself can list several topics, which can link to a user's site.

Keyword   A word or phrase entered into a search engine in an effort to get the search engine to return matching and relevant results. Many websites offer advertising based on keyword targeting so an advertiser's banner will show only when specific keywords are entered.

Keyword buys   The purchase of keywords that trigger the display of search advertising.

Keyword density   A percentage measure of the number of times a keyword is repeated within the text of a web page. Too high a density can classify a web page as spam, while too low a density can result in the page not indexed appropriately for the given keyword.

Keyword frequency   Denotes how often a keyword appears in a page or in an area of a page. In general, the higher the number of times a keyword appears in a page, the higher its ranking in the search engines.

Keyword marketing   The placement of a marketing message in front of internet users based on the keywords for which they are searching.

Keyword matching   Methods of selecting and organizing your keywords to match the user's query. Four types of keyword matching options can help you refine your ad targeting: broad match, exact match, phrase match, and negative keyword.

Keyword phrases, Keyphrases   Refers to two or more keywords combined to form a search query.

Keyword prominence   Refers to how close to the start of an area your keyword appears. The closer to the beginning your targeted keyword appears within the search results, the higher and better the prominence. Prominence applies to the words within the title, the body of the document, the meta tags, the heading tags, and the alt tags.

Keyword research   The search for keywords related to your website and the analysis of which ones yield the highest return on investment (ROI).

Keyword selector tool   A tool designed to help advertisers identify the search terms to bid on. The keyword selector tool shows the number of searches conducted in a period using keywords related to your business.

Keyword stuffing   The process of populating a page with many keywords in the meta tags or main HTML body.

Keyword tag   Meta tag used to help define the primary keywords of a web page.

Keyword weight Denotes the number of times a keyword appears in a page as a percentage of all the other words in the page. In general, the higher the weight of a particular keyword in a page, the higher the search engine ranking is for the keyword in the page. However, repeating a keyword too often in order to increase its weight can cause the page to be penalized by the search engines.

Kilobits per second (Kbps) Kilobits per second (thousands of bits per second) is a measure of bandwidth (the amount of data that can flow in a given time) on a data transmission medium. It is the standard measurement of modem speed.

Landing page The web page on which internet users will land when they click through to your website from a search listing, banner, link, or other online advertisement. ROI usually improves if your landing page directly relates to your ad and immediately presents a conversion opportunity—whether that means signing up for a newsletter, downloading a software demo, or buying a product. Also known as a destination URL or click-through URL.

Link track The process of tracking your link partners' removed links early in the game and frequently so you can react quickly without losing valuable Google page rank and link popularity.

Linkage The total number of links pointing (inbound links) at a website. Many search engines now count linkage in their algorithms.

Listings The information that appears on a search engine's results page in response to a search.

List server An automated mailing list distribution system. List servers maintain a list of email addresses to be used for mass emailing. Subscribing and unsubscribing to the list is accomplished by sending a properly formatted email message to the list server.

Local sponsored search A pay-per-click product that displays your business listing in local search results. By targeting customers who are searching for businesses in your area, local sponsored search helps to drive traffic from the web to your physical store locations.

Mailbomb The act of sending massive amounts of email to a single address with the malicious intent of disrupting the system of the recipient. Mailbombing is a serious breach of netiquette and is probably illegal.

Mail filter   A program that allows you to sort email before viewing it using the subject, date, the sender's email address, or even information in the body of the message.

Mailing Preference Service (MPS)   A database of individual home addresses where the occupiers have elected not to receive unsolicited direct (marketing) mail.

Make goods   Adjustments made by a publisher to an advertiser to make up for a shortfall in contracted ad impressions or errors.

Marketing Console   A tool that measures the effectiveness of online marketing campaigns. Marketing Console generates reports that show a company's performance in search advertising, email marketing, banner advertisements, paid inclusion, and/or affiliate programs.

Marketing information system (MIS)   A computer program that enables a business to track customers' activities from when they enter their website to when they leave. MISs track customers' click-throughs within multiple visits to the business's website and gain information about customers' buying behavior, products they are interested in purchasing, and the services they require. MISs vary in complexity from very simple systems (e.g., using a simple spreadsheet to keep track of customers) to very sophisticated systems that create sales forecasts based on previous sales data and seasonal trends.

Massively multiplayer online role-playing games (MMORPG)   Genre of online computer role-playing games (RPGs) in which a large number of players interact with one another in a virtual world. Players assume the role of a fictional character (most commonly in a fantasy setting) and take control over many of that character's actions. MMORPGs are distinguished from single-player or small multiplayer RPGs by the number of players, and by the game's persistent world, usually hosted by the game's publisher, which continues to exist and evolve while the player is away from the game.

Match types   The ways in which a searcher's keyword can be matched to an advertiser's listing.

Max bid   The maximum amount a person is willing to pay when a consumer clicks on his or her listing. This amount determines the ranking in sponsored search results.

M-commerce (mobile commerce)   The use of mobile devices, such as wireless phones, to conduct e-business.

Meta ad   Also referred to as keyword advertising, meta ads are search engine advertisements displayed on the results page of a search, specific to the searched term.

Meta description tag   Allows page authors to notate a description of their pages when listed by search engines. Not all search engines use the tag.

Meta keywords tag   Allows page authors to add text to a page to help with the search engine ranking process. Not all search engines use the tag.

Meta robots tag   Allows page authors to keep their web pages from being indexed by search engines, especially helpful for those who cannot create robots.txt files.

Meta search engine   A search engine that gets listings from two or more other search engines, rather than through its own efforts.

Meta tag generator   Tool that will output meta tags based on input page information.

Meta tags   Special HTML tags that provide information about a web page; unlike normal HTML tags, meta tags do not affect how the page is displayed in browsers.

Microsite   A separate page of a website that has a separate URL used to provide information about and promote something that is related to the main page. A microsite is also called a minisite.

Monthly impression (MI)   A term used to describe the number of impressions in one month.

Monthly rental rate (MRR)   The rate at which a given number of impressions over the period of a month are sold.

Mousetrapping   The use of browser tricks in an effort to keep a visitor captive at a site, often by disabling the back button or generating repeated pop-up windows.

Multimedia messaging service (MMS)   MMS is the next generation of short message service (SMS). It allows you to create, send, receive, and forward multimedia messages—with sound, animation, snapshots, and video clips that include text and sound to and from mobile telephones, from mobile telephones to computer, and from computers to mobile telephones.

Multiple keyword tags   Using two or three keyword meta tags to increase the relevancy of a page. This technique is considered spam by most search engines and should be avoided.

Multivariable testing   A research approach that aims to optimize performance by testing and evaluating several factors simultaneously in web pages or online advertising.

Negative keyword   Negative keywords allow you to eliminate searches that you know are not related to your message. If you add the negative keyword "-table" to your keyword "tennis shoes," your ad will not appear when a user searches on "table tennis shoes." Negative keywords should be used with caution, as they can eliminate a large portion of a desired audience if applied incorrectly.

Newsgroup   A public place where electronic messages are posted for public consumption and response.

Off-page criteria   When a search engine ranks pages by using data that is not presented on the web page itself. This could be the presence of a directory listing, or the number and quality of inbound links to a page.

Off-site optimization   Optimizing factors such as domain name, link popularity, and link reputation that cannot be changed through modifications in the HTML code.

Online Publishers Association (OPA)   Industry trade organization dedicated to representing high-quality online content providers before the advertising community, the press, the government, and the public.

Online research   Refers to investigating and accessing information over a computer network, especially the internet.

On-site optimization   Optimization by modifying page source code factors such as keyword frequency, keyword prominence, title, meta tags, body copy, alt tags, navigation, and so on.

Opt-in   The process by which a subscriber requests (by submitting electronically his or her email address and any other required information) to receive information and/or advertising via email from companies or organizations. An opt-in email list is also called a permission-based email list.

Organic listings   Listings that search engines do not sell (unlike paid listings). Instead, sites appear solely because a search engine has deemed it editorially important for them to be included, regardless of payment.

Outbound links   Links on a particular web page leading to other web pages, whether they are within the same website or other websites.

Overlaid data   A process whereby a customer file has data appended to it (such as age, income, or home value) from some external data file, also called fusion.

Page impression   Each time a particular web page is displayed by someone using the internet.

Page rank   A method developed and patented by Stanford University and Larry Page (co-founder of Google) to rank search engine results. Page rank gives a unique ranking to every page on the internet. The ranking number is based on the number and quality of inbound links pointing at a page.

Page view   Occurs when a user's browser requests a web page. A single page view may create multiple hits to the server if the page contains multiple elements.

Paid inclusion   Guaranteed inclusion on a search engine's results in exchange for payment, without any guarantee of how high the listing will appear. A paid inclusion appears to the user as an organic listing rather than as a sponsored link. Paid inclusion pricing is based on a flat fee or index fee.

Paid listings   Listings that search engines sell to advertisers, usually through paid placement or paid inclusion programs. In contrast, organic listings are not sold.

Paid placement   Guaranteed listing with high ranking among search results, usually in relation to specified keywords. Search engines clearly identify paid placements as sponsored links, listing them separately from the editorial portion of the results page. Paid placement programs are typically based on activity, such as cost-per-click (CPC), or exposure, such as cost-per-thousand (CPM).

Paid search   Paid search (also known as sponsored search) is characterized by advertiser bids on queried keywords. Paid search results appear separately from algorithmic, or natural, search results, typically along the top, down the side, and across the bottom of search results pages. Listing order is determined by the amount each advertiser has bid on keywords.

Pass-along rate   The percentage of people who pass on a message or file.

Pay-for-performance   Term popularized by some search engines as a synonym for pay-per-click.

Pay-per-click (PPC)   The payment model used for sponsored search advertising. Advertisers set bids on their keywords and pay only when searchers click the search results listings associated with those keywords.

Pay-per-click search engine (PPCSE)   Search engine where results are ranked according to the bid amount and advertisers are charged only when a searcher clicks on the search listing.

Permission marketing   Ensures that consumers permit marketers to send them online marketing communications. The process of granting permission is called opt-in.

Phrase match   A successful phrase match occurs when your ad appears if users search on the exact phrase or their search contains additional terms matching your keyword phrase in exactly the same order. Foe example, a phrase match for "tennis shoes" would include "red tennis shoes" but not "shoes for tennis."

Pixel   Short for picture element, a pixel is a measure of image size. Most ad units are measured in pixels such as the common 468 pixel by 60 pixel full banner.

Pixel tag   Used in combination with a web cookie, a pixel tag is a transparent graphic image placed on a website or in an email to monitor the behavior of the user visiting the website or sending the email.

Pop-under ads   Ads that appear in a separate browser window beneath an already open browser window.

Pop-up ads   Ads that appear in a separate window on top of content already viewable on-screen.

Post coordination of terms   The use of two or more single words to describe a document. A page about herbal cures for common ailments, for example, could be indexed under "herbal," "cures," and "remedies." The search engine would then consider that document a match to a query like "alternative remedies."

Postmaster   The name given to the person in charge of administrating email for a particular site.

Psychographics   Identification of personality characteristics and attitudes that affect a person's lifestyle and purchasing behaviors. Psychographic data points include opinions, attitudes, and beliefs about various aspects relating to lifestyle and purchasing behavior.

Query   A request for information, usually to a search engine or a database. The user types in words or topics, and the search engine returns matching results from its database. A query is at the center of every search engine's interaction.

Reach   The number of unique visitors that visited a site over the course of the reporting period, expressed as a percentage of the universe for the demographic category. Also called unduplicated audience.

Reciprocal link   A link you place on your web page with the understanding that the linked web page will create a link to your site.

Referral fees   Fees paid in exchange for delivering a qualified sales lead or purchase inquiry. For example, an affiliate drives traffic to other companies' sites, typically in exchange for a percentage of sales or a flat referral fee.

Referrer   The address (URL) of the web page a user came from before entering another site.

Referring page   The web page that a visitor was on before arriving at the current page as a result of clicking a hyperlink on the previous web page.

Refresh tag   Meta refresh tag reloads a page at a set time.

Remnant inventory   Low-cost advertising space that is relatively undesirable or otherwise unsold.

Response device   An order or donation form.

Results page   After a user enters a search query, the page that is displayed is called the results page. Sometimes it may be called a SERP, for search engine results page.

Return days   The number of days an affiliate can earn a commission on a conversion (sale or lead) by a referred visitor.

Rich media   A type of advertisement technology that often includes richer graphics, audio, or video within the advertisement. Rich media advertisements often enable users to interact with the banner without leaving the page on which it appears. Rich media ads are created with generic technologies like HTML, Shockwave, and Flash or proprietary branded units from vendors such as Eyeblaster, PointRoll, and Shoskeles.

Rotation   An ad that is in rotation on a page or group of pages will alternate with others when any of the pages are reloaded.

Run of category (ROC)   In an ROC ad campaign a banner will appear anywhere within a category on a website or ad network. More targeted than a run of site (ROS) campaign, where the banner would appear randomly on any page of the site.

Run of network (RON)   In an RON ad campaign a banner will appear on any page of any site that is part of an ad network. Since this type of buy is not targeted, it tends to be the least expensive type of advertisement that can be purchased.

Run of site (ROS)   Refers to the scheduling of ads across an entire site, often at a lower cost than the purchase of specific pages or subsections of the site. A run-of-site ad campaign is rotated on all general, nonfeatured ad spaces on a site.

Search engine marketing (SEM)   The process and strategy of using search engine results as an advertising vehicle. This may include improving rank in organic listings, purchasing paid listings, paying for inclusion, or a combination of methods, all designed to increase visibility, traffic, leads, and orders.

Search Engine Marketing Professional Organization (SEMPO) A nonprofit organization formed to increase the awareness of and educate people on the value of search engine marketing.

Search engine optimization (SEO)   The process of choosing targeted keyword phrases related to a site and ensuring that the site positions well when search results are generated from inputting those same keyword phrases during the initial web search. The planning and modifying of a website, web pages, and links to websites and web pages to improve visibility, rank, and relevance in the organic, crawler-based listings of search engines. The altering of a website, web pages, and links to websites and web pages to improve visibility, rank, and relevance in the organic, crawler-based listings of search engines.

Search engine sponsored link networks   Companies that sell and distribute search results via their own network of partners. Examples include Google Syndication, Yahoo! Search Marketing, and MSN Search.

Search engine submission The act of supplying a URL to a search engine in an attempt to make a search engine aware of a site or page.

Secure Electronic Transaction (SET) A system for encrypting e-commerce transactions, such as online credit card purchases. Developed by Visa, MasterCard, Microsoft, and several major banks, SET combines 1,024-bit encryption with digital certificates to ensure security.

Session A series of page requests by a visitor without 30 consecutive minutes of inactivity. The number 30 is arbitrary but most commonly used among web advertisers and publishers. Also called a visit.

Shockwave A browser plug-in that allows multimedia objects to appear on the web (animation, audio, and video).

Shopping bot A tool that aggregates different online stores that sell products so that a consumer can have one point of access to multiple stores to compare products, pricing, and shipping costs.

Shopping cart A feature of online stores that allows consumers to select items for purchase and to review the items placed into the shopping cart prior to finalizing the purchase.

Shopping search Shopping search engines allow shoppers to look for products and prices in a search environment. Premium placement can be purchased on some shopping search indexes.

Short message service (SMS) SMS sends messages by text and/or simple line drawings to and from mobile telephones.

Shoskeles An animated ad that moves across the browser, usually with sound effects. It animates only long enough to play a message before settling into a stationary ad on the page.

Site map A page on a website that lists and links to all the other pages on that website.

Site optimization The act of fine-tuning website content and code to perform well in search engine results.

Site promotion Site promotion includes all of the steps that a website takes to help increase traffic, name recognition, and potential business. Site promotion includes, but is not limited to, search engine optimization.

Skewing   The practice of artificially altering the search results so that certain documents will score well on certain queries; it is a technique used by search engines.

Skyscraper   An ad that has a vertically oriented image, normally 120 × 600 pixels, found on many more websites than normal horizontal ads.

Spam   The sending of unsolicited emails or newsgroup posts in bulk, often containing commercial advertising messages. Considered bad netiquette, bad business, and illegal in some U.S. states. The opposite of spam would be permission-based or opt-in email whereby customized information is emailed to individual users who have previously requested such information.

Spamdexing   All attempts to deceive search engines or gain an unfair advantage in the search results of a search engine. Spamdexing decreases the value of a search engine's index by reducing the precision with which the search engine can return relevant documents. Most search engines have measures in place to detect spamdexing.

Spider   A software program that automatically follows links on the World Wide Web. The most common types of spiders are those used by search engines for indexing web pages.

Spim   Spam that is sent to someone through an instant messaging application.

Splash page   A highly expressive page between an advertisement and an advertiser's website that often provides product information. Some splash pages automatically jump to another page on the advertiser's website after a certain amount of time has elapsed.

Split test   The testing process of sending the same advertisement to two or more groups with different headlines or copy to determine effectiveness of each.

Sponsored links   Text-based ads that often appear either from a keyword search on a search engine or from an associated site. These ads are often displayed alongside natural search results but identified under specified headers (e.g., "Paid Sponsors," "Sponsored Links," "Sponsored Sites," or "Sponsored Results").

Sponsored search   A pay-per-click product that allows your business to be featured in the sponsored search results at the top, along the side, and across the bottom of search results pages.

Sponsored search results   Search listings that are generated as a result of advertiser bids on queried keywords. Sponsored search results appear separately from algorithmic, or natural, search results, typically along the top, down the side, and across the bottom of search results pages. Listing order is determined by the amount each advertiser has bid on keywords.

Standard match type   A keyword matching option. The standard match includes an advertiser's listing in relevant searches where the bid keyword is an exact match with the search query (taking pluralization and common misspellings into account).

Static content   Content on a website that is hard coded onto the page and does not come from a database. Search engines have no difficulties indexing this content, unlike dynamic content.

Stemming   Refers to root word origins. For example, "search," "searching," and "searches" all have "search" as the root stem. Some search engines use stemming to provide results from more than just the entered search terms. A search on "boat" could return results on "boating" or "boats."

Stop words   A stop word is a word that causes an indexer to stop indexing in the current procedure and do something else. The most common instance is when an indexer encounters an adult censored word. Also referred to as filter words.

Subdomain   The traditional portion of a domain name, where the "www" location is said to be a third level or subdomain of the primary domain.

Subsegment   A grouping of advertisements according to their topic or main focus of business. The most granular competitive classification to which an advertisement can be assigned.

Subsite   A section of a website that focuses on a particular topic, function, or theme. Many subsites coincide with a directory path, although this is not required. Other considerations include breadcrumb trail and/or title bar, primary navigation bar selections, logo and branding, and description of channel(s) in media kit and/or site map.

Super affiliate   An affiliate capable of generating a significant percentage of an affiliate program's activity.

Superstitials   Ads developed by a company, Unicast, which are rich media that can be any size on the screen. Superstitials download in the background and launch a browser window only when it has completed downloading.

Surround session   Advertising sequence in which a visitor receives ads from one advertiser throughout an entire site visit.

Syndication   An option that allows you to extend your reach by distributing ads to additional partner sites.

Tagline   A slogan or phrase that conveys the most important product attribute or benefit that the advertiser wishes to convey.

Text link exchange   Network where participating sites display text ads in exchange for credits, which are converted (using a predetermined exchange rate) into ads to be displayed on other sites.

Text links   Text that is hyperlinked to another web page. Can be found on websites or in newsletters and email.

Theme engine   A search engine that indexes entire sites as one giant page. It then uses only the most relevant keywords found to determine your site's theme. By determining a theme, search engines hope to return results that are more accurate.

Third-party bidding tools   Automated bidding tools that work with advertisers to maintain their desired bids and positions in sponsored search results. These tools are also used to help advertisers adjust their bids on their accounts.

Title tag   An HTML tag used to define the text in the top line of a web browser, which is also used by many search engines as the title of search listings and for bookmark identification.

Token   A tracer or tag attached by the receiving server to the address (URL) of a page requested by a user. A token lasts only through a continuous series of requests by a user, regardless of the length of the interval between requests. Tokens can be used to count unique users.

Toolbar   With reference to search engines, toolbars are browser add-ons provided by the search engines. These toolbars often include a search box, shortcuts to the different sections of the search engine, and additional page information.

Top-level domain (TLD)   The domain name extension that follows a domain name. For example, in the United States ".com" is used for businesses, ".edu" for educational institutions, ".net" for networking companies, ".gov" for government agencies, ".mil" for the military, and ".org" for nonprofit organizations. In addition, most countries have been assigned a two-letter TLD, such as ".ca" for Canada and ".uk" for United Kingdom.

Top-level page The default page or home page of a website recognized by search engines (usually including index.html, index.htm, default.asp, etc.). "Submitting only a top-level page" means that search engines will have a spider that can locate the rest of a website's pages that are necessary. It is always a good practice to have a link from your top-level page to your site map.

Tracking Online advertising opens the opportunity to track audience response throughout the life of your campaign. Tracking and reporting tools can help marketers learn, so ad creative elements can be refined, placement options modified, and spending levels changed if expected results are not met. The ad publisher can provide reports on ad impressions and click-through rates, and for additional analysis of your traffic and actual customer conversion rates further tracking mechanisms can be built into your website.

Transitional ad Ad displayed between pages; typically seen when a user is trying to link from one page to another and the ad appears in between pages. Also known as an interstitial.

Trapdoor A type of banner advertisement that leads to a page that does not easily allow visitors to return to the previous page the banner was on. This is accomplished by using a meta refresh tag set to 0 on the destination page, immediately sending them to another page, or launching a browser window that has hidden the browser's back button.

Two-tier affiliate program Affiliate program structure whereby affiliates earn commissions on their conversions as well as the conversions of webmasters they refer to the program.

Unique ads Individual ads counted not by impression, but by their unique creative content.

Unique page view A visit that is counted the first time a unique visitor looks at a web page, no matter how many other times the visitor views the page later.

Unique visitors Describes the total number of unique visitors to a site over a certain period.

URL (Uniform Resource Locator)   The internet address of a website or web page on the World Wide Web, such as www.thearf.org. A browser requires this information in its location box in order to load a web page. Can be pronounced "you-are-ell" or "earl."

User session   A session of activity for one user on a website.

Valid hits   A term used to differentiate between successful click-throughs by individuals and those that may have resulted in a server error or been generated by some kind of automated software program (a search engine spider).

Vertical banner   A banner ad measuring 120 pixels wide by 240 pixels tall.

Viral marketing   A marketing strategy that encourages consumers to pass along messages to others in order to generate added exposure.

Webcasting   A process where sound and/or video are/is broadcasted online. The process can deliver live or prerecorded information. Often advertisements are inserted at the beginning of the broadcast.

Web copywriting   Copywriting specifically aimed at an online audience. It shares many of the ground rules of offline copywriting, but has quickly evolved to become a stand-alone discipline concerned with SEO and converting visitors to customers.

Webliography   A listing of source World Wide Web sites.

Web log   Usually shortened to "blog"; a narrative for a wide range of personal pages, journals, and diary-type entries.

Webmaster   A term used to describe an individual assigned to administering a website. Typical duties might include updating pages, correcting errors, fixing links, or responding to technical inquiries.

Webmercials   Full-screen animated ads accompanied by professional voice-over and sound effects. Usually appear between web pages for 5 to 30 seconds and used for branding purposes.

Web server   A computer connected to the internet for serving a website's web pages to visitors on the World Wide Web.

Web server log   A file that lists actions that have occurred on a user's website. With log file analysis tools, it is possible to get information of where site visitors are coming from, how often they return, and how they navigate through the site.

Website   A set of interconnected web pages, usually including a home page, generally located on the same server, that is prepared and maintained as a collection of information by a person, group, or organization. A website can be viewed by directing an internet browser to the website's address on the internet (URL).

Weighting   Describes the technique search engines use to compare the relevance of different documents to a query. Search engines effectively weigh different pages based on instances like the occurrence of keywords in the title in order to list documents in order of most to least relevant.

360i and SearchIgnite. 2006a. Giving clicks credit where they're due, part two: The value of assists for natural and paid search conversions. 360i/SearchIgnite.

360i and SearchIgnite. 2006b. Giving clicks credit where they're due: What you need to know when allocating your search budget. 360i/SearchIgnite.

Advertising Age. 2006. Interactive marketing and media fact book 2006. Crain Communications.

Advertising.com. 2005. The state of online marketing: Behavioral targeting and other key trends. September 16.

Ahrens, Frank. 2004. Circulation fraud contained, audit group says. *Washington Post*, November 12, E04.

Aldrich, Susan. 2006. The other search: Making the most of site search to optimize the total customer experience. Patricia Seybold Group.

Amazon Product Review. 2006. So far five star: Just got it. Amazon.

Anfuso, Dawn. 2004. Excellent email. iMedia Connection. www.imedia connection.com/global/5728.asp?ref=http://www.imediacon nection.com/content/4435.asp.

Anfuso, Dawn. 2005. Drilling down in behavioral targeting. iMedia Connection, April 27. www.imediaconnection.com/content/5581 .asp, accessed August 15, 2006.

Anfuso, Dawn. 2006. Contextual versus behavioral targeting. iMedia Connection. www.imediaconnection.com/global/5728.asp?ref= http://www.imediaconnection.com/content/8863.asp.

AOL. 2005. Brand new world: How the internet is changing consumer attitudes to brands, research conducted in conjunction with The Henley Center.

AOL and Nielsen. 2005. Impact of the internet on today's moviegoer: A study of consumer purchase behavior. AOL Media Networks and Nielsen Media Entertainment.

Ashford, Nickolas, and Valery Simpson. 1968. Ain't nothing like the real thing. Song.

Atkinson, Claire. 2004. People meter controversy: Nielsen local ratings under gov't scrutiny, *Advertising Age*, May 17.

AWSM Technology. 2006. An in-depth exploration: Why search advertising works. www.awsmtechnology.com/marketing/search-ad vertising-terms.htm, accessed May 31, 2006.

Baggott, Chris. 2006. 2006 Top email trends annual report: Eye-opening statistics and examples from world-class marketers. ExactTarget.

Balzer, Cam. 2006. Search's place in the purchase funnel. iMedia Connection. www.imediaconnection.com/global/5728.asp?ref=http://www.imediaconnection.com/content/7658.asp, accessed July 16, 2006.

Beck, Paul. 2006. Interview with Stephen D. Rappaport, September 19.

Belkin, Matt. 2005. Search engine marketing: Maximizing profit with web analytics. Omniture.

Berkowitz, Tobe. 1996. Political media buying: A brief guide. www.ksg.harvard.edu/case/3pt/berkovitz.html#anchor563516.

Bianco, Anthony, with Ronald Grover. 2004. How Nielsen stood up to Murdoch. *BusinessWeek*, September 20.

BL Labs. 2006. Behaviorally targeted ads work better out of context. October 16.

BoldMouth. 2006. Perceptions, practices & ethics in word-of-mouth marketing. BoldMouth.com.

Bolger, Lynn, and Marie Pauline E. Mörn. 2004. Internet audience dynamics. DoubleClick, September.

Bosman, Julie. 2006a. Hey kid, you want to buy a Scion? *New York Times*, June 14.

Bosman, Julie. 2006b. When consumers can write the ads. *International Herald Tribune*, April 5. http://iht.com/articles/2006/04/04/business/ads.php.

Boswell, Wendy. 2006. Ten steps to a well optimized site. About.com.

Box Office Mojo. 2006. *The Da Vinci Code*. BoxOfficeMojo.com, August 20. www.boxofficemojo.com/movies/?id=davincicode.htm, accessed September 30, 2006.

Briggs, Rex. 2002. Cross-media measurement: The new medium necessitates a new approach to an old problem. New York: Interactive Advertising Bureau.

Briggs, Rex. 2004. XMOS research review: The new marketing mix. Marketing Evolution (2004).

Briggs, Rex. 2005. XMOS research review: The new marketing mix. Marketing Evolution.

Briggs, Rex, et al. 2001. Hong Kong online advertising effectiveness study. Nielsen Consult.

Briggs, Rex, et al. 2005. Integrated multichannel communication strategies: Evaluating the return on marketing objectives—The case of the 2004 Ford F-150 launch. *Journal of Interactive Marketing* 19, no. 3 (Summer), published online in Wiley InterScience (www.interscience.wiley.com).

Brohan, Mark. 2006a. Bigger is better: Technobrands' FirstStreetOnline finds a search marketing strategy that fits. *Internet Retailer*. www.internetretailer.com/article.asp?id=19366, accessed July 30, 2006.

Brohan, Mark. 2006b. Omit needless words. InternetRetailer.com, February. http://internetretailer.com/printArticle.asp?id=17442, accessed October 4, 2006.

Brohan, Mark. 2006c. Racing ahead: 2006 is shaping up as another year of record sales, with retailers shifting their attention to customer retention from acquisition. *Internet Retailer*. www.internet retailer.com/printArticle.asp?id=19104, accessed August 8, 2006.

Brooks, Nico. 2005a. The Atlas rank report: How search engine rank impacts traffic. Atlas Institute.

Brooks, Nico. 2005b. The Atlas rank report II: How search engine rank impacts conversions. Atlas Institute.

Broussard, Gerard. 2000. How advertising frequency can work to build online advertising effectiveness. *International Journal of Market Research* 42, no. 4.

Broussard, Gerard, et al. 2001. Visual noise: The role of site clutter in advertising branding effectiveness. Presentation by OgilvyOne, Dynamic Logic, iVillage, and Jupiter Media Metrix, October 29.

Bruner, Rick, and Marissa Gluck. 2006. Best practices for optimizing web advertising effectiveness. DoubleClick.

Bruner, Rick, and Kathryn Koegel. 2005. Target demographics, before and after. DoubleClick.

Bruner, Rick E., and Marissa Gluck. 2005. The evolution of rich media. DoubleClick, September.

Burst! 2002. *Online Insights*. 02.4. June.

BusinessWeek. 2006a. My virtual life. May 1. www.businessweek.com/magazine/content/06_18/b3982001.htm.

BusinessWeek. 2006b. Wiser about the web. www.businessweek.com/magazine/content/06_13/b3977401.htm, accessed March 23, 2006.

Carlon, Michael, et al. 2000. The five golden rules of branding. Dynamic Logic, AdRelevance, 24/7 media white paper, October; OPA White Paper, October.

Carton, Sean. 2003. Geotargeting: Why it matters to marketers. ClickZ. www.clickz.com/experts/media/agency_strat/article.php/831601.

Chain Store Age. 2006. Albertsons to stop on-line shopping service. ChainStoreAge.com. www.chainstoreage.com/storyPrint.cfm?ID=60078UCJ, accessed July 30, 2006.

Chandler-Pepelnjak, John, and Young-Bean Song. n.d. Ad creative or media placement: Which is more important when optimizing online direct response campaigns? Atlas Institute. www.atlassolutions.com/pdf/CreativePlacements.pdf.

CheetahMail. 2005a. Email marketing creative best practices and techniques: Updated 4.11.05. CheetahMail, an Experian Company.

CheetahMail. 2005b. Recapturing customers through remarketing: Turning browsers and abandoners into buyers. CheetahMail, an Experian company.

CheetahMail. 2005c. Transactional and operational messaging. Cheetah Mail, an Experian company.

CheetahMail. 2006. Brooks Brothers case study. CheetahMail, an Experian company. www.cheetahmail.com/corp/brooks_brothers.html, accessed August 17, 2006.

CNET Networks. 2006. What creative works online? www.clickz.com/news/article.php/3615611.

Coffey, Steve, and Mainak Mazumdar. 2002. The reach and frequency approach to advertising planning on the internet. ESOMAR, Online Audience Conference, Cannes, June, 141–162.

Cohen, David. 2003. This half is wasted. ClickZ, September 3. www.clickz.com/experts/brand/emkt_strat/article.php/3071191/.

ComScore. 2002a. Advertisers beware: Media buys across fewer online networks are inefficient. ComScore Networks press release, May 1.

ComScore. 2002b. ComScore study shows strong connection between online marketing, offline buying and purchase intent: Relationships drawn between online and offline dynamics for Nestlé Purina petcare brands. April 15.

ComScore. 2003. Media Metrix 2.0 reach/frequency report user guide. ComScore Media Metrix.

ComScore. 2006. IAB and comScore research on the effectiveness of local, directory and classified advertising. www.comscore.com/press/release.asp?press=791.

ComScore Networks. 2006a. ComScore study confirms the importance of search in influencing offline buying.

ComScore Networks. 2006b. Google continues to increase search engine market share.

ComScore Networks. 2006c. Understanding consumers' shopping and buying behavior at supplier and agency travel sites: Travel industry overview and analysis. www.comscore.com.

Copeland, Chris, and Greg Rogers. 2005. The multi channel impact on shopping behavior. ShopLocal White Paper.

CoreMetrics. 2006. Increasing email relevance: Five best practices that drive ROI.

David. 2006. Sprint ambassador program—influence on the cheap. ThirdWayAdvertisingBlog.com. www.thirdwayadvertisingblog.com/?p=156, accessed September 15, 2006.

Davis, Wendy. 2006. Merrill Lynch: Online ad spend to surpass $16B. MediaPost (May 9), http://publications.mediapost.com/index.cfm?fuseaction=Articles.san&s=43135&Nid=20221&p=352249, accessed May 9, 2006.

Deal, David. 2006. Embrace interactive video now. *Avenue A | Razorfish Insight*, August.

Deierlein, Tom. 2005. Best practices in cross-media advertising measurement. Dynamic Logic, January.

Deitlinger Research Group. 2002. American interactive consumer study.

Dempsey, Brian. 2006. The art of online conversion: Four steps from interest to acquisition. MarketingProfs.com. /www.marketingprofs.com/6/dempsey1.asp?sz=10.

Digital Element. 2006a. Success stories: E4X. www.digital-element.net/success_stories/e4x.html.

Digital Element. 2006b. Success stories: Poindexter. www.digital-element.net/success_stories/pdf/de_cs_poindexter.pdf.

Dilworth, Dianna. 2006a. Etail: L'Occitane vende avec l'email, DMNews. www.dmnews.com/cms/trackback/37801-1, accessed August 9, 2006.

Dilworth, Dianna. 2006b. Lane Bryant sizes up online marketing. DMNews. www.dmnews.com/cms/dm-news/email-marketing/37800.html, accessed August 14, 2006.

Doohan, Kevin. 2006. Email newsletter marketing for CPG companies: Simple and delicious. Presentation supplied and interview with Stephen D. Rappaport.

Dou, Wenyu, and Sandeep Krishnamurthy. 2007 (in press). Using brand web sites to build brands: A product vs. service brand comparison. *Journal of Advertising Research* 47, no. 2.

DoubleClick. 2001a. Online brand effectiveness study. July.

DoubleClick. 2001b. Online branding: Executive summary. July.

DoubleClick. 2003. Cross-media reach and frequency planning studies: American Airlines, Kraft and Subaru. DoubleClick/Nielsen//NetRatings/IMS, March.

DoubleClick. 2004a. DoubleClick's Q3 2004 ad serving trend report. Smart Marketing Report. November.

DoubleClick. 2004b. Internet audience dynamics: How can you effectively use online as a reach medium? September.

DoubleClick. 2005a. DoubleClick's Touchpoints III: The internet's role in the modern purchase process.

DoubleClick. 2005b. Search before the purchase: Understanding buyer search activity as it relates to online purchase.

DoubleClick. 2005c. Search trend report DoubleClick Q3 2005.

DoubleClick. 2005d. Sixth annual consumer email study. DoubleClick Email Solutions. December.

DoubleClick. 2006a. Best practices for optimizing web advertising effectiveness. May.

DoubleClick. 2006b. Search trend report DoubleClick Q4 2005.

Dugan, Kevin. 2006. P&G expands word-of-mouth efforts. ClickZ. www.webpronews.com/blogtalk/blogtalk/wpn-58-20060417PG ExpandsWordofMouthEfforts.html, accessed September 15, 2006.

Duncan, Apryl. 2005. Paris Hilton's controversial new commercial. About.com. http://advertising.about.com/b/a/165351.htm, accessed September 15, 2006.

Dynamic Logic. 2001. Ad unit effectiveness study. Dynamic Logic on behalf of IAB, March–June.

Dynamic Logic. 2004. Consumer perceptions of various web ad formats. March.

Eisenberg, Bryan. 2006a. Conversion funnel folly, part 2. ClickZ Network. www.clickz.com/experts/crm/traffic/article.php/3588626, accessed June 11, 2006.

Eisenberg, Bryan, 2006b. Do you want traffic or business? ClickZ Network. www.clickz.com/experts/crm/traffic/article.php3609086, accessed May 26, 2006.

Eisenberg, Bryan, and Jim Novo. 2002. The marketer's common sense guide to e-metrics. *Future Now*.

Elliott, Stuart. 2006. More agencies investing in marketing with a click. *New York Times* (March 14). www.nytimes.com/2006/03/14/business/media/14adco.html?ei=5089&en=6fcd30ba68dd1312&ex=1299992400&partner=rssyahoo&emc=rss&pagewanted=print, accessed March 14, 2006.

Email Experience Council. 2006. eNews you can use: The top 10 for '07 in August 2006 Newsletter, Email Experience Council.

eMarketer. 2006a. Email and word-of-mouth: Connect with your best customers.

eMarketer. 2006b. Internet advertising revenues soar to a new record in 2005. www.emarketer.com/Articles/Print.aspx?1003854, accessed March 3, 2006.

eMarketer. 2006c. Local advertising: Measuring the potential.

eMarketer. 2006d. Multi-channel marketing: The rise of the retail chains.

eMarketer. 2006e. New ways to target your customer. April. www.emarketer.com/Articles/Print.aspx?1003937.

eMarketer. 2006f. Online ad targeting: Engaging the audience. May. www.emarketer.com/Report.aspx?targeting_may06.

eMarketer. 2006g. Search marketing: Players and problems.

eMarketer. 2006h. Search marketing: Spending and metrics.

eMarketer. 2006i. US retail e-commerce.

Enquiro, Eyetools, and Did-it. 2005. Google eye tracking report.

Ephron, Erwin. 2005. The CPM below: User targeting can discover TV program value. October.

Epsilon Interactive. 2006. Epsilon Interactive's research shows major retail brands are missing opportunities to grow sales and build customer loyalty online. www.bigfootinteractive.com/eisite/press room/press_releases/pr2006/pr-04-12-06.htm, accessed September 17, 2006.

ESPN.com. 2004. Tylenol 8 Hour: A crossmedia advertising case study. October.

Estrada, Lydia. 2005. Six principles of effective online advertising. iMedia Summit.

ExactTarget. 2006a. Motorcycle Superstore: Paving the road to email success.

ExactTarget. 2006b. Wild Oats marketplace sows the seeds for email marketing success.

Experian. 2003. Advanced contact strategies for multichannel merchants.

Eyeblaster. 2002. Florida orange juice, the best start under the sun: Case study. Presented at iMedia Summit, May.

Eyeblaster. 2005. Click-thru and interaction rates: By ad format and ad category.

Fallon Worldwide. 2006. Holiday Inn Express: Showerhead. Gold Medal Effie Award brief, American Marketing Association, New York.

Fallows, Deborah. 2005. Search engine users. Pew Internet & American Life Project.

Fathom Online. 2006. Fathom Online reports first quarter search marketing keyword prices ease. April 17.

Fine, Jon. 2006. Rise of the lowly search ad. Business Week Online. businessweek.com/print/magazine/content/06_17/b3981022.htm?chan=gl, accessed June 2, 2006.

Fisk, Linda. 2006. "Who" is the first step before "how." MediaPost. http://publications.mediapost.com/index.cfm?fuseaction=Articles.showArticle&art_aid=41393, accessed March 24, 2006.

Folkenflik, David. 2005. Report details dropping circulation for newspapers. NPR, May 3. www.npr.org/templates/story/story.php?storyId=4628368, accessed September 6, 2006.

Forman, Tami Monahan. 2005. Beyond clicks, opens and bounces: Metrics that reveal the path to optimal email performance. ReturnPath.

Forrester Research. 2004. Selecting a site analytics product. June.

Forrester Research. 2006a. The state of consumers and technology: benchmark 2006.

Forrester Research. 2006b. The state of retail online.

Freedman, Lauren. 2006. Measured growth via marketing and email: 5th annual merchant survey 1st quarter 2006. The E-tailing Group. www.e-tailing.com/newsandviews/details/Merch_Measured_Grow_2_2.pdf, accessed July 25, 2006.

Gabler, Ellen. 2005. Car dealers ramp-up online spending. *Minneapolis/St. Paul Business Journal*, September 5. http://twincities.bizjournals.com/twincities/stories/2005/09/05/story1.html.

GameSpot. 2005. Bringing Starch to the internet.

Gartner, John. 2007. Taking it off-line: Juggling both real-world and virtual marketing can be tricky. *Revenue*, January/February, 74–78.

Glover, Tony. 2006. Google aims to take over your TV screen. *The Business*, May 28.

Gluck, Marissa, and Adam Sinnreich. 2006. Clumsy to cool: Branded entertainment and the rules of in-games ads. *iMedia-Post Publications*.

Goldman, Aaron. 2006. Why can't everything be searchable? *Media Post Search Insider*. http://publications.mediapost.com/index.cfm?fuseaction=Articles.showArticle&art_aid=44605, accessed June 16, 2006.

Goldman Sachs, Nielsen//NetRatings, Harris Interactive. 2005. More than half of online shoppers finish shopping the week prior to the holidays; Total holiday spending hits $25 billion, according to holiday espending report. Nielsen//NetRatings. www.nielsen-netratings.com/pr/pr_051222.pdf, accessed July 29, 2006

Goodman, Alistair. 2006. Online session depth and user response. Presentation to the ARF ReThink Conference, March 20. www.ephrononmedia.com/article_archive/articleViewer.asp?origin=AR&articleID=145&categoryID=22&categoryName=Planning.

Google AdWords Help Center. 2006. How do I choose a daily budget for my cost-per-click campaign? https://adwords.google.com/support/bin/answer.py?answer=6386&ctx=sibling, accessed May 10, 2006.

Google. 2005a. Google log analysis.

Google. 2005b. Millward Brown consumer study: Search in the business technology purchase process.

Google. 2006a. From personal communication with Stephen D. Rappaport.

Google. 2006b. Google advertising: Search advertising glossary of terms. www.google.com/ads/glossary.html, accessed March 14, 2006.

Google. 2006c. Google study: Internet directs moviegoers. Online Media Daily, September 22. http://publications.mediapost.com/index.cfm?fuseaction=Articles.showArticle&art_aid=48550, accessed September 30, 2006.

Google. 2006d. National Instruments (NI) uses non-traditional marketing to accomplish its goals in a cost-efficient manner. Google AdWords Case Study—Business and Industrial.

Google. 2006e. The role of search in consumer buying: Executive summary.

Google. 2006f. Zeitgeist this week. www.google.com/press/zeitgeist .html, accessed May 15, 2006.

Grau, Jeffrey. 2006a. Multi-channel shopping: The rise of the retail chains. eMarketer.

Grau, Jeffrey. 2006b. Online travel sales to boom. iMedia Connection. www.imediaconnection.com/global/5728.asp?ref=http://www .imediaconnection.com/content/9953.asp, accessed July 21, 2006.

Green, Heather. 2006. It takes a web village. *BusinessWeek* Online, September 4. www.businessweek.com/magazine/content/06_36/ b3999076.htm; GSD&M, personal communication, 2006.

Greenspan, Robyn. 2004. Search individualized by demographics. ClickZ News, www.clickz.com/news/article.php/3391251, accessed May 15, 2006.

Gupta, Shankar. 2005. Study: Best online ads draw on print techniques. *iMediaPost Publications*, April 25.

Gupta, Shankar. 2006a. Microsoft plans to extend paid search platform to games, IPTV, other media. MediaPost. publications.mediapost .com/index.cfm?fuseaction=Articles.san&s=44262&Nid=20809& p=352249, accessed June 8, 2006.

Gupta, Shankar. 2006b. Sony traffic surges with Google promo. Online Media Daily, May 12. http://publications.mediapost.com/index .cfm?fuseaction=Articles.showArticle&art_aid=43295, accessed September 30, 2006.

Gupta, Shankar. 2007. Getting a jump on free games. *OMMA* Magazine, January, 6.

Hallerman, David. 2006. Search marketing, players and problems. eMarketer.

Hansell, Saul. 2006. Yahoo! is unleashing a new way to turn ad clicks into ka-ching. *New York Times* (May 8).

Harris, Stephen, 2006. Online marketing for brand building. *Media-Post Publications Search Insider*, May 26.

Harvey, Bill. 2006. The advantage of behavior targeting increases dramatically with frequency. TACODA.

Healthy Mom, The. 2006. Please vote for my margarita masterpiece! The Healthy Mom Blog (April), www.thehealthymom.com/ 2006/04/, accessed September 26, 2006.

Heath, R. G. 2001. Low involvement processing—A new model of brand communication. *Journal of Marketing Communications* 7, no. 1: 27–34.

Helfand, Jeremy. 2005. The true dynamics of on-line targeting. iMedia Connection, October 24. www.imediaconnection.com/content/7057.asp.

Heyman, Bob. 2006. Search marketing spotlight: Search is "Element"-al for Honda. *MediaPost Search Insider* (May 17).

Hitwise. 2006a. Best practices for search engine brand management.

Hitwise. 2006b. Search brand management white paper.

Holland, Anne. 2005. Search engine marketing: Top five eye-tracking laboratory test results. *Chief Marketer*.

Holland, Anne. 2006. The annoying precision of email open rate metrics. MarketingSherpa. www.marketingsherpa.com/sample.cfm?ident=29670#, accessed August 15, 2006.

Hong, James. n.d. How HotOrNot got started. HotOrNot.com. www.hotornot.com/pages/about.html, accessed October 6, 2006.

Horrigan, John. 2006. Home broadband adoption 2006. Pew Internet & American Life Project, May 28.

Hotchkiss, Gord. 2004. Flying blind? Search marketing metrics. WebProNews. www.webpronews.com/ebusiness/seo/wpn-42004 0602FlyingBlindSearchMarketingMetrics.html, accessed June 12, 2006.

Hotchkiss, Gord. 2006. Interview with Stephen D. Rappaport.

Hotel Online. 2005. The Holiday Inn Express brand completing roll-out of shower initiative; $20 million bathroom upgrade at 1,300 North American properties. www.hotel-online.com/News/PR 2005_1st/Mar05_SimplySmart.html, accessed September 24, 2006.

Hunt, Bill, and Mike Moran. 2005. Branding tactics of search. Search Engine Strategies Conference Presentation.

Hutchinson, Whitney. 2005. Best practices for email deliverability. Avenue A | Razorfish.

IAB. 2006a. Impacts and ROI of internet local, classifieds and directory advertising. Interactive Advertising Bureau. www.iab.net/resources/admin/downloads/IAB_comScoreExecPreso.ppt.

IAB. 2006b. Interactive advertising revenues grow 30% to a record $12.5 billion in '05. Interactive Advertising Bureau. http://iab .printthis.clickability.com/pt/cpt?action=cpt&title=IAB+Press+ Release&expire=&urlID=17977334&fb=Y&url=http://www.iab .net/news/pr_2006_04_20.asp&partnerID=297, accessed April 22, 2006.

IAB. 2006c. Internet advertising revenue report: An industry survey conducted by PricewaterhouseCoopers and sponsored by the IAB; 2005 full year results. Interactive Advertising Bureau, April.

IAB. 2006d. Internet advertising revenues continue to accelerate at an unprecedented rate with a 36% increase for first half of '06. Interactive Advertising Bureau. http://www.iab.net/news/pr_2006 _09_25.asp, accessed January 16, 2007.

IAB. 2006e. Measurement guidelines and measurement certification: Overview. www.iab.net/standards/measurement.asp, last accessed September 8, 2006.

iCrossing. 2006. How America searches. *Reverse Direct Marketing*, Issue 1.

iMedia Connection. 2002. Purina.com's Betsy Cohen. iMedia Connec tion.com (March 14). www.imediaconnection.com/global/5728 .asp?ref=http://www.imediaconnection.com/content/1348.asp, accessed September 28, 2006.

iMedia Connection. 2003. Case studies show definite lift. August 18. www.imediaconnection.com/news/1954.asp.

Integration. 2006. MCA calibration. www.integration-imc.com/ Mca-Calibration.htm, last accessed September 11, 2006.

Interactive Advertising Bureau (IAB). 2005a. XMOS case study: All new 2004 Ford F-150—Driving sales online.

Interactive Advertising Bureau (IAB). 2005b. XMOS case study: All new 2004 Ford F-150 brand launch, Ford tough.

Interactive Advertising Bureau. 2006. Standards and guidelines: Interactive marketing units. www.iab.net/standards/adunits.asp.

Internet Retailer. 2005a. HomeDepot.com blends search, navigation functions; sees conversion lift. www.internetretailer.com/ internet/marketing-conference/32164129-HomeDepot com-blends-search-navigation-functions-sees-conversion-lift .html, accessed July 27, 2006.

Internet Retailer. 2005b. Internet Retailer 2005: Report from the conference (review of Site Search: The underutilized super tool presentation by Nate Miller, director of e-commerce, Northern Tool and Equipment and Geoffrey Smith, president of e-commerce and new business development, Personal Creations). www.internet retailer.com/printArticle.asp?id=15641, accessed July 13, 2006.

Internet Retailer. 2005c. NewEgg cracks the $1 billion club. Internet Retailer.com (March).

Internet Retailer. 2005d. NewEgg's new private label card boosts order size. InternetRetailer.com (October 13).

Internet Retailer. 2006a. Calling all web sites. Internet Retailer.com (May 1).

Internet Retailer, 2006b. Home décor retailer Chiasso polishes up site search. April 6.

iProspect. 2006. Search engine marketing firm iProspect study reveals search engine marketers wear too many hats.

Jaffe, Joseph. 2003a. Dominate online share of voice. iMedia Connection, February 23. www.imediaconnection.com/content/1050.asp, accessed October 5, 2006.

Jaffe, Joseph. 2003b. The potential of affinity marketing. iMedia Connection, March 24. www.imediaconnection.com/global/5728 .asp?ref=http://www.imediaconnection.com/content/1054.asp.

Jaffe, Joseph. 2005. *Life after the 30-second spot: Energize your brand with a bold mix of alternatives to traditional advertising.* New York: John Wiley & Sons.

Jansen, Jim. 2005. Consumers suspicious of sponsored links. Pennsylvania State University. http://live.psu.edu/story/12348, accessed February 26, 2006.

Jarvis, Jeff. 2006. Smart Sprint's unadvertisement. BuzzMachine. www .buzzmachine.com/index.php/2006/01/06/smart-sprints-unad vertisement, accessed September 16, 2006.

Jasra, Manod. 2005. Measuring key performance indicators. *Enquiro Marketing Monitor*.

JupiterResearch. 2005a. Demographic profile, search users.

JupiterResearch. 2005b. The ROI of email relevance: Improving campaign results through targeting.

JupiterResearch. 2005c. Shopping cart abandonment.

JupiterResearch. 2006. Integrated marketing: The evolving role of email marketing.

Kann, Michele. 2004. Rich media market trends. AdTech, May.

Kaye, Katy, 2006. Virgin Mobile users: Will watch for minutes. www. clickz.com/showPage.html?page=3609896, accessed May 30.

Kearon, Paul. Predictive markets—A fresh approach to concept testing: How to get more research for less time and money. Brain Juicer White Paper. www.brainjuicer.com/download/papers/Predictive Markets—AFreshApproachtoConceptTesting.pdf.

Keller Fay Group. 2006a. Keller Fay's TalkTrack reveals consumer word of mouth features 56 brand mentions per week in ordinary conversations. www.kellerfay.com/news/TalkTrack5-15-06.pdf, accessed September 12, 2006.

Keller Fay Group. 2006b. The steak is the sizzle: A study on product attributes that drive word-of-mouth success. Keller Fay Group in cooperation with BzzAgent.

Kelsey Group. 2004. Local search and online shopping among leading online consumer behaviors. Kelsey Group, October 28. www.kelseygroup.com/press/pr041028.asp.

Khandelwal, Manjima, David Boyd, and Kenneth Greenberg. 2004. Closed-loop marketing solution for CPG online advertising. *ESOMAR Newsletter*, September.

Kim, Peter. 2006. Peter Kim, senior analyst, Forrester Research, personal communication with Stephen D. Rappaport, September 18.

Klaassen, Abbey. 2007. Dynamic Logic study looks into what works. AdAge, January 16.

Knopper, Doug. 2003. Rich media trends and insights. DoubleClick, September.

Krol, Carol. 2006. Email marketing gains ground with integration. BtoBOnline. www.btobonline.com/printwindow.cms?articleId=27608&pageType=article&logopath=/images/index, accessed July 29, 2006.

Krugman, Herbert. 1972. Why three exposures may be enough. *Journal of Advertising Research* 12, no. 6, 11–14.

Kuchinskas, Susan. 2005. New Responsys release tightens focus. Internet News (2005), www.internetnews.com/ec-news/print.php/3525781, accessed September 7, 2006.

LA Business Journal. 2006. Newegg.com hatches growth with tech-savvy customers. *Los Angeles Business Journal*, March 27.

Lanctot, Jeff. 2005. The truth about broadband video: Unleashing the value of an old medium in a new channel. *Avenue A | Razorfish Insight*, April.

Latzman, Andrew, and Mark Ryan. 2003. Branding and cost effectiveness of rich media in online advertising. Presentation to ESOMAR by Dynamic Logic and Nielsen//NetRatings, June.

Leavitt, Neal. 2005a. Audi's art of the heist captured leads. iMedia Connection (July 26). www.imediaconnection.com/content/6386.asp, accessed October 2, 2006.

Leavitt, Neal. 2005b. No degrees of separation—from Tide. IMedia Connection. www.imediaconnection.com/global/5728.asp?ref=http://www.imediaconnection.com/content/5062.asp, accessed August 30, 2006.

Lee, Kevin. 2002. The overlooked killer app: Paid inclusion. ClickZ (September 18). www.clickz.com/experts/search/opt/article.php/1464891, accessed May 12, 2006.

Lee, Kevin. 2004a. Buying brand keywords: A case study. ClickZ. www.clickz.com/experts/search/strat/article.php/3387751, accessed June 14, 2006.

Lee, Kevin. 2004b. Yes Virginia, there is SEM brand lift, Part 2. ClickZ. www.clickz.com/experts/search/strat/article.php/3384681, accessed June 13, 2006.

Lee, Kevin. 2005. Paid search ads and site-side brand metrics. ClickZ (July 8). www.clickz.com/experts/search/strat/article.php/3518026, accessed June 12, 2006.

Lee, Kevin. 2006. Interview with Stephen D. Rappaport.

Lieb, Rebecca. 2006. No one said this would be easy. ClickZ. www.clickz .com/experts/brand/buzz/print.php/3605696, accessed May 12, 2006.

Linares, Gabriela. 2002. Advanced email marketing strategies, presented to eMarketing Association Conference. L-Soft International.

Loyalty Lab. 2006. Loyalty Lab introduces "Loyalty 2.0" for grocers & retailers seeking to upgrade tired discount programs. August 8. www.loyaltylab.com/news_item.asp?articleID=757, accessed October 4, 2006.

L-Soft. 2002. Successful email marketing practices. L-Soft International.

Maddox, Kate. 2005. Online video ads prove effective: Advertisers see lift in brand awareness, message association and purchase intent. B to B Online, January 17. www.btobonline.com/article .cms?articleId=23009.

Maddox, Kate. 2006. Klipmart introduces new online video unit. B to B Online, April 5. www.btobonline.com/toc.cms?productId=4.

Magill, Ken. 2005a. Crew to launch discount website. MultiChannel Merchant. http://multichannelmerchant.com/news/crew_discount _site_0822/index.html, accessed July 23, 2006.

Magill, Ken. 2005b. J. Crew previews growth strategy. Direct. http://bg .directmag.com/microsites/magazinearticle.asp?mode=print& magazinearticleid=227994&releaseid=&srid=11317&magazine id=151&siteid=2, accessed July 31, 2006.

Magill, Ken. 2005c. Wedgwood goes direct to consumers. MultiChannel Merchant. www.multichannelmerchant.com/news/Wedgwood _direct_0928, accessed July 30, 2006.

Magill, Ken. 2006. Your email drives more responses than you think. DirectMag.com. http://directmag.com/magilla/email-drives-0822 06/index.html, accessed August 30, 2006.

Mandese, Joe. 1999. They didn't get SMART: The television industry looks to digital measurement. *American Demographics*, August.

Mandese, Joe. 2006. Nielsen extends its reach. *Broadcasting & Cable*, April 17. www.broadcastingcable.com/article/CA6325127.html?display=Feature&referral=SUPP, last accessed August 31, 2006.

Marckini, Fredrick. 2004. Paid inclusion beats PPC in many markets. ClickZ. www.clickz.com/experts/search/results/article.php/3415741, accessed May 12, 2006.

Marketing Evolution. 2004. The five platinum rules to online advertising creative.

MarketingExperiments.com. 2004. Natural search engines tested. *Marketing Experiments Journal*. www.marketingexperiments.com/ppc-seo-optimization/natural-search-engines.html, accessed January 16, 2007.

MarketingExperiments.com. 2005. PPC ad copy tested. *Marketing Experiments Journal*.

MarketingExperiments.com. 2006a. Essential Metrics for Online Marketers. *Marketing Experiments Journal*. www.marketingexperiments.com/improving-website-conversion/online-marketing-metrics.html, accessed January 16, 2007.

MarketingExperiments.com. 2006b. How to use pay-per-click (PPC) search campaigns to boost website traffic and maximize profits from day one: A 90-day plan. *Marketing Experiments Journal*. www.marketingexperiments.com/ppc-seo-optimization/90-day-ppc-plan.html, accessed May 17, 2006.

MarketingExperiments.com. 2006c. The power of small changes: How minor changes to your website can have a major impact on your conversion rate. *Marketing Experiments Journal*. www.marketingexperiments.com/see/1131, accessed March 30, 2006.

Marketing Management Analytics. 2005. IAB draft deck 9/28/05 working final update with appendix.

MarketingSherpa. 2006d. Travel marketing online—Lead generation & email campaign test results. MarketingSherpa.com (August 1). www.marketingsherpa.com/barrier.cfm?ident=29661, accessed August 1, 2006.

MarketingSherpa. 2006a. *Ecommerce Benchmark Guide 2006*.

MarketingSherpa. 2006b. Executive summary: 4 key email marketing alerts for 2006.

MarketingSherpa. 2006c. How to get thousands of prospects to examine new products—the split second you launch. www .marketingsherpa.com/barrier.cfm?ident=29674, accessed August 18, 2006.

MBP. 2005. Classifieds to drive local online ad growth to $3.2 billion. *MediaBuyerPlanner*, September 21, 2005. www.mediabuyer planner.com/2005/09/21/classifieds_to_drive_local/index .php.

MBP. 2006. Scion campaign lets users choose ads they see. *Media BuyerPlanner*, June 23.

McDonald, Loren. 2005a. Kick your email marketing program up a notch, in *Best practices: A collection of articles on email marketing*, 2nd edition. EmailLabs.

McDonald, Loren. 2005b. 28 ways to build permission-based email lists, in *Best practices: A collection of articles on email marketing*, 2nd edition. EmailLabs.

McKinney-Silver. 2005. The art of the h3ist: Case study (2005).

Measuring success: An advertising effectiveness series from the IAB. 2005. Vol. 1, no. 3.

Meskaukas, Jim. 2003. Spotlight on automotive advertisers. *Media Post*, November 12. www.imediaconnection.com/global/5728.asp ?ref=http://www.imediaconnection.com/content/2186.asp.

Microsoft Corporation. 2006. Microsoft previews new Windows Live and Office Live services. www.microsoft.com/presspass/press/ 2005/nov05/11-01PreviewSoftware., accessed May 11.

Miller, Stephanie. 2006. Email marketing trends and impact: Consumers and marketers speak. Presentation to Email Experience Council, August 24, 2006, ReturnPath and Email Experience Council).

Mills, Elinor. 2006. Google's market lead widens. CNET News.com (March 28). news.com.com/Googles+market+lead+widens/ 2100-1030_3-6054990.html, accessed March 29, 2006.

Mills, Jeff. 2006. Interview with Stephen D. Rappaport, August 29.

Moorhead, Patrick J. 2006. VOD—The big picture: Understanding the landscape of video on demand. *Avenue A|Razorfish Insight*, May.

Moran, Mike. 2005. Branding tactics for search. Summary of Search Engine Strategies 2005 presentation. www.mikemoran.com/ search/branding.htm, accessed June 12, 2006.

Morrissey, Brian. 2004. Jupiter: 3 of 4 search marketers unsophisticated. DMNews (October 27). www.dmnews.com/cms/dm-news/search-marketing/30850.html, accessed June 13, 2006.

MSN. 2003. Objective: Customer acquisition, lead generation strategy; Marketing strategy tactic: Search engine marketing—targeted search text ads. MSN Interactive Best Practices.

MSN, IAB, ARF. 2002. Dove Nutrium bar cross media case study 2002.

MSN. 2004. MSN-Harris interactive survey asks: What is America searching for? Internet users polled on their search engine habits. Microsoft Corporation.

Mullen, Jeanniey. 2005. Navigating eight landmines to achieve success with email. OgilvyOne.

Mullen, Jeanniey. 2006a. Interview with Stephen D. Rappaport.

Mullen, Jeanniey. 2006b. Navigating the rain: Real life—email best practices and recommendations from the RAKMF. Email Experience Council.

Nail, Jim. 2002. When online branding works. Forrester Research.

Neff, Jack. 2006. Five years in the making, Tide gets a new ad campaign. AdAge.com. http://adage.com/print?article_id=48441, accessed September 11, 2006.

Nestle. 2006. 2005 Full year results roadshow (February/March). www.ir.nestle.com/NR/rdonlyres/D8D02100-718E-4C89-A5 FD-455E10871F66/0/2005_FYRoadshow.pdf, accessed September 28, 2006.

Newcomb, Kevin. 2005a. HGTV supports TV giveaway with web. ClickZ (December 5). www.clickz.com/showPage.html?page =3568321, accessed September 26, 2006.

Newcomb, Kevin. 2005b. Quova updates geo-targeting products with ads in mind. *ClickZ News*, November 30. www.clickz.com/news/article.php/3567206.

Newcomb, Kevin. 2006a. Scion campaign has personality-driven ads. ClickZ, June 23.

Newcomb, Kevin. 2006b. Study: Top 4 percent of queries matter most. ClickZ. www.clickz.com/news/article.php/3611296, accessed June 6, 2006.

Nielsen BuzzMetrics. 2006. History of Nielsen BuzzMetrics. www .nielsenbuzzmetrics.com/history.asp, last accessed September 10, 2006.

Nielsen Consult. 2001a. Australia online advertising effectiveness study 2001: Summary.

Nielsen Consult. 2001b. New Zealand online effectiveness study 2001: Summary.

Nielsen, Jakob. 2006a. Email usability study: Executive summary. www.nngroup.com/reports/newsletters/summary.html, accessed September 16, 2006.

Nielsen, Jakob. 2006b. F-shaped pattern for reading web content. Jakob Nielsen's Alertbox, April 17.

Nielsen//NetRatings. 2004. IAB issues new research from Nielsen// NetRatings on branding value of sponsored text advertising.

Nielsen//NetRatings. 2006b. Online searches grow 55 percent year over year to nearly 5.1 billion searches in December 2005 (February).

Nielsen//NetRatings. 2006c. Sponsored link advertising on Google and Yahoo! grows 16 percent in six months: Yahoo's sponsored links rise 21 percent, Google's 14 percent, according to Nielsen//NetRatings.

Nielsen//NetRatings. 2006a. NIELSEN//NetRatings announces November U.S. search share rankings. December 16. www.nielsennet ratings.com/pr/pr_061219.pdf, accessed January 16, 2007.

Nielsen//NetRatings AdRelevance. 2006a. Most popular ad sizes. Data glance. March 13–March 19, 2006 www.adrelevance.com/ intelligence/intel_dataglance.jsp?sr=89654&flash=false.

Nielsen//NetRatings AdRelevance. 2006b. Top site genres ranked by impressions: April 24–April 30, 2006. www.adrelevance.com/ intelligence/intel_dataglance.jsp?sr=36808&flash=false, accessed May 9, 2006.

Nimetz, Jody. 2006. Determining proper key performance indicators. *Enquiro Marketing Monitor*.

NTT DoCoMo.com. 2006. Company overview. www.nttdocomo.com/ about/company/index.html.

Nussey, Bill, and David Hallerman. 2005. Email marketing: How to improve ROI. eMarketer and Silverpop.

Obringer, Lee Ann. 2003. How Marketing Plans Work. http:// money.howstuffworks.com/marketing-plan.htm/printable.

OneStat. 2005. Less people use 1 word phrase in search engines according to OneStat.com. www.onestat.com/html/aboutus_press box39.html, accessed May 16, 2006.

OPA. 2002a. Audience affinity study. Online Publishers Association in conjunction with Millward Brown IntelliQuest and ComScore Networks, October.

OPA. 2002b. Topline summary: Media consumption study. OPA White Papers.

OPA. 2003a. At-work audience media consumption study. Online Publishers Association in conjunction with Millward Brown IntelliQuest.

OPA. 2003b. The existence and characteristics of dayparts on the internet. OPA White Papers 1, no. 3. www.online-publishers .org/pdf/opa_dayinthelife_anethnographicstudyofmedia consumption.pdf.

OPA. 2003c. The impact of audience affinity on advertising performance. OPA White Papers, June. www.online-publishers .org/pdf/opa_affinity_impact_study_jun03.pdf.

OPA. 2005. Drivers and barriers to online video viewing. Online Publishers Association, February.

OPA. 2006. A day in the life: An ethnographic study of media consumption. The OPA White Paper.

Optimost. 2006. Dale and Thomas Popcorn: Homepage optimization. www.optimost.com/customers/casestudies/DaleThomas0106.pdf, accessed June 12, 2006.

Palumbo, Paul. 2006. Streaming video advertising guide 2006. Accu Stream iMedia Research, April.

ParisInfo.com. 2006. Paris at the heart of the Da Vinci Code. www .parisinfo.com/paris_sightseeing/rub5910.html, accessed September 30, 2006.

Pepelnjak, John Chandler, and Young-Bean Song. 2006. Optimal frequency—The impact of frequency on conversion rates. Atlas Institute.

Pew. 2005. September 2005 tracking survey, reported in Lee Rainie and Jeremy Sharnak, Pew Internet & American Life Project and comScore Media Metrix, *Search engine use*, November 2005.

Pew. 2006. Home broadband adoption up 40 percent in past year. Pew Charitable Trusts, May 29. www.pewtrusts.org/ideas/ideas_item .cfm?content_item_id=3383&content_type_id=7&issue_name= Society%20and%20the%20Internet&issue=10&page=7&WT.mc _id=06/05/2006, accessed June 5, 2006.

PhoCusWright. 2005. U.S. online travel market fueled by supplier sites, though growth slows. www.phocuswright.com/modules .php?op=modload&name=News&file=article&sid=252.

Pilotta, Joe. 2006a. 5 tips from BigResearch's Joe Pilotta. Word of Mouth Marketing Association. www.womma.org/wombat/blog/ 2006/07/howto_synthesiz.htm, accessed September 14, 2006.

Pilotta, Joe. 2006b. Personal communication with Stephen D. Rappaport.

Ponemon Institute. 2004. The 2004 survey of internet ads. Ponemon Institute with Chapell & Associates and Revenue Science.

Porres, Eric. 2003. Reaching the at-work audience. iMediaConnection, March 5. www.imediaconnection.com/global/5728.asp?ref =http://www.imediaconnection.com/content/1996.asp, accessed January 9, 2006.

Porres, Eric. 2005. Sugarshots: Targeting challenges. iMedia Connection, June 24. www.imediaconnection.com/content/6194.asp.

Position Research. 2002. Search engine optimization for managers.

Posman, Adam. 2001. The benefits of geotargeting. ClickZ. www .clickz.com/experts/media/agency_strat/article.php/831601.

Prescott, LeeAnn. 2005. Case study: Tide boosts traffic 9-fold. iMedia Connection. www.imediaconnection.com/global/5728.asp?ref= http://www.imediaconnection.com/content/7406.asp, accessed July 21, 2006.

Prescott, LeeAnn. 2006. Searching your customer's mind. iMedia Connection. www.imediaconnection.com/content/8148.asp, accessed July 21, 2006.

Procter & Gamble. 2006. P&G delivers results above expectations— raises fiscal year outlook: Strong sales growth on P&G and Gillette drives higher EPS results. PR Newswire. http://sev .prnewswire.com/household-consumer-cosmetics/20060127/ CLF00427012006-1.html, accessed September 11, 2006.

Promo Magazine. 2005. P&G reaches 1 million mark for Tide Coldwater. PromoMagazine.com. http://promomagazine.com/news/pg _tidecoldwater_051005/index.html, accessed September 11, 2006.

Punch, Linda. 2006. Reviving the web sites: Federated puts its faith— and $130 million—into online stores. www.internetretailer.com/ article.asp?id=17760, accessed July 30, 2006.

Queer as Folk. 2006. A Canadian dedication page. www.queeras folk.ca/.

Quinton, Brian. 2005. Live from Ad:Tech: iProspect launches offline conversion tracking. *Direct* Magazine. directmag.com/news/adtech-iprospect-launches-offline-110905/index.html, accessed July 23, 2006.

Quinton, Brian. 2006a. Newegg speaks geek. iMedia Connection (May).

Quinton, Brian. 2006b. StepUp makes the local connection for web searchers. *Direct* Magazine, http://directmag.com/searchline/7-05-06-StepUp/, accessed July 26, 2006.

Raitt, Bonnie. 1991. Something to talk about. Lyrics from "Luck of the Draw" album.

Ramos, Patty. 2005. Website redesign adding SEO rich content and PPC campaign greatly increases captured leads to security business. SEMP.

Red. 2005. Tide Coldwater launch backed by direct response TV advertising from Red. PRWeb (August 3).

ReturnPath. 2006. Results summary.

Revenue Science. 2005a. Case study: American Airlines and WSJ.com.

Revenue Science. 2005b. Case study: NTT DoCoMo and FT.com.

Reverse Direct Marketing. 2005. How America searches: Online shopping. iCrossing.

Richards Group. 2006. Florida Department of Citrus breaks new advertising with the Richards Group: "Florida orange juice, the best start under the sun." www.richards.com/default.asp?S=0665&ST=A, accessed October 9, 2006.

Rodgers, Zachary. 2006a. Advertising.com launches pre-roll video network. *ClickZ News*. www.clickz.com/news/article.php/3596626.

Rodgers, Zachary. 2006b. Scion offers virtual car loans at Whyville. ClickZ (July 18). www.clickz.com/news/article.php/3620606, accessed September 25, 2006.

Romeo, Anthony, et al. 2004. Maturity matters: How and why online advertising has been getting better over time. Dynamic Logic, June.

Ryan, Kevin. 2006. Are users ignoring paid search listings? iMedia Connection. www.imediaconnection.com/global/5728.asp?ref=http://www.imediaconnection.com/content/8953.asp, accessed April 5, 2006.

Saunders, Christopher. 2002. Study finds banners brand. InternetNews.com (April 17).

Schionning, Raz. 2006. Second Life panel on virtual marketing. MIT AdvertisingLab Blog, June 6. http://adverlab.blogspot.com/2006/06/second-life-panel-on-virtual-world.html, accessed January 18, 2007.

SEMPO. 2005. Survey of SEM agencies and advertisers, global results. Search Engine Marketing Professional Organization.

Shamdasani, Prem N., et al. 2001. Location, location, location: Insights for advertising placement on the web. *Journal of Advertising Research* 41, no. 4.

Sherman, Chris. 2005. Survey: Searchers are confident, satisfied & clueless. ClickZ Networks (January 24). http://searchenginewatch.com/searchday/article.php/3462911, accessed May 15, 2006.

Sherman, Lee. 2004. Online targeting and personalization: Harnessing customer-level data for greater relevance. *Avenue A | Razorfish Insight.*

ShopLocal. 2005. Web2Store presentation. ShopLocal, LLC. www.shoplocalllc.com/documents/Web2Store%20Presentation.ppt, accessed July 28, 2006.

Sicilia, Maria, et al. 2006. Attitude formation online: How the consumer's need for cognition affects the relationship between attitude towards the website and attitude towards the brand. *International Journal of Market Research* 48, no. 2, 139–154.

Silverpop. 2005. 2005 broken link study: What do recipients really see? Silverpop Systems.

Silverpop. 2006a. HoneyBaked Ham: HoneyBaked Ham and Spunlogic savor unprecedented success with Silverpop: A Silverpop case study. www.silverpop.com/practices/casestudies/honeybaked.html, accessed July 7, 2006.

Silverpop. 2006b. 2006 Email list growth survey.

Simpson, George. 2006. Relevance—The cure for clutter. Media Post, April 3. http://publications.mediapost.com/index.cfm?fuseaction=Articles.showArticle&art_aid=41693.

Skeen, Dan. 2006. SEO copywriting: Does "search friendly" mean "human readable"? MarketingProfs.com. www.marketingprofs.com/print.asp?source=/6/skeen1.asp, accessed May 22, 2006.

Skylist. 2006. Email marketing survey results.

Smith, Steve. 2006a. In search of behavioral targeting. Media Post, February 17. http://publications.mediapost.com/index.cfm?fuseaction=Articles.showArticle&art_aid=39925.

Smith, Steve. 2006b. Laser-target the creative; Micro-measure your results. Media Post, March 3. http://publications.mediapost .com/index.cfm?fuseaction=Articles.showArticle&art_aid=40537.

Spiderhelp. 2006. Why search engine promotion works. Spiderhelp .com. www.spiderhelp.com, accessed June 14, 2006.

Springs, Kabibi. 2006. Geotargeting in 10 minutes. iMedia Connection, April 10. www.imediaconnection.com/content/8988.asp.

Stewart, Morgan. 2006. Email marketing: 2005 response rate study. ExactTarget.

Strong, Esco. n.d. Online media conversion rates by daypart. *Digital Marketing Insights*. Atlas Institute. www.atlassolutions.com/pdf/ DaypartAnalysisDMI.pdf.

Sullivan, Andrew. 2006. The future of interactive lies in its past. Media Post (March 9). http://publications.mediapost.com/index.cfm ?fuseaction=Articles.san&s=40707&Nid=18951&p=352249, accessed March 9, 2006.

Sullivan, Laurie. 2006. New service offers online video syndication. TechWeb.com, April 20. www.informationweek.com/story/show Article.jhtml?articleID=186500313.

Tancer, Bill. 2006. Google Pontiac: A search call to action. Hitwise. http://weblogs.hitwise.com/bill-tancer/2006/01/google_ pontiac.html, accessed July 25, 2006.

Tedeschi, Bob. 2006. Salesmanship comes to the online stores, but please call it a chat. *New York Times* (August 7), C9.

Thurow, Shari. 2006. Analyzing search behavior for SEO. ClickZ. www.clickz.com/experts/search/results/article.php/3607336, accessed June 2, 2006.

Treacy, Michael, and Fred Wiersema. 1997. *The discipline of market leaders*. Perseus Books Group; Expanded E Edition.

Turow, Joseph. 2006. *Niche envy: Marketing discrimination in the digital age*. Cambridge, MA: MIT Press.

Tweedy, Todd. 2006. Personal communication with Stephen D. Rappaport, October 6.

U.S. Census Bureau. 2006a. IDB summary demographic data. Population Division/International Programs Center. www.census.gov/ cgi-bin/ipc/idbsum.pl?cty=US, accessed September 25, 2006.

U.S. Census Bureau. 2006b. Unadjusted and adjusted estimates of monthly retail and food services sales by kind of business: 2005. www.census.gov/mrts/www/data/html/nsal05.html, accessed July 26, 2006.

Usborne, Nick. 2005. Add newsletter signup forms at the end of related content pages. Excess Voice newsletter. www.excessvoice.com/web-copywriting-tip50.htm, accessed January 16, 2007.

Volt, Lester. 2004. Internet impact on offline spending at all-time high, Axcess News. www.axcessnews.com/technology_100604.shtml, accessed July 25, 2006.

Wakeling, Patti, and Brian Murphy. 2007. E-ad works. Internet Advertising Effectiveness Consortium.

WebSideStory. 2006. Site search for e-commerce web sites.

Wharton, Alexandra. 2007. Online is sweet: Food marketers have a hearty appetite for the web. *Revenue*, January/February.

White, Roderick. 2005. Measuring campaign ROI: Ford's next F-150, World Advertising Research Center, Henley-on-Thames, UK.

Whyville. 2006. Whyville sponsorships. www.whyville.com, accessed September 25, 2006.

Wikipedia. 2006. *The Apprentice: Martha Stewart*. http://en.wikipedia.org/wiki/The_Apprentice:_Martha_Stewart, accessed June 5, 2006.

Wikipedia. 2007. MMORPG. http://en.wikipedia.org/wiki/MMORPG, accessed January 21, 2007.

Wood, Cara. 2006a. Borders emails drive store sales, overcome data gap. DMNews. www.dmnews.com/cms/trackback/37388-1, accessed August 14, 2006.

Wood, Cara. 2006b. Coke, Sprint spread news of word-of-mouth efforts. DMNews. www.dmnews.com/cms/dm-news/shows-assns/37609.html, accessed July 25, 2006.

Yahoo! 2004. The role of search in the consumer buying cycle.

Yahoo! 2006a. Angler's Vice lures marketing customers with Yahoo! Search Marketing.

Yahoo! 2006b. Long and winding road: Route to the cash register. Yahoo! Summit Series.

Yahoo! 2006c. Yahoo! and OMD study reveals online tesearch plays critical role in consumers' offline purchases; online price comparisons and "communal shopping" create trust and drive decision making.

Yahoo! Buzz Index. 2006. Top overall searches. http://buzz.yahoo.com/overall/, accessed June 18, 2006.

Yahoo! Buzz Index. 2007. Top overall searches. http://buzz.yahoo.com/overall/, accessed January 16, 2007.

Joseph Plummer

Dr. Joseph Plummer is the Chief Research Officer at The Advertising Research Foundation.

Previous to his appointment at The ARF, Joe was Executive Vice President, Director of Research and Insight Development for McCann-Erickson WorldGroup. In this post, he was WorldGroup's top knowledge officer with regard to insight-development methods, strategic research quality, and employee training and standards.

Previously at McCann, Joe was Executive Vice President, Director of Brand Strategy on Global Accounts for McCann-Erickson WorldGroup. Prior to joining McCann-Erickson in 1997, he was Vice Chairman and Worldwide Planning Director at DMB&B and Executive Vice President of Young & Rubicam advertising agencies. Earlier, from 1995 to 1997, he was Vice Chairman of ASW, a worldwide research firm, and a Board Director of the firm from 1995 to 1999. He started his career in advertising with the Leo Burnett Company in Chicago. Joe earned a BA from Westminster College and a master's and doctorate from Ohio State University. He has served as chairman of the Research Committees for the American Association of Advertising Agencies and the American Marketing Association, and as a trustee of the Marketing Science Institute. Dr. Plummer is currently Adjunct Professor at the Columbia Business School.

Steve Rappaport

Stephen D. Rappaport is Director, Knowledge Solutions at The ARF. Steve's contributions to the *Playbook* are informed by his decades as a researcher, forecaster, and strategist for Interpublic, McCann World Group, BBDO, and DMB&B. Since the late 1970s, Steve has explored the implications of new electronic technologies and their impacts on advertising and marketing practice. As the chief marketer for several business-to-business and consumer packaged goods companies, Steve applied those insights to the marketing and advertising of new and in-market products and services. Steve's undergraduate and graduate education, at Stony Brook University and the University of Pennsylvania, respectively, concentrated on communications and society.

Taddy Hall

Ridgway "Taddy" H. Hall is the Chief Strategy Officer for The Advertising Research Foundation (ARF). He is a recognized authority in the fields of innovation, branding, and competitive strategy and has held senior management positions in U.S. and Latin American companies in both private equity investment firms and operational companies such as Au Bon Pain.

His recent articles on innovation have appeared in the *Harvard Business Review* (December 2006), the *Wall Street Journal*, and *CMO Magazine*.

Taddy holds a bachelor of arts degree from Yale University and an MBA from Harvard University.

Robert Barocci

In September 2003, Bob Barocci was named President and CEO of The Advertising Research Foundation.

Bob brings a long corporate advertising career to The ARF, headed by 21 years with Leo Burnett, culminating in the position of President of Leo Burnett International. After he left Leo Burnett, he was founder/CEO of McConnaughy Barocci Brown and was then invited by Alex Kroll to become Director of Central/East Europe for Young & Rubicam shortly after the wall fell.

Just prior to joining The ARF, Bob was part of Bob Kerrey's leadership team at New School University, serving as Director of Communications.

Bob holds an MBA from Harvard University and a Phi Beta Kappa mathematics degree from the University of Wisconsin.